Kritische Studien zur Demokratie

Herausgegeben von
Prof. Dr. Gary S. Schaal: Helmut-Schmidt-Universität/
Universität der Bundeswehr Hamburg, Deutschland

Dr. Claudia Ritzi: Helmut-Schmidt-Universität/
Universität der Bundeswehr Hamburg, Deutschland

Dr. Matthias Lemke: Helmut-Schmidt-Universität/
Universität der Bundeswehr Hamburg, Deutschland

Die Erforschung demokratischer Praxis aus normativer wie empirischer Perspektive zählt zu den wichtigsten Gegenständen der Politikwissenschaft. Dabei gilt es auch, kritisch Stellung zum Zustand und zu relevanten Entwicklungstrends zeitgenössischer Demokratie zu nehmen. Besonders die Politische Theorie ist Ort des Nachdenkens über die aktuelle Verfasstheit von Demokratie. Die Reihe *Kritische Studien zur Demokratie* versammelt aktuelle Beiträge, die diese Perspektive einnehmen: Getragen von der Sorge um die normative Qualität zeitgenössischer Demokratien versammelt sie Interventionen, die über die gegenwärtige Lage und die künftigen Perspektiven demokratischer Praxis reflektieren. Die einzelnen Beiträge zeichnen sich durch eine methodologisch fundierte Verzahnung von Theorie und Empirie aus.

Gregor Wiedemann

Text Mining for Qualitative Data Analysis in the Social Sciences

A Study on Democratic Discourse in Germany

Springer VS

Gregor Wiedemann
Leipzig, Germany

Dissertation Leipzig University, Germany, 2015

Kritische Studien zur Demokratie
ISBN 978-3-658-15308-3 ISBN 978-3-658-15309-0 (eBook)
DOI 10.1007/978-3-658-15309-0

Library of Congress Control Number: 2016948264

Springer VS

Printed on acid-free paper

This Springer VS imprint is published by Springer Nature
The registered company is Springer Fachmedien Wiesbaden GmbH
The registered company address is: Abraham-Lincoln-Strasse 46, 65189 Wiesbaden, Germany

Preface

Two developments in computational text analysis widen opportunities for qualitative data analysis: amounts of digital text worth investigating are growing rapidly, and progress in algorithmic detection of semantic structures allows for further bridging the gap between qualitative and quantitative approaches. The key factor here is the inclusion of context into computational linguistic models which extends simple word counts towards the extraction of meaning. But, to benefit from the heterogeneous set of text mining applications in the light of social science requirements, there is a demand for a) conceptual integration of consciously selected methods, b) systematic optimization of algorithms and workflows, and c) methodological reflections with respect to conventional empirical research.

This book introduces an integrated workflow of text mining applications to support qualitative data analysis of large scale document collections. Therewith, it strives to contribute to the steadily growing fields of digital humanities and computational social sciences which, after an adventurous and creative coming of age, meanwhile face the challenge to consolidate their methods. I am convinced that the key to success of digitalization in the humanities and social sciences not only lies in innovativeness and advancement of analysis technologies, but also in the ability of their protagonists to catch up with methodological standards of conventional approaches. Unequivocally, this ambitious endeavor requires an interdisciplinary treatment. As a political scientist who also studied computer science with specialization in natural language processing, I hope to contribute to the exciting debate on text mining in empirical research by giving guidance for interested social scientists and computational scientists alike.

Gregor Wiedemann

Contents

List of Figures

List of Tables

List of Abbreviations

AAD	Analyse Automatique du Discours
BMBF	Bundesministerium für Bildung und Forschung
BfV	Bundesamt für Verfassungsschutz
BMI	Bundesministerium des Innern
CA	Content Analysis
CAQDA	Computer Assisted Qualitative Data Analysis
CATA	Computer Assisted Text Analysis
CCA	Computational Content Analysis
CDA	Critical Discourse Analysis
CLARIN	Common Language Resources and Technology Infrastructure
MP	Manifesto Project
CTM	Correlated Topic Model
DARIAH	Digital Research Infrastructure for the Arts and Humanities
DASISH	Digital Services Infrastructure for Social Sciences and Humanities
DH	Digital Humanities
DKP	Deutsche Kommunistische Partei
DTM	Document-Term-Matrix
DVU	Deutsche Volksunion
ESFRI	European Strategic Forum on Research Infrastructures
EU	European Union
FAZ	Frankfurter Allgemeine Zeitung
FdGO	Freiheitlich-demokratische Grundordnung
FQS	Forum Qualitative Social Research
FRG	Federal Republic of Germany
GDR	German Democratic Republic

GTM	Grounded Theory Methodology
IDF	Inverse Document Frequency
IR	Information Retrieval
JSD	Jensen–Shannon Divergence
KPD	Kommunistische Partei Deutschlands
KWIC	Key Word in Context
LDA	Latent Dirichlet Allocation
LL	Log-likelihood
LSA	Latent Semantic Analysis
ML	Machine Learning
MAXENT	Maximum Entropy
MAP	Mean Average Precision
MDS	Multi Dimensional Scaling
MWU	Multi Word Unit
NB	Naive Bayes
NER	Named Entity Recognition
NLP	Natural Language Processing
NPD	Nationaldemokratische Partei Deutschlands
NSDAP	Nationalsozialistische Deutsche Arbeiterpartei
OCR	Optical Character Recognition
OLAP	Online Analytical Processing
ORC	Open Research Computing
OWL	Web Ontology Language
PAM	Partitioning Around Medoids
PCA	Principal Component Analysis
PDS	Partei des Demokratischen Sozialismus
PMI	Pointwise Mutual Information
POS	Part of Speech
QCA	Qualitative Content Analysis
QDA	Qualitative Data Analysis
RAF	Rote Armee Fraktion
RDF	Resource Description Framework
RE	Requirements Engineering
REP	Die Republikaner
RMSD	Root Mean-Square Deviation

SE	Software Engineering
SECG	Semantically Enriched Co-occurrence Graph
SED	Sozialistische Einheitspartei Deutschlands
SOM	Self Organizing Map
SPD	Sozialdemokratische Partei Deutschlands
SRP	Sozialistische Reichspartei
SVM	Support Vector Machine
TF-IDF	Term Frequency–Inverse Document Frequency
TM	Text Mining
TTM	Term-Term-Matrix
UN	United Nations
VSM	Vector Space Model
WASG	Wahlalternative Arbeit und Soziale Gerechtigkeit
XML	Extensible Markup Language

1. Introduction: Qualitative Data Analysis in a Digital World

Digitalization and informatization of science during the last decades have widely transformed the ways in which empirical research is conducted in various disciplines. Computer-assisted data collection and analysis procedures even led to the emergence of new subdisciplines such as bioinformatics or medical informatics. The humanities (including social sciences)[1] so far seem to lag somewhat behind this development—at least when it comes to analysis of textual data. This is surprising, considering the fact that text is one of the most frequently investigated data types in philologies as well as in social sciences like sociology or political science. Recently, there have been indicators that the digital era is constantly gaining ground also in the humanities. In 2009, fifteen social scientists wrote in a manifesto-like article in the journal "Science":

> "The capacity to collect and analyze massive amounts of data has transformed such fields as biology and physics. But the emergence of a data-driven 'computational social science' has been much slower. [...] But computational social science is occurring – in internet companies such as Google and Yahoo, and in government agencies such as the U.S. National Security Agency" (Lazer et al., 2009, p. 721).

In order not to leave the field to private companies or governmental agencies solely, they appealed to social scientists to further embrace computational technologies. For some years, developments marked by

[1] In the German research tradition the disciplines of social sciences and other disciplines of the humanities are separated more strictly (*Sozial- und Geisteswissenschaften*). Thus, I hereby emphasize that I include social sciences when referring to the (digital) humanities.

popular buzzwords such as *digital humanities*, *big data* and *text and data mining* blaze the trail through the classical publications. Within the humanities, social sciences appear as pioneers in application of these technologies because they seem to have a 'natural' interest for analyzing semantics in large amounts of textual data, which firstly is nowadays available and secondly rises hope for another type of representative studies beyond survey research. On the other hand, there are well established procedures of manual text analysis in the social sciences which seem to have certain theoretical or methodological prejudices against computer-assisted approaches of large scale text analysis. The aim of this book is to explore ways of systematic utilization of (semi-)automatic computer-assisted text analysis for a specific political science research question and to evaluate on its potential for integration with established manual methods of qualitative data analysis. How this is approached will be clarified further in Section 1.4 after some introductory remarks on digital humanities and its relation to social sciences.

But first of all, I give two brief definitions on the main terms in the title to clarify their usage throughout the entire work. With *Qualitative Data Analysis* (QDA), I refer to a set of established procedures for analysis of textual data in social sciences—e.g. Frame Analysis, Grounded Theory Methodology, (Critical) Discourse Analysis or (Qualitative) Content Analysis. While these procedures mostly differ in underlying theoretical and methodological assumptions of their applicability, they share common tasks of analysis in their practical application. As Schönfelder (2011) states, "qualitative analysis at its very core can be condensed to a close and repeated review of data, categorizing, interpreting and writing" (§ 29). Conventionally, this process of knowledge extraction from text is achieved by human readers rather intuitively. QDA methods provide systematization for the process of structuring information by identifying and collecting relevant textual fragments and assigning them to newly created or predefined semantic concepts in a specific field of knowledge. The second main term *Text Mining* (TM) is defined by Heyer (2009, p. 2) as a set of "computer based methods for a semantic analysis of text that help to automatically, or semi-automatically, structure text, particularly very large amounts of text". Interestingly, this definition comprises of some analogy to procedures of QDA with respect to structure identification by repeated data exploration and categorization. While manual and (semi-)automatic methods of structure identification differ largely with respect to certain aspects, the hypothesis of this study is that the former may truly benefit from the latter if both are integrated in a well-specified methodological framework. Following this assumption, I strive for developing such a framework to answer the question

1. How can the application of (semi-)automatic TM services support qualitative text analysis in the social sciences, and

2. extend it with a quantitative perspective on semantic structures towards a mixed method approach?

1.1. The Emergence of "Digital Humanities"

Although computer assisted content analysis already has a long tradition, so far it did not prevail as a widely accepted method within the QDA community. Since computer technology became widely available at universities during the second half of the last century, social science and humanities researchers have used it for analyzing vast amounts of textual data. Surprisingly, after 60 years of experience with computer-assisted automatic text analysis and a tremendous development in information technology, it still is an uncommon approach in the social sciences. The following section highlights two recent developments which may change the way qualitative data analysis in social sciences is performed: firstly, the rapid growth of the availability of digital text worth to investigate and, secondly, the improvement of (semi-)automatic text analysis technologies which allows for further bridging the gap between qualitative and quantitative text analysis. In consequence, the use of text mining cannot be characterized only as a further development of traditional quantitative content analysis beyond communication and media studies. Instead, computational linguistic models aiming towards the extraction of meaning comprise opportunities for the coalescence of former opposed research paradigms in new mixed method large-scale text analyses.

Nowadays, Computer Assisted Text Analysis (CATA) means much more than just counting words.[2] In particular, the combination of pattern-based and complex statistical approaches may be applied to support established qualitative data analysis designs and open them up to a quantitative perspective (Wiedemann, 2013). Only a few years ago, social scientists somewhat hesitantly started to explore its opportunities for their research interest. But still, social science truly has much unlocked potential for applying recently developed approaches to the myriads of digital texts available these days. Chapter 2 introduces an attempt to systematize the existing approaches of CATA from the perspective of a qualitative researcher. The suggested typology is based not only on the capabilities contemporary computer algorithms provide, but also on their notion of context. The perception of context is essential in a two-fold manner: From a qualitative researcher's perspective, it forms the basis for what may be referred to as meaning; and from the Natural Language Processing (NLP) perspective it is the decisive source to overcome the simple counting of character strings towards more complex models of human language and cognition. Hence, the way of dealing with context in analysis may act as decisive bridge between qualitative and quantitative research designs.

Interestingly, the quantitative perspective on qualitative data is anything but new. Technically open-minded scholars more than half a century ago initiated a development using computer technology for textual analysis. One of the early starters was the Italian theologist Roberto Busa, who became famous as "pioneer of the digital humanities" for his project "Index Thomasticus" (Bonzio, 2011). Started in 1949—with a sponsorship by IBM—this project digitalized and indexed the complete work of Thomas Aquinas and made it publicly

[2] In the following, I refer to CATA as the complete set of software-based approaches of text analysis, not just Text Mining.

available for further research (Busa, 2004). Another milestone was the software THE GENERAL INQUIRER, developed in the 1960s by communication scientists for the purpose of computer-assisted content analysis of newspapers (Stone et al., 1966). It made use of frequency counts of keyword sets to classify documents into given categories. But, due to a lack of theoretical foundation and exclusive commitment to deductive research designs, emerging qualitative social research remained skeptical about those computer-assisted methods for a long time (Kelle, 2008, p. 486). It took until the late 1980s, when personal computers entered the desktops of qualitative researchers, that the first programs for supporting qualitative text analysis were created (Fielding and Lee, 1998). Since then, a growing variety of software packages, like MAXQDA, ATLAS.ti or NVivo, with relatively sophisticated functionalities, became available, which make life much easier for qualitative text analysts. Nonetheless, the majority of these software packages has remained "truly qualitative" for a long time by just replicating manual research procedures of coding and memo writing formerly conducted with pens, highlighters, scissors and glue (Kuckartz, 2007, p. 16).

This once justified methodological skepticism against computational analysis of qualitative data might be one reason for qualitative social research lagging behind in a recent development labeled by the popular catchword Digital Humanities (DH) or 'eHumanities'. In contrast to DH, which was established at the beginning of the 21st century (Schreibman et al., 2004), the latter term emphasizes the opportunities of computer technology not only for digitalization, storage and management of data, but also for analysis of (big) data repositories.[3]

Since then, the digitalization of the humanities has grown in big steps. Annual conferences are held, institutes and centers for DH are founded and new professorial chairs have been set up. In 2006, a group

[3] A third term, "computational humanities", is suggested by Manovich (2012). It emphasizes the fact that additionally to the digitalized version of classic data of the humanities, new forms of data emerge by connection and linkage of data sources. This may apply to 'retro-digitalized' historic data as well as to 'natively digital' data in the worldwide communication of the 'Web 2.0'.

of European computer linguists developed the idea for a long-term project related to all aspects of language data research leading to the foundation of the *Common Language Resources and Technology Infrastructure* (CLARIN)[4] as part of the *European Strategic Forum on Research Infrastructures* (ESFRI). CLARIN is planned to be funded with 165 million Euros over a period of 10 years to leverage digital language resources and corresponding analysis technologies. Interestingly, although mission statements of the transnational project and its national counterparts (for Germany CLARIN-D) speak of humanities *and* social sciences as their target groups[5], few social scientists have engaged in the project so far. Instead, user communities of philologists, anthropologists, historians and, of course, linguists are dominating the process. In Germany, for example, a working group for social sciences in CLARIN-D concerned with aspects of computational content analysis was founded not before late 2014. This is surprising, given the fact that textual data is one major form of empirical data many qualitatively-oriented social scientists use. Qualitative researchers so far seem to play a minor role in the ESFRI initiatives. The absence of social sciences in CLARIN is mirrored in another European infrastructure project as well: the *Digital Research Infrastructure for the Arts and Humanities* (DARIAH)[6] focuses on data acquisition, research networks and teaching projects for the Digital Humanities, but does not address social sciences directly. An explicit QDA perspective on textual data in the ESFRI context is only addressed in the *Digital Services Infrastructure for Social Sciences and Humanities* (DASISH).[7] The project perceives digital "qualitative social science data", i.e. "all non-numeric data in order to answer specific research questions" (Gray, 2013, p. 3), as subject for quality assurance, archiving and accessibility. Qualitative researchers in the DASISH context acknowledge that "the inclusion of qualitative data represents

[4]http://clarin.eu

[5]"CLARIN-D: a web and centres-based research infrastructure for the social sciences and humanities" (http://de.clarin.eu/en/home-en.html).

[6]http://dariah.eu

[7]http://dasish.eu

an important opportunity in the context of DASISH's focus on the development of interdisciplinary 'cross-walks' between the humanities and social sciences" reaching out to "quantitative social science", while at the same time highlighting their "own distinctive conventions and traditions" (ibid., p. 11) and largely ignoring opportunities for computational analysis of digitized text.

Given this situation, why has social science reacted so hesitantly to the DH development and does the emergence of 'computational social science' compensate for this late-coming? The branch of qualitative social research devoted to understanding instead of explaining avoided mass data—reasonable in the light of its self-conception as a counterpart to the positivist-quantitative paradigm and scarce analysis resources. But, it left a widening gap since the availability of digital textual data, algorithmic complexity and computational capacity has been growing exponentially during the last decades. Two humanist scholars highlighted this development in their recent work. Since 2000, the Italian literary scholar Franco Moretti has promoted the idea of "distant reading." To study actual world literature, which he argues is more than the typical Western canon of some hundred novels, one cannot "close read" all books of interest. Instead, he suggests making use of statistical analysis and graphical visualizations of hundreds of thousands of texts to compare styles and topics from different languages and parts of the world (Moretti, 2000, 2007). Referring to the Google Books Library Project the American classical philologist Gregory Crane asked in a famous journal article: "What do you do with a Million Books?" (2006). As possible answer he describes three fundamental applications: digitalization, machine translation and information extraction to make the information buried in dusty library shelves available to a broader audience. So, how should social scientists respond to these developments?

1.2. Digital Text and Social Science Research

It is obvious that the growing amount of digital text is of special interest for the social sciences as well. There is not only an ongoing stream of online published newspaper articles, but also corresponding user discussions, internet forums, blogs and microblogs as well as social networks. Altogether, they generate tremendous amounts of text impossible to close read, but worth further investigation. Yet, not only current and future social developments are captured by 'natively' digital texts. Libraries and publishers worldwide spend a lot of effort retro-digitalizing printed copies of handwritings, newspapers, journals and books. The project Chronicling America by the Library of Congress, for example, scanned and OCR-ed[8] more than one million pages of American newspapers between 1836 and 1922. The Digital Public Library of America strives for making digitally available millions of items like photographs, manuscripts or books from numerous American libraries, archives and museums. Full-text searchable archives of parliamentary protocols and file collections of governmental institutions are compiled by initiatives concerned with open data and freedom of information. Another valuable source, which will be used during this work, are newspapers. German newspaper publishers like the *Frankfurter Allgemeine Zeitung*, *Die Zeit* or *Der Spiegel* made all of their volumes published since their founding digitally available (see Table 1.1). Historical German newspapers of the former German Democratic Republic (GDR) also have been retro-digitized for historical research.[9]

Interesting as this data may be for social scientists, it becomes clear that single researchers cannot read through all of these materials. Sampling data requires a fair amount of previous knowledge on the topics of interest, which makes especially projects targeted to a long investigation time frame prone to bias. Further, it hardly enables

[8] Optical Character Recognition (OCR) is a technique for the conversion of scanned images of printed text or handwritings into machine-readable character strings.

[9] http://zefys.staatsbibliothek-berlin.de/ddr-presse

Table 1.1.: Completely (retro-)digitized long term archives of German newspapers.

Publication	Digitized volumes from
Die Zeit	1946
Hamburger Abendblatt	1948
Der Spiegel	1949
Frankfurter Allgemeine Zeitung	1949
Bild (Bund)	1953
Tageszeitung (taz)	1986
Süddeutsche Zeitung	1992
Berliner Zeitung	1945–1993
Neue Zeit	1945–1994
Neues Deutschland	1946–1990

researchers to reveal knowledge structures on a collection-wide level in multi-faceted views as every sample can only lead to inference on the specific base population the sample was drawn from. Technologies and methodologies supporting researchers to cope with these mass data problems become increasingly important. This is also one outcome of the KWALON Experiment the journal Forum Qualitative Social Research (FQS) conducted in April 2010. For this experiment, different developer teams of software for QDA were asked to answer the same research questions by analyzing a given corpus of more than one hundred documents from 2008 and 2009 on the financial crisis (e.g. newspaper articles and blog posts) with their product (Evers et al., 2011). Only one team was able to include all the textual data in its analysis (Lejeune, 2011), because they did not use an approach replicating manual steps of qualitative analysis methods. Instead, they implemented a semi-automatic tool which combined the automatic retrieval of key words within the text corpus with a supervised, data-driven dictionary learning process. In an iterated coding process, they "manually" annotated text snippets suggested by the computer, and they simultaneously trained a (rather simple) retrieval algorithm generating new suggestions. This procedure of "active learning" enabled them to process much more data than all other teams, making pre-selections on the corpus unnecessary. However, according to their own assessment they only conducted a more or less exploratory analysis which was not able to dig deep into the data. Nonetheless, while Lejeune's approach points into the targeted direction, the present study focuses on exploitation of more sophisticated algorithms for the investigation of collections from hundreds up to hundreds of thousands of documents.

The potential of TM for analyzing big document collections has been acknowledged in 2011 by the German government as well. In a large funding line of the German Federal Ministry of Education and Research (BMBF), 24 interdisciplinary projects in the field of eHumanities were funded for three years. Research questions of the humanities and social science should be approached in joint cooperation with computer scientists. Six out of the 24 projects have a dedicated social science background, thus fulfilling the requirement of the funding line which explicitly had called qualitatively researching social scientists for participation (BMBF, 2011).[10] With their methodological focus on eHumanities, all these projects do not strive for standardized application of generic software to answer their research questions. Instead, each has to develop its own way of proceeding, as

[10] *Analysis of Discourses in Social Media* (http://www.social-media-analytics.org); *ARGUMENTUM* – Towards computer-supported analysis, retrieval and synthesis of argumentation structures in humanities using the example of jurisprudence (http://argumentum.eear.eu); *eIdentity* – Multiple collective identities in international debates on war and peace (http://www.uni-stuttgart.de/soz/ib/forschung/Forschungsprojekte/eIdentity.html); *ePol* – Post-democracy and neoliberalism. On the usage of neoliberal argumentation in German federal politics between 1949 and 2011 (http://www.epol-projekt.de); *reSozIT* – "Gute Arbeit" nach dem Boom. Pilotprojekt zur Längsschnittanalyse arbeitssoziologischer Betriebsfallstudien mit neuen e-Humanities-Werkzeugen (http://www.sofi-goettingen.de/index.php?id=1086); *VisArgue* – Why and when do arguments win? An analysis and visualization of political negotiations (http://visargue.uni-konstanz.de)

well as to reinvent or adapt existing analysis technologies for their specific purpose. For the moment, I assume that generic software for textual analysis usually is not appropriate to satisfy specific and complex research needs. Thus, paving the way for new methods requires a certain amount of willingness to understand TM technologies together with open-mindedness for experimental solutions from the social science perspective. Ongoing experience with such approaches may lead to best practices, standardized tools and quality assurance criteria in the nearby future. To this end, this book strives to make some worthwhile contribution to the extension of the method toolbox of empirical social research. It was realized within and largely profited from the eHumanities-project *ePol – Post-democracy and Neoliberalism* which investigated aspects of qualitative changes of the democracy in the Federal Republic of Germany (FRG) using TM applications on large newspaper collections covering more than six decades of public media discourse (Wiedemann et al., 2013; Lemke et al., 2015).

1.3. Example Study: Research Question and Data Set

The integration of QDA with methods of TM is developed against the background of an exemplary study concerned with longitudinal aspects of democratic developments in Germany. The political science research question investigated for this study deals with the subject of "democratic demarcation". Patterns and changes of patterns within the public discourse on this topic are investigated with TM applications over a time period of several decades. To introduce the subject, I first clarify what "democratic demarcation" refers to. Then, I introduce the data set on which the investigation is performed.

1.3.1. Democratic Demarcation

Democratic political regimes have to deal with a paradox circumstance. On the one hand, the democratic ideal is directed to allow as much freedom of political participation as possible. On the other hand, this freedom has to be defended against political ideas, activities or groups who strive for abolition of democratic rights of participation. Consequently, democratic societies dispute on rules to decide which political actors and ideas take legitimate positions to act in political processes and democratic institutions and, vice versa, which ideas, activities or actors must be considered as a threat to democracy. Once identified as such, opponents of democracy can be subject to oppressive countermeasures by state actors such as governmental administrations or security authorities interfering in certain civil rights. Constitutional law experts as well as political theorists point to the fact that these measures may yield towards undemocratic qualities of the democratic regime itself (Fisahn, 2009; Buck, 2011). Employing various TM methods in an integrated manner on large amounts of news articles from public media this study strives for revealing how democratic demarcation was performed in Germany over the past six decades.

1.3.2. Data Set

The study is conducted on a data set consisting of newspaper articles of two German premium newspapers – the weekly newspaper *Die Zeit* and the daily newspaper *Frankfurter Allgemeine Zeitung (FAZ)*. The *Die Zeit* collection comprises of the complete (retro-)digitized archive of the publication from its foundation in 1946 up to 2011. But, as this study is concerned with the time frame of the FRG founded on May 23rd 1949, I skip all articles published before 1950. The FAZ collection comprises of a representative sample of all articles published between 1959 and 2011.[11] The FAZ sample set was drawn from the

[11]The newspaper data was obtained directly from the publishers to be used in the ePol-project (see Section 1.2). The publishers delivered Extensible Markup Language (XML) files which contained raw texts as well as meta data for

Table 1.2.: Data set for the example study on democratic demarcation.

Publication	Time period	Issues	Articles	Size
Die Zeit	1950–2011	3,398	384,479	4.5 GB
FAZ	1959–2011	15,318	200,398	1.1 GB

complete data set of all articles published during the aforementioned time period by the following procedure:

1. select all articles of category "Meinung" (op-ed commentaries) published in the sections "Politik" (politics), "Wirtschaft" (economics) and "Feuilleton" (feature) and put them into the sample set; then
2. select all articles published in the sections "Politik", "Wirtschaft" and "Feuilleton"
   - which do not belong to the categories "Meinung" or "Rezension" (review),
   - order them by date, and
   - put every twelfth article of this ordered list into the sample set.

The strategy applied to the FAZ data selects about 15 percent of all articles published in the three newspaper sections taken into account. It guarantees that there are only sections included in the sample set which are considered as relevant, and that there are many articles expressing opinions and political positions. Furthermore, it also ensures that the distribution of selected articles over time is directly proportional to the distribution of articles in the base population. Consequently, distributions of language use in the sample can be regarded as representative for all FAZ articles in the given sections over the entire study period.

each article. Meta data comprises of publishing date, headline, subheading, paragraphs, page number, section and in some cases author names.

1.4. Contributions and Structure of the Study

Computer algorithms of textual analysis do not understand texts in a way humans do. Instead they model meaning by retrieving patterns, counting of events and computation of latent variables indicating certain aspects of semantics. The better these patterns overlap with categories of interest expressed by human analysts, the more useful they are to support conventional QDA procedures. Thus, to exploit benefits from TM in the light of requirements from the social science perspective, there is a demand for

1. conceptual integration of consciously selected methods to accomplish analysis specific research goals,
2. systematic adaptation, optimization and evaluation of workflows and algorithms, and
3. methodological reflections with respect to debates on empirical social research.

On the way to satisfy these demands, this introduction has already shortly addressed the interdisciplinary background concerning the *digitalization* of the humanities and its challenges and opportunities for the social sciences. In Chapter 2, methodological aspects regarding qualitative and quantitative research paradigms are introduced to sketch the present state of CATA together with new opportunities for content analysis. In Section 2.2 of this chapter technological foundations of the application of text mining are introduced briefly. Specifically, it covers aspects of representation of semantics in computational text analysis and introduces approaches of (pre-)processing of textual data useful for QDA. Section 2.3 introduces exemplary applications in social science studies. Beyond that, it suggests a new typology of these approaches regarding their notion of context information. This aims to clarify why nowadays TM procedures may be much more compatible with manual QDA methods than earlier approaches such as computer assisted keyword counts dating back to the 1960s have been.

Chapter 3 introduces an integrated workflow of specifically adapted text mining procedures to support conventional qualitative data analysis. It makes a suggestion for a concrete analysis process chain to extract information from a large collection of texts relevant for a specific social science research question. Several technologies are adapted and combined to approach three distinctive goals:

1. *Retrieval of relevant documents:* QDA analysts usually are faced with the challenge to identify document sets from large base populations relevant for rather abstract research questions which cannot be described by single keywords alone. Section 3.1 introduces an Information Retrieval (IR) approach for this demand.

2. *Inductive exploration of collections:* Retrieved collections of (potentially) relevant documents are still by far too large to be read closely. Hence, Section 3.2 provides exploratory tools which are needed to extract meaningful structures for 'distant reading' and good (representative) examples of semantic units for qualitative checks to fruitfully integrate micro- and macro-perspectives on the research subject.

3. *(Semi-)automatic coding:* For QDA categories of content usually are assigned manually to documents or parts of documents. Supervised classification in an active learning scenario introduced in Section 3.3 allows for algorithmic classification of large collections to validly measure category proportions and trends. It especially deals with the considerably hard conditions for machine learning in QDA scenarios.

Technologies used in this workflow are optimized and, if necessary, developed further with respect to requirements from the social science perspective. Among other things, applied procedures are

- key term extraction for dictionary creation,
- document retrieval for selection of sub-corpora,
- thematic and temporal clustering via topic models,

- co-occurrence analysis enriched with sentiment, controversy and keyness measures, and
- (semi-)supervised classification for trend analysis

to extract information from large collections of qualitative data and quantify identified semantic structures. A comprehensive analysis on the basis of such a process chain is introduced in Chapter 4. In an exemplary study, the public discourse on *democratic demarcation* in Germany is investigated by mining through sixty years of newspaper data. Roughly summarized, it tries to answer the question which political or societal ideas or groups have been considered a threat for democracy in a way that the application of non-democratic countermeasures was considered as a legitimate act. Chapter 5 draws conclusions on the results of the example study with respect to methodological questions. Insights based on requirements, implementation and application of the exemplary analysis workflow are generalized to a methodological framework to support QDA by employing various types of TM methods. The proposed V-TM framework covers research design recommendations together with evaluation requirements on hierarchical abstraction levels considering technical, methodical and epistemological aspects. Finally, Chapter 6 gives a summary of this interdisciplinary endeavor.

2. Computer-Assisted Text Analysis in the Social Sciences

Despite there is a long tradition of Computer Assisted Text Analysis (CATA) in social sciences, it followed a rather parallel development to QDA. Only a few years ago, realization of TM potentials for QDA started to emerge slowly. In this chapter, I reflect on the debate of the use of software in qualitative social science research together with approaches of text analysis from the NLP perspective. For this, I shortly elaborate on the quality versus quantity divide in social science methods of text analysis (2.1). Subsequently, perspectives and technologies of text analysis from NLP perspective are introduced briefly (2.2). Finally, I suggest a typology of computer-assisted text analysis approaches utilized in social science based on the notion of context underlying the analysis methods (2.3). This typology helps to understand why developments of qualitative and quantitative CATA have been characterized by mutual neglect for a long time, but recently opened perspectives for integration of both research paradigms—a progress mainly achieved through advancements in Machine Learning (ML) for text. Along with the typology descriptions example studies utilizing different kinds of CATA approaches are given to introduce on related work to this study.

2.1. Text as Data between Quality and Quantity

When analyzing text, social scientists strive for inference on social reality. In contrast to linguists who mainly focus on description of language regularities itself, empirical language use for sociologists or political scientists is more like a window through which they try to reconstruct the ways speaking actors perceive themselves and the world around them. Systematic reconstruction of the interplay between language and actors' perception of the world contributes to much deeper understanding of social phenomena than purely quantitative methods of empirical social research, e.g. survey studies, could deliver. Consequently, methodical debates on empirical social research distinguish between reconstructivist and hypothesis testing approaches (Bohnsack, 2010, p. 10). While research approaches of hypothesis testing aim for intersubjectively reliable knowledge production by relying on a quantitative, statistical perspective, reconstructivist approaches share a complicated relationship with quantification. As already mentioned in the introduction, it is a puzzling question why social science, although having put strong emphasis on analyzing textual data for decades, remained skeptical for so long about computer-assisted approaches to analyze large quantities of text. The answer in my opinion is two-fold, comprising a methodological and a technical aspect. The methodological aspect is reflected in the following, while I highlight on the technical obstacles in Section 2.3.

In the German as well as in the Anglo-Saxon social research community a deep divide between quantitative and qualitative oriented methods of empirical research has evolved during the last century and is still prominent. This divide can be traced back to several roots, for example the Weberian differentiation between explaining versus understanding as main objectives of scientific activity or the conflict between positivist versus post-positivist research paradigms. Following a positivist epistemological conceptualization of the world, media scientists up to the mid 20th century perceived qualitative data only as a sequence of symbols, which could be observed and processed as unambiguous analysis units by non-skilled human coders or computers to produce scientific knowledge. Analyses were run on a large numbers of cases, but tended to oversimplify complex societal procedures by application of fixed (deductive) categories. As a counter model, during the 1970s, the post-positivist paradigm led to the emergence of several qualitative text analysis methodologies seeking to generate an in-depth comprehension of a rather small number

Table 2.1.: Examples for two kinds of software products supporting text analysis for linguistic and social research.

Data management	Data processing
Atlas.ti, MAXQDA, QDA-Miner, NVivo, QCAmap, CATMA, LibreQDA	MAXDictio, WordStat (QDAMiner), WordSmith, Alceste, T-LAB, Lexico3, IRaMuteQ, Leipzig Corpus Miner

of cases. Knowledge production from text was done by intense close reading and interpretation of trained human analysts in more or less systematic ways.

Computer software has been utilized for both paradigms of text analysis, but of course, provided very distinct functions for the analysis process. Analogous to the qualitative-quantitative divide, two tasks for Computer Assisted Text Analysis can be distinguished:

- data management, and
- data processing.

Table 2.1 illustrates examples of software packages common in social science for qualitative and quantitative text analysis.

Data processing of large document sets for the purpose of quantitative content analysis framed the early perception of software usage for text analysis from the 1960s onward. For a long time, using computers for QDA appeared somehow as retrogression to protagonists of truly qualitative approaches, especially because of their awareness of the history of flawed quantitative content analysis. Software for *data management* to support qualitative analysts by annotating parts of text with category codes has been accepted only gradually since the late 1980s. On the one hand, a misunderstanding was widespread that such programs, also referred to as Computer Assisted Qualitative Data Analysis (CAQDA), should be used to analyze text, like SPSS is used to analyze numerical data (Kelle, 2011, p. 30). Qualitative researchers intended to avoid a reductionist positivist epistemology, which they associated with such methods. On the other hand, it was not seen as advantageous to increase the number of cases in qualitative research designs by using computer software. To generate insight into their subject matter, researchers should not concentrate on as many cases as possible, but on as most distinct cases as possible. From that point of view, using software bears the risk of exchanging creativity and opportunities of serendipity for mechanical processing of some code plans on large document collections (Kuckartz, 2007, p. 28). Fortunately, the overall dispute for and against software use in qualitative research nowadays is more or less settled. Advantages of CAQDA for data management are widely accepted throughout the research community. But there is still a lively debate on how software influences the research process—for example through its predetermination of knowledge entities like code hierarchies or linkage possibilities, and under which circumstances quantification may be applied to coding results.

To overcome shortcomings of both, the qualitative and the quantitative research paradigm, novel 'mixed method' designs are gradually introduced in QDA. Although the methodological perspectives of quantitative content analysis and qualitative methods are almost diametrically opposed, application of CATA may be fruitful not only as a tool for exploration and heuristics. Functions to evaluate quantitative aspects of empirical textual data (such as the extension MAXDictio for the software MAXQDA), have been integrated in all recent versions of the leading QDA software packages. Nevertheless, studies on the usage of CAQDA indicate that qualitative researchers usually confine themselves to the basic features (Kuckartz, 2007, p. 28). Users are reluctant to naively mixing qualitative and quantitative methodological standards of both paradigms—for example, not to draw general conclusions from the distribution of codes annotated in a handful of interviews, if the interviewees have not been selected by representative criteria (Schönfelder, 2011, § 15). Quality criteria well established for quantitative (survey) studies like validity, reliability and objectivity do not translate well for the manifold approaches of qualitative research. The ongoing debate on quality of qualitative research generally concludes that those criteria have to be reformulated differently. Possible aspects are a systematic method design, traceability of the research process, documentation of intermediate results, permanent self reflection and triangulation (Flick, 2007). Nonetheless, critics of qualitative research often see these rather 'soft' criteria as a shortcoming of QDA compared to what they conceive as 'hard science' based on knowledge represented by numeric values and significance measures.

Proponents of 'mixed methods' do not consider both paradigms as being contradictory. Instead, they stress advantages of integration of both perspectives. Udo Kuckartz states: "Concerning the analysis of qualitative data, techniques of computer-assisted quantitative content analysis are up to now widely ignored" (2010, p. 219; translation GW). His perspective suggests that qualitative and quantitative approaches of text analysis should not be perceived as competing, but as complementing techniques. They enable us to answer different questions on the same subject matter. While a qualitative view may help us to understand which categories of interest in the data exist and how they are constructed, quantitative analysis may tell us something about the relevance, variety and development of those categories. I fully agree with Kuckartz advertising the advantages a quantitative perspective on text may contribute to an understanding—especially to integrate micro studies on text with a macro perspective.

In contrast to the early days of computer-assisted text analysis which spawned the qualitative-quantitative divide, in the last decades computer-linguistics and NLP have made significant progress incorporating linguistic knowledge and context information into its analysis routines, thereby overcoming the limitations of simple "term based analysis functions" (ibid., p. 218). Two recent developments of computer-assisted text analysis may severely change the circumstances which in the past have had been serious obstacles to a fruitful integration of qualitative and quantitative QDA. Firstly, the availability and processability of full-text archives enables researchers to generate insight from quantified qualitative analysis results through comparison of different sub populations. A complex research design as suggested in this study is able to properly combine methodological standards of both paradigms. Instead of a potentially biased manual selection of a small sample ($n < 100$) from the population of all documents, a statistical representative subset ($n \approx 1,000$) may be drawn, or even the full corpus ($n >> 100,000$) may be analyzed. Secondly, the epistemological gap between how qualitative researchers perceive their object of research compared to what computer algorithms are able to identify is constantly narrowing. The key factor here is the algorithmic extraction of *meaning*, which is approached by the inclusion of different levels of *context* into a complex analysis workflow integrating systematically several TM applications of distinct types. How meaning is extracted in NLP will be introduced in the next section. Then, I present in detail the argument why modern TM applications contribute to bridge the seemingly invincible qualitative-quantitative divide.

2.2. Text as Data for Natural Language Processing

For NLP, text as data can be encoded in different ways with respect to the intended algorithmic analysis. These representations model semantics distinctively to allow for the extraction of meaning (2.2.1). Moreover, textual data has to be preprocessed taking linguistic knowledge into account (2.2.2), before it can be utilized as input for TM applications extracting valuable knowledge structures for QDA (2.2.3).

2.2.1. Modeling Semantics

If computational methods should be applied for QDA, models of semantics of text are necessary to bridge the gap between research interests and algorithmic identification of structures in textual data. Turney and Pantel (2010, p. 141) refer to semantics as "in a general sense [...] the meaning of a word, a phrase, a sentence, or any text in human language, and the study of such meaning". Although there was some impressing progress in the field of artificial intelligence and ML in recent decades, computers still lack of intelligence comparable to humans regarding learning, comprehension and autonomous problem solving abilities. In contrast, computers are superior to human abilities when it comes to identify structures in large data sets systematically. Consequently, to utilize computational powers for NLP we need to link computational processing capabilities with analysis requirements of human users. In NLP, three types of semantic representations may be distinguished:

1. patterns of character strings,
2. logical rule sets of entity relations, and
3. distributional semantics.

Text in computational environments generally is represented by *character strings* as primary data format, i.e., sequences of characters from a fixed set which represent meaningful symbols, e.g., letters of an alphabet. The simplest model to process meaning is to look for fixed, predefined patterns in these character sequences. For instance, we may define the character sequence *United States* occurring in a text document as representation of the entity 'country United States of America'. By extending this single sequence to a set of character strings, e.g. "United States", "Germany", "Ghana", "Israel", ..., we may define a representation of references to the general entity 'country'. Such lists of character sequences representing meaningful concepts, also called 'dictionaries', have a long tradition in communication science (Stone, 1996). They can be employed as representations of meaningful concepts to be measured in large text collections. By using regular expressions[1] and elaborated dictionaries it is possible to model very complex concepts.[2] In practice, however, success of this

[1] Regular expressions are a formal language to fulfill 'search and replace' operations. With a special syntax complex search patterns can be formulated to identify matching parts in a target text.

[2] The pattern `\d+ (protester|people|person)[\w\s]*(injured|hurt|wounded)`, for example, would match text snippets containing a number (`\d+`) followed by mentioning of a group together with verbs indicating injury in any permutation where only word characters or spaces are located between them (`[\w\s]*`).

approach still depends on the skill and experience of the researcher who creates such linguistic patterns. In many cases linguistic expressions of interest for a certain research question follow rather fixed patterns, i.e. repeatedly observable character strings. Hence, this rather simple approach of string or regular expression matching can already be of high value for QDA targeted to manifest content.

A much more ambitious approach to process semantics is the employment of *logic frameworks*, e.g., predicate logic or first-order logic, to model relations between units represented by linguistic patterns. Instead of just searching for patterns as representatives for meaning in large quantities of text, these approaches strive for inference of 'new' knowledge not explicitly contained in the data basis. New knowledge is to be derived deductively from an ontology, i.e., a knowledge base comprising of variables as representatives of extracted linguistic units and well-formed formulas. Variables may be formally combined by functions, logical connectives and quantifiers that allow for reasoning in the ontology defined. For example, the set of two rules 1) $car(b) \wedge red(b)$, 2) $\forall x(car(x) \rightarrow vehicle(x))$ would allow to query for the red vehicle b, although the knowledge base only contains explicit information about the red car b (rule 1), because the second rule states that all cars are vehicles. Setting up a formal set of rules and connections of units in a complete and coherent way, however, is a time consuming and complex endeavor. Quality and level of granularity of such knowledge bases are insufficient for the most practical applications. Nevertheless, there are many technologies and standards such as Web Ontology Language (OWL) and Resource Description Framework (RDF) to represent such semantics with the objective to further develop the internet to a 'semantic web'. Although approaches employing logic frameworks definitely model semantics closer to human intelligence, their applicability for QDA on large data sets is rather limited so far. Not only that obtaining knowledge bases from natural language text is a very complex task. Beyond manifest expressions content analytic studies are also interested in latent meaning. Modeling latent semantics by formal logic frameworks is a very tricky task, so far not solved for NLP applications in a satisfying manner.

Most promising for QDA are distributional approaches to process semantics because they are able to cover both, manifest and latent aspects of meaning. *Distributional semantics* is based on the assumption that statistical patterns of human word usage reveal what people mean, and “words that occur in similar contexts tend to have similar meanings” (Turney and Pantel, 2010). Foundations for the idea that meaning is a product of contextual word usage have been established already in the early 20th century by emerging structural linguistics (Saussure, 2001; Harris, 1954; Firth, 1957). To employ statistical methods and data mining to language, textual data needs to be transformed into numerical representations. Text no longer is comprehended as a sequence of character strings, instead character strings are chopped into lexical units and transformed into a numerical vector. The Vector Space Model (VSM), introduced for IR (Salton et al., 1975) as for many other NLP applications, encodes counts of occurrences of single terms in documents (or other context units, e.g., sentences) in vectors of the length of the entire vocabulary V of a modeled collection. If there are $M = |V|$ different word types in a collection of N documents, then the counts of the M word types in each of the documents leads to N vectors which can be combined into a $N \times M$ matrix, a so-called Document-Term-Matrix (DTM). Such a matrix can be weighted, filtered and manipulated in multiple ways to prepare it as an input object to many NLP applications such as extraction of meaningful terms per document, inference of topics or classification into categories. We can also see that this approach follows the ‘bag of words’ assumption which claims that frequencies of terms in a document mainly indicate its meaning; order of terms in contrast is less important and can be disregarded. This is certainly not true for most human real world communication, but works surprisingly well for many NLP applications.[3]

[3]The complete loss of information on word order can be mitigated by observing n-grams, i.e. concatenated ongoing sequences of n terms instead of single terms while creating a DTM.

2.2.2. Linguistic Preprocessing

Analyzing text computationally in the sense of distributional semantics requires the transformation of documents, i.e. sequences of character strings, into numerical data suitable for quantifying evaluation, statistical inference or modeling. Usually, for such a transformation documents need to be separated into single lexical units, which then are counted. Depending on the application, the analysis unit for counts may be altered from documents to paragraphs or single sentences to narrow down certain contexts, or document sets for aggregating information on higher discursive levels. After definition of the analysis unit and its corresponding data separation, e.g. detecting sentence boundaries in documents, single lexical units, also known as *tokens*, need to be identified. This process, called 'tokenization', separates all distinct word forms present in the entire text corpus. Such distinct word forms are called *types*. Again, counts of types for every analysis unit can be encoded and stored in a vector—collections in a DTM respectively.

The way in which text is tokenized mainly influences posterior analysis steps as it defines the atomic representatives of semantics. Tokens might be single terms, punctuation marks, multi-word units, or concatenations of n tokens, so called n-grams encoding different aspects of semantics numerically. Computer linguistics comprises of a variety of procedures to preprocess textual data before encoding it in a DTM. After initial encoding, the DTM may be further preprocessed mathematically, e.g. to weight terms by their contribution to document meaning. Linguistic and mathematical preprocessing of the DTM prepare subsequent TM analysis. The following list briefly introduces the most common preprocessing steps:

- Sentence segmentation: For certain TM applications, single sentences need to be identified in documents. The simplest approach would be to separate by locating punctuation marks or full stops. However, this produces false separations in certain cases, e.g. abbreviations or date formats. More sophisticated approaches utilize probabilistic models to determine whether punctuation marks indicate ends of sentences by observing their context (Reynar and Ratnaparkhi, 1997).

- Tokenization: Separation of text into single tokens can be achieved in many languages simply by separating at white space characters. However, this base line approach misses separation of punctuation marks from single terms or does not cover recognition of Multi Word Units (MWUs). Again, more sophisticated approaches utilize probabilistic models trained on manually tokenized data to decide on boundaries of lexical units more accurately.
- Cleaning: For specific use cases, not all identified types of lexical units contribute to the desired level of meaning. For example, stop words such as articles or pronouns often do not cover relevant aspects of meaning in a 'distant reading' perspective. The same can be valid for punctuation marks or numbers in the text. If useful, such types of lexical units can be omitted to reduce the amount of data and concentrate on the most meaningful language aspects for subsequent analysis.
- Unification: Lexical units occur in different ways of spelling and syntactical forms. Variants of the same noun may occur in singular, plural or different cases, verbs may be inflected. Unification procedures reduce such forms to a single basic form, to treat occurrences of variances in the data as identical event for all further applications. Common forms of unification are reduction of characters to lowercase, stemming and lemmatization. For stemming word stems of terms are guessed by cutting suffixes from tokens according to a language specific rule set. For lemmatization, large language specific lists which contain assignments of inflected forms to corresponding dictionary forms are utilized to look up and replace any occurrence of a token by its lemma.
- Part of Speech (POS): In POS-tagging any token in a sequence of tokens, e.g. in a sentence, is labeled with a part of speech label, e.g. NN for nouns, ADJ for adjectives, VA for auxiliary verb (Heyer

et al., 2006, p. 126). POS labels may be utilized as filter during preprocessing, e.g. to just concentrate on nouns for certain analysis. They also can be helpful for disambiguation of homonyms (e.g. *can_VA* versus *can_NN*), hence, contributing to capture desired semantics more accurately.

- Pruning: Characteristics of term distributions in natural language can be formally described by Zipf's law (Heyer et al., 2006, p. 87). From Zipf's law it can be inferred that most frequent types do not contribute much to specific constitution of meaning in a text, and that roughly half of the types only occur once in the entire corpus. Hence, pruning the most and least frequent terms for DTM generation while preprocessing helps to keep data objects manageable in size and concentrate on the most meaningful lexical units. Pruning can be done in absolute manner (omitting terms occurring more or less than n times in the corpus) or relative manner (omitting terms occurring in more or less than p percent of documents of the corpus).

These procedures of preprocessing distinctively shape the set of types to be counted to prepare a DTM by identifying, transforming and filtering lexical units with respect to linguistic knowledge. There is no ideal or correct configuration of such a preprocessing chain. Instead, each application demands its own parameter settings to yield optimal results. For example, in QDA scenarios stemming might contribute to performance gains in a classification task through extensive feature unification while it produces artificial homonymy and unpleasant term stubs in co-occurrence analysis. Often it is necessary to experiment with different parameters for preprocessing before deciding which results fit best to study requirements.

2.2.3. Text Mining Applications

Once a document collection is encoded in a numerical DTM format, it can be utilized as input for various TM applications. Regarding TM applications, I distinguish in lexicometric and Machine Learning approaches. Lexicometric approaches calculate statistics on closed data sets, rank observed events and highlight on those where observations deviate from expectations. ML approaches 'learn' data regularities by inferring discriminative or generative probabilistic models. Such models can be applied to previously unseen data to identify structures or patterns. Within this study, I refer to both, lexicometric and ML applications, as Text Mining applications.

Lexicometrics

Lexicometric analysis on digital text has been utilized since the early beginning of computational text processing and is widely used in corpus linguistics. Over the decades the method toolbox has been extended from simple frequency counts to more elaborated statistical methods:

- *Frequency analysis:* In this application observations of events, e.g. specific terms or concepts occurring in documents, are counted and counts are compared across dimensions, e.g. time. Observing term frequencies in a longitudinal view over several decades may reveal peaks and dips in term usage, and corresponding concepts. Events for observation can be defined in distinguished ways, e.g. as raw term frequencies or as document frequencies where multiple occurrences of one term in the same document are counted only once. Beyond just single terms, more meaningful concepts can be counted by defining sets of terms as events which either must occur together in a specific context unit, or are treated as a list of synonyms. Utilization of such lists is also called dictionary analysis (Stone et al., 1966).
- *Key term extraction:* This application identifies important terms in documents or entire collections by applying statistical measures (Archer, 2008). The established method of difference analysis compares term frequencies in a target text (or an entire collection) to frequencies in a reference corpus, e.g. a collection of general texts of

the same language without a bias to any topic. Deviations between expectations based on the comparison text and observations in the target text are evaluated by a statistical test resulting in lists of terms ranked by 'keyness'. Terms of such lists can be displayed in Key Word in Context (KWIC) views which allow for quick qualitative assessment of usage contexts of terms in a collection (Luhn, 1960).

- *Co-occurrence analysis:* For co-occurrence analysis[4], joint occurrence of events in a well defined context unit is observed and evaluated by a statistical test (Bordag, 2008; Büchler, 2008). For any word type it reveals a ranked list of other words which co-occur with it, e.g. in a sentence or as its left / right neighbor, more often than expected under the assumption of independence. In accordance with structuralist linguistic theory, this reveals semantic fields of syntagmatically related terms. Comparing and ranking such semantic fields by similarity further may reveal paradigmatically related terms, i.e. words occurring in similar contexts (Heyer et al., 2006, p. 19ff).
- *Dimension reduction:* The idea of co-occurrence of two terms can be extended to observation of co-occurrence of multiple terms to infer on latent structures. For this, various methods of dimension reduction from data mining are also applicable to DTMs extracted from text collections. In Principal Component Analysis (PCA), Multi Dimensional Scaling (MDS) or Correspondence Analysis continuous or categorical data incorporated in a DTM can be reduced to its main components or projected into a two-dimensional space. The reduced two dimensions of the vocabulary, for example, may be utilized to visualize semantic proximity of terms. A higher number of reduced dimensions may be utilized to infer on similarity of documents in a latent semantic space. As Latent Semantic Analysis (LSA), dimension reduction has also been utilized in Information Retrieval (Deerwester et al., 1990).

[4]In linguistic contexts it is also referred to as collocation analysis.

Machine learning

While lexicometric approaches are widely used in corpus linguistics, the exploration of ML applications for QDA in social science is just at its beginning. Tom Mitchell formally defines ML as follows: "A computer program is said to learn from experience E with respect to some class of tasks T and performance measure P, if its performance at tasks in T, as measured by P, improves with experience E" (1997, p. 2). While lexicometric measures lack of the 'learning' property through ongoing 'experience' of data observation, ML incorporates such experience in model instances. Model parameters can be updated with new units of observed data which make the concept interesting especially for large data sets and streaming data. For analyzing textual data, several kinds of ML applications have been developed.

Analogue to data mining, we can distinguish *unsupervised* from *supervised* methods for data analysis. Unsupervised, data-driven approaches identify previously unknown patterns and structures emerging from the data itself. They provide a clustering of data points satisfying certain similarity criteria (e.g. similarity of documents based on word usage, or similarity of terms based on their contexts). Supervised classification methods in contrast utilize document external knowledge, e.g. information on class membership of a document, to model the association between that external observation and features of the document. This allows to assign category labels to new, unknown documents (or document fragments), analogously to manual coding in a content analysis procedure. These methods resemble research paradigms in data analysis for social sciences. While the unsupervised methods help to explore structures in large amounts of unknown data, thus supporting *inductive* research approaches of text analysis, supervised methods may take into account external, theory-led knowledge to realize *deductive* research workflows.

Useful Text Mining applications for QDA following the paradigm of *unsupervised learning* are:

- *Document clustering:* For cluster analysis, context units such as sentences or documents have to be grouped according to similarity of their content, e.g. based on common term usage (Heyer et al., 2006, p. 195ff). Clusters should have the property of optimal similarity of documents within the cluster and maximum difference of documents between clusters. Variants exist for strict partitioning versus hierarchical or overlapping (soft) clustering. For some algorithms the number of clusters for partitioning has to be given as external parameter, some try to identify an optimal number of clusters on their own. With the help of clustering analysts can separate large collections into manageable sub-collections, explore collections by semantic coherence and concentrate on the most meaningful ones.

- *Topic Models:* refer to a set of "algorithms for discovering the main themes that pervade a large and otherwise unstructured collection of documents [...] topic models can organize the collection according to the discovered themes" (Blei, 2012, p. 77). Since the initial Latent Dirichlet Allocation (LDA) model developed by Blei et al. (2003) a variety of more complex topic models has been introduced (Blei and Lafferty, 2006; Mcauliffe and Blei, 2008; Grimmer, 2010; Mimno et al., 2011). All these models assume a generative process of text production governed by a probability distribution of topics within a document and a probability distribution of terms for each topic. Via a complex inference mechanism on the observed words per document in a collection, they infer on semantic coherent terms representing topics, and proportions of topics contained in each document as latent variables. In analogy to LSA, "LDA can also be seen as a type of principal component analysis for discrete data" (Blei, 2012, p. 80). Among other things, topic models provide two valuable matrices as a result of the inference process:
  - matrix $\boldsymbol{\beta}$ of the dimensions $|V| \times K$ containing a posterior probability distribution over the entire vocabulary V for each of the K modeled topics,
  - matrix $\boldsymbol{\theta}$ of the dimensions $N \times K$ containing a posterior probability distribution over all K topics for each of the N documents in a collection.

With these results analysts can reveal thematic structures, filter large document collections or observe changes in topic proportions over time. Consequently, topic models can be seen as a kind of soft or fuzzy clustering giving the likelihood of a document belonging to a certain thematic cluster.

- *Dimensional Scaling:* Especially for political science analysis, dimensional scaling strives for assigning a measurement to documents of a collection representing a relative position on a one-dimensional scale (Benoit and Laver, 2012). For thematically coherent collections, e.g. parliamentary speeches on a single draft bill or party manifestos, this measurement shall represent political position between a left and a right pole of the spectrum. Based on word usage, centrist or outer political positions of single speeches, parliamentarians or parties may be determined.

Useful Text Mining applications for QDA following the paradigm of *supervised learning* are:

- *Classification:* While clustering assigns any unit of analysis to a group of other units based on the emergent structure from within the data itself, supervised classification relies on external information to group the units. This external knowledge usually is a set of categories (classes) and assignments of these categories to a set of training data entities, e.g., documents. Based on this knowledge supervised ML algorithms can learn to predict which category a new unobserved document belongs to (Sebastiani, 2002). Again, instead of documents also paragraphs, sentences or terms may be useful context units for classification. For QDA, e.g. sentence classification can be a worthwhile extension to manual content analysis in which human coders assign category labels to texts.
- *Named Entity Recognition / information extraction:* This application strives for the identification of person names, organizations or locations in a document. Usually, it is realized by probabilistic sequence classification determining the most probable category for

any token in a sentence (Finkel et al., 2005). For QDA, Named Entity Recognition (NER) is useful to identify actors or places associated with any other information identified in a text, e.g. certain vocabulary use, an activity or a quote. The method of sequence classification surely is not restricted to named entities. It may be applied to any other information occurring in a contextual sequence in a structural way, e.g. currency amounts or dates.

- *Sentiment Analysis:* A specific application for supervised classification is sentiment analysis, the identification of subjective information or attitudes in texts (Pang and Lee, 2008). It may be realized as a ML classification task assigning either a positive, neutral, or negative class label to a document. Another wide-spread approach is the use of so-called sentiment lexicons or sentiment dictionaries which are basically word lists with additionally assigned sentiment weights on a positive–negative scale (Remus et al., 2010).

While such applications represent deeply studied problems in NLP and computer linguistics, only few studies exist so far which apply such techniques for social science. Moreover, little knowledge exists on their systematic and optimal integration for complex analysis workflows.

2.3. Types of Computational Qualitative Data Analysis

So far, the TM applications briefly introduced above have been utilized for social science purposes with varying degrees of success and in a rather isolated manner. The method debate in social science tries to identify different types of their usage by constructing method typologies. In the literature on Computer Assisted Text Analysis (CATA), several typologies of software use to support QDA can be found. The aim of this exercise usually is to draw clear distinctions between capabilities and purposes of software technologies and to give guidance for possible research designs. By the very nature of the matter, it is obvious that these typologies have short half-life periods due to the ongoing technological progress. A very first differentiation of CATA dates back to the *Annenberg Conference on Content Analysis* in the late 1960s. There Content Analysis (CA) methods were divided into exploration of term frequencies and concordances without theoretical guidance on the one hand, and hypothesis guided categorizations with dictionaries on the other hand (Stone, 1997). More fine grained, a famous text book on Content Analysis (CA) by Krippendorff suggests the differentiation into three types: 1. retrieval functions for character strings on raw text, 2. Computational Content Analysis (CCA) with dictionaries and 3. Computer Assisted Qualitative Data Analysis (CAQDA) for data management supporting purely manual analysis. Although published recently in its third edition (2013), it largely ignores latest developments of Machine Learning (ML). The typology from Lowe (2003) additionally incorporates computer-linguistic knowledge by covering aspects of linguistics and distributional semantics. Algorithmic capabilities are differentiated into 1. dictionary based CCA, 2. parsing approaches, and 3. contextual similarity measures. Scharkow (2012, p. 61) proposes the first typology including ML distinctively. He distinguishes three dimensions of computational text analysis: 1. unsupervised vs. supervised approaches. Within the supervised approaches he distinguishes 2. statistical vs. linguistic, and 3. deductive vs. inductive approaches. Unquestionably, this typology covers important characteristics of CATA approaches used for QDA. Yet, the assignments of single techniques to the introduced categories of his typology is not convincing in all cases. For example, he categorizes supervised text classification supporting manual CA as inductive approach (p. 89) although it is described as a process of subsuming contents into previously defined content categories. On the other hand, full-text search is categorized as deductive approach (p. 81), although it remains unclear to which extent document retrieval contributes to a deductive research design as isolated technique. Last but not least, the rather arbitrary distinction between statistical and linguistic approaches does not cover the fact that most TM applications combine aspects of both, for example in linguistic preprocessing and probabilistic modeling of content.

The difficulty in constructing a convincing typology for CATA is that the technical perspective and the applied social science perspective are intermingling. While the distinctions *supervised* versus *unsupervised* as well as *statistical* versus *linguistic* relate to technical aspects of NLP algorithms, the distinction *inductive* versus *deductive* captures methodological aspects. Although there might be some overlapping of category dimensions from both disciplines, they do not give guidance for clear separation.[5] To capture important characteristics of recent CATA approaches from an application perspective of social science research, I suggest another typology along two dimensions: complexity of meaning and textual quantity. As displayed in Figure 2.1, I distinguish between four types of CATA:

1. frequency observations of manifest expressions (fixed character strings) for CCA in large collections,

2. data management tools supporting manual coding of local contexts within single documents (CAQDA),

3. lexicometric approaches capturing aspects of (latent) meaning on a collection level, and, finally,

4. machine learning approaches incorporating characteristics of all three aforementioned types.

The horizontal dimension of this typology highlights the complexity of meaning extraction capabilities. It visualizes the progress that has been made from observation of document surfaces by simple word counts in CCA to more complex lexicometric approaches seeking to identify meaningful structures in document collections. Manually

[5] There are conceptual parallels between the pairs unsupervised/inductive and supervised/deductive with respect to usage of prior knowledge for structure identification. Nevertheless, NER, for instance, is technically realized as a supervised ML approach based on previously annotated training data. The results, however, lists of named entities associated to certain context units, can be employed methodologically in an exploratory step of QDA as well as for deductive hypothesis testing.

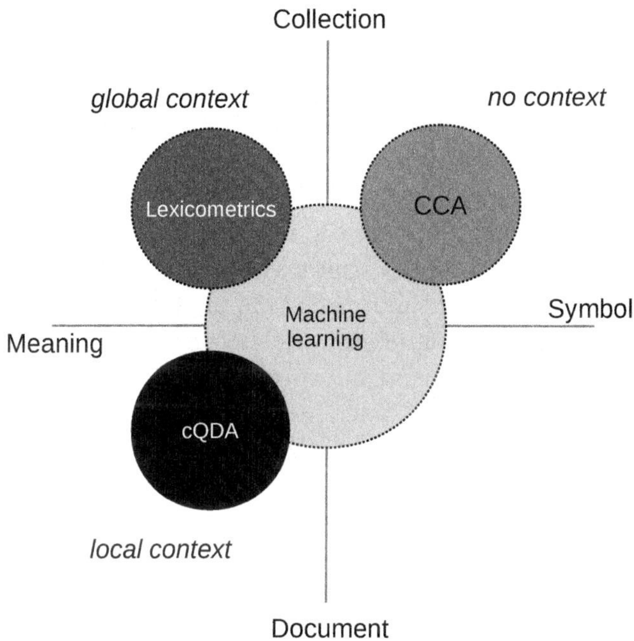

Figure 2.1.: Two-dimensional typology of analysis software for text.

conducted CAQDA, of course, strives for inference of meaningful structures identified in close reading processes on the document level. On the quantitative dimension CAQDA operates on small corpora manually manageable, while CCA and lexicometrics extract their structures from large collections. Machine learning approaches encompass an interesting intermediate position along these two dimensions as they operate on single documents and large collections at the same time by modeling single document contents with respect to collection-wide observations. This characteristic can be described further by the character of 'context' incorporated into the analysis.

At the beginning of the quantitative–qualitative divide, Kracauer (1952) criticized the methodological neglect of substantial meaning in quantitative CA. Content analysis, especially its computer-assisted version, observed the occurrence of specific sets of terms within its analysis objects, but systematically ignored its contexts. To generate understanding out of the analysis objects in favor to gain new insights, counting words did not prove as adequate to satisfy more profound research interests. In this respect, upcoming methods of qualitative CA were not conceptualized to substitute its quantitative counterparts, but to provide a systematic method for scientific rule-based interpretation. One essential characteristic of these methods is the embedded inspection and interpretation of the material of analysis within its communication contexts (Mayring, 2010, p. 48). Thus, the systematic inclusion and interpretation of contexts in analysis procedures is essential to advance from superficial counts of character strings in text corpora to the extraction of meaning from text.

Since the linguistic turn took effect in social science (Bergmann, 1952), it became widely accepted that structures of meaning are never fully fixed or closed. Instead, they underlie a permanent evolvement through every speech act which leaves its traces within the communicative network of texts of a society. Hence, meaning can be inferred only through the joint observation of the differential relations of linguistic structures in actual language use. At the same time, it always stays preliminary knowledge (Teubert, 2006). For CATA this can be translated into the observation of networks of simple lexical or more complex linguistic units within digitalized speech. The underlying assumption is that structures of meaning evolve from the interplay of these units, measurable for example in large text collections. Luckily, identifying patterns in digital data is one major strength of computers.

However, not all types of approaches are able to capture context or patterns of language use alike. Boyd and Crawford (2012) even warn that big data is losing its meaning, if taken out of context. Hence, concentrating on this important aspect, all four distinguished types of CATA capture aspects of context in their own way with severe consequences for their utilization in QDA:

1. Early approaches of Computational Content Analysis (CCA) just observed character strings in digital text for frequency analysis,

while largely ignoring context at all. More complex definitions for event observation, e.g. occurrence of term x near to term y in a distance of d or less terms, may include simple context aspects.

2. CAQDA software for *manual coding* of carefully selected small document sets allows for comprehensive consideration of linguistic and situational contexts. Understanding of expressed meaning is achievable through cognitive abilities of the human coder who also includes text external knowledge for interpretation. Analysis primarily concentrates on deep understanding of single cases through investigation of their *local context.*

3. Lexicometric applications such as key term extraction, co-occurrence analysis or LSA allow for inductive *exploration* of statistically prominent patterns of language data. Instead of local contexts in single documents, they extract *global context* observable only through examination of an entire document collection.

4. Characteristics of context extracted via Machine Learning (ML), both supervised and unsupervised, reside in an interesting middle positions between the other three types. ML works on the basis of local context by observing textual events in single documents or smaller sequences (e.g. sentences). Through aggregation and joint observation of multiple text instances, knowledge conceivable only on the collection-level is learned and incorporated into model instances representing global context. At the same time, learned global knowledge again is applied on individual text instances, e.g. by assigning globally learned categories to documents.

Through consideration of context defined as surrounding language patterns of observed events, lexicometric as well as ML approaches are able to capture more complex semantics than CCA. Combined observation of linguistic units overcomes isolated counting of overt meanings in manifest expressions. Instead, it digs down into 'latent meaning' either represented as statistical co-occurrence significance measure relating an observed linguistic unit to multiple other ones, or as non-observable variables from statistical dimension reduction on observable variables. The special characteristics of ML approaches in the two-dimensional typology positioned between symbol observation and meaning extraction, as well as between document and collection level, makes it a perfect connective link to the other three CATA approaches. On the one hand, the visualization contributes to understanding why utilization of CCA and lexicometrics was spurned longtime in the QDA community, since they all operate on different levels of context and semantics. On the other hand, it helps to understand that with the advancement in ML for text, QDA is definitely confronted with a new technology bridging the gap between such formerly rather parallel developments of text analysis. ML models oscillate between local and global contexts on document and collection level to learn characteristics from individual analysis units, while also applying globally learned knowledge to them. Technically these algorithms comply with human cognitive procedures of generating textual understanding better than any prior approach.

In the following section, I will explain characteristics of these types in detail and give examples of social science studies applying such kinds of methods.

2.3.1. Computational Content Analysis

Quantitative approaches of content analysis first originated in media studies. As a classic deductive research design, CA aims at a data-reducing description of mass textual data by assigning categories on textual entities, such as newspaper articles, speeches, press releases etc. The set of categories, the code hierarchy, usually is developed by domain experts on the basis of pre-existing knowledge and utilized for hypothesis testing of assumptions on proportions or quantitative developments of code frequencies in the data. Categories may be assigned on several dimensions, like occasion of a topic (e.g. mentioning ethical, social or environmental standards in business reports), its share of an analyzed text (once mentioned, higher share or full article) or its valuation and intensity (e.g. overall/mainly pro, contra or neutral). Codebooks explain these categories in detail and give examples to enable trained coders to conduct the data collection of the study by hand. Following a rather nomothetic research paradigm, CA is described by Krippendorff as "a research technique for making replicable and valid inferences from texts [...] to the contexts of their use" (Krippendorff, 2013, p. 24). Replicability is to be achieved by determining highest possible inter- and intracoder-reliability—two metrics which calculate the matches of code assignments between several coders or the same coder in repeated coding processes.

Automatic CCA has to operationalize its categories in a different way. Already in 1955, a big conference on CA marked two main trends in the evolvement of the method: 1. the shift from analysis of contents to broader contexts and conditions of communication which led to more qualitative CA, and 2. counting of symbol frequencies and co-occurrences instead of counting subject matters (ibid., p. 19). The latter strand paved the way for the overly successful CCA software THE GENERAL INQUIRER during the 1960s (Stone et al., 1966). While neglecting implicit meaning through concentration on linguistic surfaces, CCA simply observed character string occurrences and their combinations in digital textual data. Researchers therefore create lists of terms, so called *dictionaries*, describing categories of interest. A search algorithm then processes large quantities of documents looking for those category-defining terms and in case of detection, increases a category counter. The process can be fine-tuned by expanding or narrowing the dictionary, applying pattern rules (e.g. observation of one, several or all category-defining terms; minimum $1 \ldots n$ times per document). Category counts in the end allow for assertions on the quantitative development of the overall subject-matter. Thus, developing valid dictionaries became the main task of the research process in a CCA designs.

In social science research, the method is applicable when large corpora of qualitative data need to be investigated for rather manifest content expressions. Züll and Mohler (2001) for example have used the method to summarize open questions of a survey study on the perception of aspects of life in the former GDR. Tamayo Korte et al. (2007) evaluated tens of thousands of forum postings of a public campaign on bioethics in Germany. The project is interesting insofar as it embeds CCA in a framework of discourse analysis. The development of the categories of interest was conducted in an abductive manner. At first, recurring discourse and knowledge structures were inferred from observed lexical units inductively. These structures, operationalized as dictionaries in MAXDictio, then were tested as hypothesis against the empirical data. The project shows that CCA is not constrained to a pure nomothetic research paradigm.

Scharloth et al. (2013) have classified newspaper articles from a complete time indexed corpus of the German magazine *Die Zeit* between 1949 and 2011 by applying a dictionary approach with rather abstract categories. Using selected parts of an onomasiological dictionary, they identified and annotated the mentioning of tropic frames (e.g. health, criminality, family, virtue, order) in more than 400,000 articles. The increases and decreases, as well as the co-occurrences of these frames over time give some interesting insights: Their method reveals long-term developments in societal meta-discourses in Germany. At the same time, results of the rather data-driven study are hard to interpret qualitatively due to the fact that causes of the identified long-term trends remain obscure.[6]

Because of serious methodical concessions, CCA is comprised with several obstacles. Researchers need a detailed comprehension of their subject matter to construct dictionaries which deliver valid results. If not developed abductively, their categories need to "coincide well with those of the author" of the analyzed document (Lowe, 2003, p. 11). In fact, a lot of effort has been made during last decades by exponents of CCA to develop generic dictionaries applicable to various research projects. The project Linguistic Inquiry and Word

[6] In fact, dictionary application itself cannot be considered as a data-driven approach. But selection of interesting tropic frames to describe discourse developments in the FRG was realized in a data-driven manner by ranking time series of all frames with respect to best compliance with ideal long-term trends, e.g. steady in-/decreases during the investigated time period.

Count[7], for example, provides dictionaries for linguistic and psychological processes like swear words, positive emotions or religion related vocabulary. But, having the above-mentioned constraint in mind, experience has demonstrated that these general dictionaries alone are of little use for generating insights in QDA. Although often freely available, dictionaries were almost never re-used outside the research projects for which they were developed originally (Scharkow, 2012, p. 79). Furthermore, studies comparing different versions of the same translated texts from one language into the other have shown that vocabulary lists of single terms are not necessarily a good indicator for similar content (Krippendorff, 2013, p. 239). The deterministic algorithmic processing of text guarantees optimum reliability (identical input generates identical output), but poor validity due to incomplete dictionaries, synonyms, homonyms, misspellings and neglect of dynamic language developments. Hence, CCA bears the risk to "end up claiming unwarranted generalizations tied to single words, one word at a time" (ibid., p. 264). The systematic omission of contexts limits the method to "very superficial meanings" with a tendency to "follow in the footsteps of behaviourist assumptions" (ibid.).

2.3.2. Computer-Assisted Qualitative Data Analysis

As a counter-model to CCA and its methodological flaws, methods of QDA have emerged followed by corresponding software to support it. For this, software packages like MAXQDA, NVivo or ATLAS.ti have been developed since the 1980s. They provide functions for document management, development of code hierarchies, annotation of text segments with codes, writing memos, exploring data and text retrieval as well as visual representations of data annotations. The major characteristic of this class of CAQDA software is that

> "none of these steps can be conducted with an algorithm alone. In other words, at each step the role of the computer remains restricted to an intelligent archiving ('code-and-retrieve') system, the analysis itself is always done by a human interpreter" (Kelle, 1997, § 5.7).

[7] http://www.liwc.net

Most of the software packages are relatively flexible concerning the research methodologies they are employed with. Early versions usually had concrete QDA methodologies in mind which should be mapped onto a program-guided process. Data representations and analysis functions in ATLAS.ti for example were mainly replicating concepts known from Grounded Theory Methodology (GTM) (Mühlmeyer-Mentzel, 2011). Later on, while the packages matured and integrated more and more functions, they lost their strict relations to specific qualitative methods. Although differences are marginal, debates on which software suits which method best persist in the qualitative research community (Kuş Saillard, 2011). Nonetheless, the use of CAQDA software in social science is nowadays widely accepted. Anxious debates from the 1980s and early 1990s, whether or not computers affect qualitative research negatively *per se*, have been settled. A study by Fielding and Lee (1998) suggested

> "that users tend to cease the use of a specific software rather than adopt their own analysis strategy to that specific software. There seem to be good reasons to assume that researchers are primarily guided by their research objectives and analysis strategies, and not by the software they use" (Kelle, 1997, § 2.9).

The KWALON experiment conducted by the journal FQS in 2010 largely confirmed this assumption. The experiment sought to investigate the influence of different CAQDA programs on research results in a laboratory research design (same data, same questions, but different software packages and research teams). Regarding the results, Friese (2011) concluded that the influence of software on the research process is more limited when the user has fundamental knowledge of the method he/she applies. Conversely, if the user has little methodological expertise, he/she is more prone to predefined concepts the software advertises.

Taking context of analysis objects into account is not determined by CAQDA programs, but by the applied method. Due to its focus on support of various manual analysis steps, it is flexible in methodological regard. Linguistic context of units of interest are part of the analysis simply because of the qualitative nature of the research process itself.

Situational contexts, such as historic circumstances during times of origin of the investigated texts, may be easily integrated into the analysis structure through memo functions or linkages with other texts. However, this kind of CATA limits the researcher to a narrow corpus. Although CAQDA software guidance may increase transparency and traceability of the research process, as well as possibilities for teamwork in research groups, it does not dissolve problems of quality assurance of qualitative research directly related to the rather small number of cases investigated. Analyzing larger, more representative amounts of text to generate more valid results and dealing with reliability in the codification process is the objective of the other types of CATA, strongly incorporating a quantitative perspective on the qualitative data. The current method debate on CATA highlights this trade-off between qualitative deep understanding of small corpora and the rather shallow analysis capabilities of automatic big data analysis (Boyd and Crawford, 2012; Fraas and Pentzold, 2015). Taking the best of both worlds, more and more researchers advocate for combined analysis approaches of 'close' and 'distant' reading (Lemke and Stulpe, 2015; Lewis et al., 2013; Wettstein, 2014).

2.3.3. Lexicometrics for Corpus Exploration

As a critical reaction to nomothetic, deductive and behaviorist views on social research with linguistic data, notably in France the emergence of (post-)structuralism had sustainable impact on CATA. In the late sixties, the historian Michel Pêcheux (1969) published his work "Analyse automatique du discours" (AAD) which attracted much attention in the Francophone world, but remained largely ignored in the English speaking world due to its late translation in 1995 (Helsloot and Hak, 2007, § 3). While the technical capacities of computational textual analysis did not allow realizing his ideas during that time, AAD was conceptualized as a theoretical work. Pêcheux generally accepted the need of analyzing large volumes of text for empirical research, but rejected the methods of CCA, because of the ideological distortions by naively applying dictionary categories onto the data:

> "Given the volume of material to be processed, the implementation of these analyses is in fact dependent upon the automatization of the recording of the discursive surface. In my view [...] any preliminary or arbitrary reduction of surface [...] by means of techniques of the 'code résume' type is to be avoided because it presupposes a knowledge of the very result we are trying to obtain [...]" (Pêcheux et al., 1995, p. 121).

With Saussure's distinction of signifier and signified he argues that discourse has to be studied by observing language within its contexts of production and its use with as little pre-assumptions as possible. Approaches which just count predefined symbol frequencies assigned to categories suffer from the underlying (false) assumption of a bi-unique relation between signifier and signified—thus are considered as "pre-Saussurean" (Pêcheux et al., 1995, p. 65). Meaning instead is "an effect of metaphoric relations (of selection and substitution) which are specific for (the conditions of production of) an utterance or a text" (Helsloot and Hak, 2007, § 25). In the 1970s and following decades, Analyse Automatique du Discours (AAD) was developed further as a theoretical framework of discourse study as well as an empirical tool to analyze texts. This class of text analysis tools is often labeled lexicometrics.

Lexicometric approaches in discourse studies aim to identify major semantic structures inductively in digital text collections. Linguists apply lexicometric measures in the field of corpus linguistics to quantify linguistic data for further statistical analysis. Other social scientists who are interested in analyzing texts for their research adapted these methods to their needs and methodologies. Dzudzek, Glasze, Mattissek, and Schirmel (2009) identify four fundamental methods of lexicometrics: 1. frequency analysis for every term of the vocabulary in the collection to identify important terms, 2. concordance analysis to examine local contexts of terms of interest,[8] 3. identification/measuring of characteristics of sub-corpora which are selected

[8]Results usually are returned as Key Word in Context (KWIC) lists (Luhn, 1960), which display n words to the left and to the right of each occurrence of an examined key term.

by meaningful criteria (e.g. different authors, time frames etc.), and finally 4. co-occurrence analysis to examine significant contexts of terms on a global (collection) level. Dzudzek (2013) extends this catalog by applying the dimension reduction approaches Principal Component Analysis (PCA) and Correspondence Analysis on the vocabulary of an investigated corpus. By aggregating documents of one year from a diachronic corpus into meta-documents, she visualizes semantic nearness of terms as well as their correspondence with years in two-dimensional plots displaying the two principal components of the investigated semantic space.

In contrast to CCA, where development of categories, category markers, code plans etc. takes place before the automated analysis, the interpretive part of lexicometric text analysis is conducted after the computational part. Compared to CCA, the exchange of these steps in the research process allows the researcher a chance to understand how meaning is constructed in the empirical data. This makes these tools compatible with a range of poststructuralist methodological approaches of text analysis such as (Foucauldian) Discourse Analysis, Historical Semantics, Grounded Theory Methodology, or Frame Analysis.

Especially in France (and other French speaking countries), discourse studies combining interpretive, hermeneutic approaches with lexicometric techniques are quite common (Guilhaumou, 2008). In the Anglo-Saxon and German-speaking qualitative research community, the methodical current of Critical Discourse Analysis (CDA) has developed a branch which incorporates lexicometric methods of corpus linguistics successfully into its analysis repertoire:

> "The corpus linguistic approach allows the researcher to work with enormous amounts of data and yet get a close-up on linguistic detail: a 'best-of-both-worlds' scenario hardly achievable through the use of purely qualitative CDA, pragmatics, ethnography or systemic functional analysis" (Mautner, 2009, p. 125).

In a lexicometric CDA study of the discourse on refugees and asylum seekers in the UK the authors conclude on their mixed method:

> "The project demonstrated the fuzzy boundaries between 'quantitative' and 'qualitative' approaches. More specifically, it showed that 'qualitative' findings can be quantified, and that 'quantitative' findings need to be interpreted in the light of existing theories, and lead to their adaptation, or the formulation of new ones" (Baker et al., 2008, p. 296).

For a study of the (post-)colonial discourse in France, Georg Glasze (2007) suggested a procedure to operationalize the discourse theory of Ernesto Laclau and Chantal Mouffe by combining interpretive and lexicometric methods. With rather linguistic research interest Noah Bubenhofer (2009) sketched a framework of purely data-driven corpus linguistic discourse analysis which seeks to identify typical repetitive patterns of language use in texts. In his view, extracted patterns of significant co-occurrences provide the basis for intersubjectively shared knowledge or discursive narratives within a community of speakers. For political scientists of special interest is the project PolMine[9] which makes protocols of German federal and state parliaments digitally available and provides lexicometric analysis functions over an R interface. In a first exploratory study, Blätte (2012) investigated empirically overlaps and delimitations of policy fields with this data and compared his findings with theoretical assumptions on policy fields in political science literature. Lemke and Stulpe (2015) study the change of meaning of the political concept 'social market economy' in the German public discourse over the last six decades by exploring frequencies and co-occurrences of the term in thousands of newspaper articles.

Although these examples show that lexicometric approaches gain ground in QDA, they have lived a marginalized existence in the social science method toolbox for a long time. Their recent awakening largely is an effect of manageable complexity by nowadays software packages[10] together with the availability of long-term digital corpora allowing for tracing change of words and concepts in new ways.

[9] http://polmine.sowi.uni-due.de

[10] Popular programs are for example Alceste, WordSmith or TextQuest as well as the packages *tm* (Feinerer et al., 2008) and *PolmineR* for R.

Besides the fact that no methodological standard yet exists, these methods require a certain amount of technical understanding, which excludes quite a bit of social scientists not willing to dive into this topic. Yet, lexicometric approaches are quite flexible to be integrated into different research designs and are compatible with epistemological foundations of well-established manual QDA approaches. In addition to traditional manual QDA approaches, lexicometrics are able to enlighten constitution of meaning on a global context level augmenting insights from hermeneutic-interpretive analysis of single paradigmatic cases.

2.3.4. Machine Learning

The cognitive process of extracting information represented and expressed within texts is achieved by trained human readers very intuitively. It can be seen as a structuring process through identifying of relevant textual fragments and assigning them to predefined or newly created concepts, by and by forming a cognitive map of knowledge. Analogue to human processing, TM can be defined as a set of methods that (semi-)automatically structure very large amounts of text. ML approaches for TM brought *syntactic* and *semantic* analysis of natural language text decisive steps forward (McNamara, 2011).

Important computer-linguistic applications to identify syntactic structures are POS-tagging, sentence chunking or parsing to identify meaningful constituents (e.g. subject, predicate, object) or information extraction (e.g. NER to identify person names or locations). Sequence classification allows for analysis beyond the 'bag of words'-assumption by taking order of terms into account through conjoint sequence observation. These computer-linguistic procedures by themselves are not really useful for QDA as single analysis. Instead, they may contribute to subsequent analysis as useful preprocessing steps to filter desired contexts by syntactic criteria.[11]

[11]Part-of-speech tagging for example can be utilized to filter document contents for certain word types before any subsequent TM application. Term extraction or topic models then can just concentrate on nouns or verbs, for example.

Semantic structures directly useful for QDA can be inferred by procedures of clustering and classification, e.g. to identify thematic coherences or label units of analysis with specific content analytic codes. Units of analysis can be of different granularity, e.g. single terms, phrases, sentences, paragraphs, documents or sub-collections. As introduced in Section 2.2.3, ML approaches can be distinguished in unsupervised clustering and supervised classification. ML approaches try to infer on knowledge structures interpretable as representations of global context by joint observation of the entire set of analysis units. At the same time, the learned model is applied to each individual unit of analysis, either by assigning it to a cluster or a classification category. For structure inference, not only linguistic contexts of modeled analysis units can be taken into account. Additionally, various kinds of external data might be included into models—for instance, time stamps of documents allowing for the data-driven identification of evolvement-patterns of linguistic data, or manually annotated category labels per analysis unit such as sentiment or valence scales. This interplay between local document contexts, global collection contexts together with possibilities of integrating external knowledge provides genuinely novel opportunities for textual analysis. For a few years now, pioneering studies utilizing ML have entered social science research.

QDA and Clustering

Thematic structures within document collections and characteristic similarities between documents can be inferred in a purely data-driven manner by clustering algorithms. Clustering for a dedicated qualitative research interest has been employed by Janasik et al. (2009). They studied interviews conducted in a small Finnish coffee firm with self organizing maps (SOM). With the help of SOMs they visually arranged their interview data by textual similarity on a two-

Syntactic parsing may be utilized to identify desired subject-object relations to differentiate between certain contents dependent on word order ("In America, you watch Big Brother." versus "In Soviet Russia, Big Brother watches you!").

dimensional map to disclose the topological structure of the data and infer data-driven "real types" (in contrast to theory-led "ideal types") of their interviewees. Methodologically, the authors argue for parallels of their approach with GTM (Janasik et al., 2009, pp. 436f).

Topic models as a variant of soft clustering have been recognized for their potential in the Digital Humanities (Meeks and Weingart, 2012), but also have received criticism from the DH community for lacking coherence and stability (Schmidt, 2012; Koltcov et al., 2014). Experience so far suggests not to apply clustering algorithms naively onto text collections, but rather to acquire decent knowledge of the algorithm along with its parameter adjustments and to critically evaluate its results. Early applications of topic models simply described topics and evaluated on thematic coherence of their highest probable terms. For example, Hall et al. (2008) investigate a large collection of historical newspapers from the USA to study topic trends over time. Another model for political science studies, incorporating authors as observed variable in addition to word usage in documents, has been introduced by Grimmer (2010). He analyzes more than 25,000 press releases from members of the US Congress. By also modeling authorship of parliamentarians, topics could be correlated with external information such as partisanship and rural versus urban election districts. Incorporating such external information allowed for a hypothesis testing research design. A more inductive study with topic models is done by Evans (2014) who analyzed US newspapers on issues denoted as "unscientific" in public discourse. A broad sample of articles selected by key terms such as "not scientific", "non-science" etc. was clustered by a topic model revealing intepretable topics such as "evolution", "climate change", or "amateur sports" as issues where allegations of unscientific knowledge seem to play a major role. Slowly topic model results are not only evaluated on their own, but integrated with other TM methods for more complex analysis. With a dedicated research interest in "net policy" as an emerging policy field Hösl and Reiberg (2015) utilize topic models in combination with a dictionary approach to identify core topics with respect to their degree of politicization.

A special kind of ML clustering for political science use is dimensional scaling (Benoit and Laver, 2012) which relates texts or corresponding authors to each other on a one-dimensional scale, e.g. to determine their political left/right attitude. But, as prerequisites on text collections for valid scaling models are rather hard (collections need to be very coherent thematically) and information reduction through one-dimensional scaling is severe, benefits of methods such as *Wordscores* (Laver et al., 2003; Lowe, 2008) or *Wordfish* (Slapin and Proksch, 2008) are not clear—at least from QDA perspective targeted towards deepening of understanding instead of mere quantification.

QDA and Classification

Much more useful for QDA are approaches of classification of documents, or parts of documents respectively. *Classification of documents* into a given set of categories is a standard application of media and content analysis. Methodically the combination of manual CA with supervised ML into a semi-automatic process is, for example, reflected in Wettstein (2014). Using Support Vector Machine (SVM) (2012) and Naive Bayes (2013) approaches for classification, Scharkow has shown that for simple category sets of news-article types (e.g. "politics," "economy," "sports,") automatic classification achieves accuracy up to 90 % of correct document annotations. Unfortunately, conditions for successful application of classification in typical QDA environments are somewhat harder than in Scharkow's exemplary study (see Section 3.3). Hillard et al. (2008) applied a variety of classifiers on Congressional bills for classification of 20 thematic policy issues. They also report on accuracy up to 90 % using ensemble classification with three learning algorithms (SVM, Maximum Entropy and BoosTexter). Moreover, they showed that SVM classification alone is able to predict category proportions in their data set relatively well. For semi-automatic classification of a much more complex category, 'neoliberal justifications of politics' in newspaper data of several decades, Lemke et al. (2015) applied an approach of active learning within the aforementioned *ePol*-project. In iterated steps of manual annotation followed by automatic classification, we extended an initial training set of around 120 paragraphs to more than 600 paragraphs representing our desired category. This training set provides a valid basis to measure the category in various sub-populations of complete newspaper archives. With the trained model we are able to identify trends of usage of "neoliberal justifications" in different policy fields. Exemplary studies utilizing syntactic information from parsing for classification have been conducted on large text collections as well. To extract semantic relations between political actors in Dutch newspapers, van Atteveldt et al. (2008) used a parsing model which grouped identified actors with respect to their syntactic role along with certain activities (e.g. "Blair *trusts* Bush"). Kleinnijenhuis and van Atteveldt (2014) employed parsing information on news coverage of the middle east conflict to distinguish speech acts expressing Israel as an aggressor against Palestine or vice versa.

Recently, classification of online communication such as Twitter posts became a popular field of interest especially in computational social science. For example, Johnson et al. (2011) analyzed around 550,000 twitter posts on Barack Obama and cross-correlated their findings with national survey data on popularity of the president. Their findings suggest that short term events affecting Twitter sentiments do not necessarily relate to president's popularity in a sense of significant correlation. Tumasjan et al. (2010) classified sentiment profiles of politicians and parties of the German parliamentary elections in 2010 by analyzing sentiments in more than 100,000 Twitter posts. Surprisingly, they also claimed that mere frequency of mentioning of major parties pretty accurately predicted election results. Since then, a bunch of studies using Twitter as primary data source have been published. From QDA perspective, these early studies based on social media data are questionable, as most of them rely on overly simple categories or try to reproduce measurements formerly collected in quantitative (survey) studies. As long as they do not strive for a more complex investigation of textual meaning they do not contribute to a deeper understanding of communication contents in a qualitative sense.

But not only the result of a classification process, i.e. labels for individual documents, can be used for qualitative analysis. The global knowledge inferred from a collection incorporated in an ML model can also deliver interesting information for investigation. Pollak et al. (2011) study a document set with rule based classifiers (J48, decision tree). Their document set consists of two classes: local and international media articles on the Kenyan elections in 2008. For their analysis, they investigate the rules learned by the classifier to distinguish between the two text sets. The most discriminating features allow for intriguing insights into the differences of Kenyan news framing and its reception in the Anglo-Saxon world.

For social science purpose, Hopkins and King point to the fact that CA studies often are not primarily interested in correct classification of single documents (Hopkins and King, 2010). Instead they want to infer generalization on the whole document set like proportions of the identified categories. This introduces additional problems: "Unfortunately, even a method with a high percent of individual documents correctly classified can be hugely biased when estimating category proportions" (ibid. p. 229). To address this problem, they introduce an approach which does not aggregate results of individual document classification, but estimates proportions directly from feature distributions in training and test collections via regression calculus. With this method they measured the sentiments (five classes ranging from extremely negative to extremely positive) on more than 10,000 blog posts reporting on candidates of the 2008 US-American presidential election. Their proportion prediction is more accurate than aggregating individual classification results.[12] My suggested procedure for application of classification in an active learning paradigm presented in Section 3.3 also deals with the question of reliable measurement of category proportions, but further extends it to the reliable measurement of category trends.

[12] Actually, their method need severe conditions to be fulfilled to produce accurate results (ibid. 242). Complying with these prerequisites leads to the consequence that their method is not much more useful than random sampling for proportion estimation (see Section 3.3 for more information on this problem).

3. Integrating Text Mining Applications for Complex Analysis

The last chapter already has demonstrated that Text Mining (TM) applications can be a valid approach to social science research questions and that existing studies employ single TM procedures to investigate larger text collections. However, to benefit most effectively from the use of TM *and* to be able to develop complex research designs meeting requirements of established QDA methodologies, one needs specific adaptions of several procedures as well as a systematic integration of them. Therefore, this chapter introduces an integrated application of various TM methods to answer a specific political science research question. Due to the rather abstract character of the research question, customarily it would be a subject to manual qualitative, interpretive analysis on a small sample of documents. Consequently, it would aim for extensive description of the structures found in the data, while neglecting quantitative aspects. One meta-objective of this study is to show that also TM methods can contribute to such qualitative research interests and, moreover, that they offer opportunities for quantification. To guide the analysis for the research question on *democratic demarcation* briefly introduced in Section 1.3, I propose a workflow of three complementary tasks:

1. document retrieval to identify (potentially) relevant articles from a large corpus of newspaper data (Section 3.1),
2. (unsupervised) corpus exploration to support identification and development of categories for further analysis (Section 3.2),

3. classification of context units into content analytic categories for trend analysis, hypothesis testing and further information extraction (Section 3.3).

Each task of this workflow is described by its motivation for a QDA scenario, its specific implementation or adaptation, its optimal application with respect to requirements of the example study, and approaches for evaluation to assure quality of the overall process.

3.1. Document Retrieval

3.1.1. Requirements

When exploring large corpora, analysts are confronted with the problem of selecting relevant documents for qualitative investigation and further quantitative analysis. The newspaper corpus under investigation $\mathcal{D}$ comprises of several hundreds of thousands of articles (see Section 1.3). The absolute majority of them might be considered as irrelevant for the research question posed. Thus, the first of the three tasks introduced in this analysis workflow is concerned with the objective to reduce a large data set to a smaller, manageable set of potentially relevant documents. This can be related clearly to an *ad hoc* task of IR comparable to search applications such as library systems or web search engines:

> "The ad hoc task investigates the performance of systems that search a static set of documents using new topics. This task is similar to how a researcher might use a library—the collection is known but the questions likely to be asked are not known" (Voorhees and Harman, 2000, p. 2).

Nonetheless, IR for QDA differs in some respects from standard applications of this technology. In standard scenario of ad hoc IR, users generally have a specific, well defined information need around specific topics or concrete (named) entities. This information need can be described with a small set of concrete key terms for querying a collection. Furthermore, the information need can be satisfied with a relatively small number of documents to be retrieved. Search engine users rarely have a look on more than the first page of a retrieval result, usually displaying the ten most relevant items matching a query (Baeza-Yates and Ribeiro-Neto, 2011, p. 267). Thus, most retrieval systems are optimized with regard to precision[1] among the top ranks of a result while recall[2] might be neglected.

In contrast to this standard scenario of IR, I identify different requirements when applying it for large scale QDA concerned with rather abstract research questions:

- Research interests in QDA often cannot be described by small keyword queries.[3] How to formulate a reasonable query for *documents containing expressions of democratic demarcation*? The information need of my example study rather is contained in motifs, language regularities and discourse formations spread over multiple topics which require an adapted approach of IR.
- While standard IR focuses on precision, an adapted QDA procedure has to focus on recall as well. The objective of this task is the reduction of the entire collection of a newspaper to a set of documents which contains most of the documents relevant to the research question while keeping the share of documents not related to it comparatively small.
- Related to this, we also need to know, how many documents from the entire collection should be selected for further investigations.

To meet these special requirements of QDA, this section proposes a procedure of IR using *contextualized dictionaries*. In this approach, a

[1] Precision is considering the share of actual relevant documents among all documents retrieved by an IR system.

[2] Recall expresses the share of relevant documents retrieved by an IR system among all relevant documents in the searchable collection.

[3] Doubtlessly, there are examples for QDA information needs which work well with simple keyword queries. For example, an analysis of political debates on the introduction of a legal minimum wage in Germany certainly can query an indexed corpus for the term *Mindestlohn* and try to filter out not domestically related retrieval results afterwards.

query is not based on single terms compiled by the content analyst. Instead, the query is automatically built from a set $\mathcal{V}$ of reference documents. Compared to the problem of determining concrete key terms for a query, it is rather easy for analysts to manually compile a collection of 'paradigmatic' documents which reflect topics or language use matching their research objective. Retrieval for a set of documents $\mathcal{D}' \subseteq \mathcal{D}$ with such a reference collection $\mathcal{V}$ is then performed in three steps:

1. Extract a substantial set of *key terms* from the reference collection $\mathcal{V}$, called dictionary. Terms in the dictionary are ranked by weight to reflect difference in importance for describing an analysis objective.
2. Extract term *co-occurrence statistics* from the reference collection $\mathcal{V}$ and from an additional generic comparison corpus $\mathcal{W}$ to identify language use specific to the reference collection.
3. *Score relevancy* of each document in the entire global collection $\mathcal{D}$ on the basis of dictionary and co-occurrence statistics to create a ranked list of documents and select a (heuristically retrieved) number of the top ranked documents for $\mathcal{D}'$.

Related Work

Heyer et al. (2011) and Rohrdantz et al. (2010) introduce approaches of interactive exploratory search in large document collections using data-driven methods of pattern identification together with complex visualizations to guide information seekers. Such contemporary approaches to IR also address some of the requirements described above. Nevertheless, in their data-driven manner they allow for identification of interesting anomalies in the data, but are less suited to integrate prior knowledge of social scientists to select document sets specific to a research question. To include prior knowledge, the approach of using documents for query generation is a consequent idea within the VSM of IR, where key term queries are modeled as document vectors for comparison with documents in the target collection (Salton et al., 1975). The proposed approach extends the standard VSM approach by additionally exploiting aspects of meanings of topic defining terms captured by co-occurrence data. Co-occurrence data has been used in standard IR tasks for term weighting as well as for query expansion with mixed results (van Rijsbergen, 1977; Wong et al., 1985; Peat and Willett, 1991; Holger Billhardt et al., 2000). These applications differ from the approach presented here, as they want to deal with unequal importance of terms in a single query due to term correlations in natural language. The method presented in this chapter does not globally weight semantically dependent query terms by co-occurrence information. Instead, in CA analysts are often interested in certain aspects of meaning of specific terms. Following the distributional semantics hypothesis (see Section 2.2.1), meaning may be captured by contexts better than just by isolated terms. Therefore, relevancy is scored based on similarity of individual contexts of single query terms in sentences of the target documents in $\mathcal{D}$ compared to observed contexts from the reference collection $\mathcal{V}$. In case of my example study, this approach may, for example, not only capture the occurrence of the key term "order" in a document contributing to its relevancy score. In addition, it captures whether the occurrence of the term "order" is accompanied by terms like "liberal", "democratic" or "socialist" which describes contents of interest much more precisely than just the single term.

This section describes the details of this adapted IR approach and is organized as follows: After having clarified the motivation, the next section presents different approaches of dictionary extraction for automatic query generation. The subsequent parts explain how to utilize ranked dictionaries together with co-occurrence data for document retrieval. Finally, an evaluation of the approach is presented.

3.1.2. Key Term Extraction

The generation and usage of dictionaries is an important part of quantitative CA procedures (Krippendorff, 2013). Dictionaries in the context of CA are basically controlled lists of key terms which are semantically coherent with respect to a defined category (e.g. terms expressing religious beliefs, emotions or music instruments). These lists provide the basis of code books and category systems within CA studies. Usually dictionaries are crafted by analysts in manual processes. Yet, their creation also can be supported by computational methods of key term extraction. For the proposed approach of document retrieval, I utilize automatically extracted dictionaries describing characteristic vocabulary extracted from a reference collection. To exploit dictionaries for document retrieval different methods of key term extraction might be used. Each method puts emphasis on different text statistical aspects of the vocabulary which, of course, leads to different lists of extracted key terms as well as to different levels of semantic coherence between them. Consequently, we can expect varying results for the retrieval process when utilizing such dictionaries. To evaluate which method of key term extraction produces the most valuable result for our IR task, three methods are compared:

- Term Frequency–Inverse Document Frequency (TF-IDF),
- Topic Models, and
- Log-likelihood (LL).

But first of all, I describe how I compiled the reference collection $\mathcal{V}$ for key term extraction to retrieve documents related to the subject of democratic demarcation.

Compiling a Reference Collection about Democratic Demarcation

The objective of compiling a collection of reference documents is to create a knowledge resource to support the process of IR for complex, rather abstract research interests on qualitative data. Not only vocabulary in form of a dictionary is extracted from this collection, but also co-occurrence statistics of terms, which yield a more meaningful description of typical language use within the collection. Thus, the collection should match the research interest of the content analyst in the best possible way. It should be representative in vocabulary and contextual meaning of terms for the content, which is targeted in the later IR process. Therefore, reference documents should be selected carefully by the analysts in consideration of representing domain knowledge and specific language use of interest. The selection of documents needs to be justified as an important initial step throughout the overall process. Moreover, one has to consider shifts in language use over time as well as between different genres of text. For example, it makes a difference of taking scientific or administrative documents for a reference collection to retrieve newspaper articles, instead of using also newspaper articles. The decision to use documents of a different genre (as done in this example study) may be made consciously to cover influences of language use specific to certain actors from other discourse arenas. For retrieval of documents from a long time period, the reference collection should also contain documents from a similar time frame to capture shifts and developments of language use appropriately.

For my example study on "democratic demarcation", I decided to rely on five editions of the "Verfassungsschutzbericht" as a basis for the reference collection—one of each decade since the first report from 1969/70. "Verfassungsschutzberichte" are official administrative reports of the German domestic intelligence service Bundesamt für Verfassungsschutz (BfV) published by the Bundesministerium des Innern (BMI). They report on developments, actors and topics state officials perceive as threat to the constitutional democratic order of the FRG (Murswiek, 2009). In this respect they are an excellent source to extract language of "democratic demarcation" within the German discourse on internal security and democracy. The compiled reference collection consists of:

- Verfassungsschutzbericht 1969/1970, (BMI 1971)
- Verfassungsschutzbericht 1979, (BMI 1980)
- Verfassungsschutzbericht 1989, (BMI 1990)
- Verfassungsschutzbericht 1998, (BMI 1999)

- Verfassungsschutzbericht 2009, (BMI 2010)

All reports were scanned and OCR-ed. Then, the following preprocessing steps (see Section 2.2.2) were applied: Sentences were separated and tokenized, tokens were lemmatized and transformed to lower case. For IR purpose, I need a reasonable number of reference documents in length comparable to newspaper articles. For this, I split the five rather long documents (50–200 pages per report) into smaller pseudo-documents. Sequences of 30 successive sentences were pooled to pseudo-documents to mimic boundaries of contextual coherence for the term extraction approaches via TF-IDF and topic models. The final reference collection $\mathcal{V}$ consists of 137,845 tokens in 15,569 sentences and 519 pseudo-documents.

TF-IDF

The TF-IDF measure is a popular weighting scheme in IR (Baeza-Yates and Ribeiro-Neto, 2011) to express how informative a single term is to describe specific content of a document, or in our case the whole reference collection $\mathcal{V}$. For this, each term t is weighted by its frequency tf within the entire collection on the one hand, and inverse document frequency on the other hand:

$$w_t = \text{tf}(t, \mathcal{V}) \times \log \frac{|\mathcal{V}|}{\text{df}(t, \mathcal{V})} \tag{3.1}$$

The underlying assumption is that a term t is more important if it is more frequent within the reference collection. At the same time, t is more informative to describe a document if it is present only in few documents, instead of (nearly) every document of the entire reference collection. This is expressed by the inverse of the document frequency $\text{df}(t, \mathcal{V})$.

Topic Models

Statistical topic models infer groups of thematically coherent terms (see Section 2.2.3) which can be used to extract relevant vocabulary from a collection $\mathcal{V}$ of paradigmatic documents (Wiedemann and Niekler, 2014). Topic models infer probability distributions of terms in topics $\boldsymbol{\beta}$ and topic distributions in documents $\boldsymbol{\theta}$. Topics in the LDA model (Blei et al., 2003) are assumed as a fixed number K of underlying latent semantic structures. Posterior probabilities $P(t|\beta_k)$ for each word t from the entire vocabulary of collection $\mathcal{V}$ can be inferred for any of the topics $k \in (1, \ldots, K)$ by sampling-based inference. Terms with a high probability in the kth topic represent its determining terms and allow for interpretation of the meaning of an underlying thematic coherence. In contrast to TF-IDF, the topic model approach for term extraction can take account of the fact that terms do not occur independently of each other. Thus, highly probable topic terms may be utilized to compile another valuable dictionary of keywords from a collection.

Probability distributions from $\boldsymbol{\beta}$ can easily be transformed into weights to receive a ranked list of terms describing the reference collection $\mathcal{V}$. In the simplest case the weight of a term in the dictionary can be defined as the sum of its probability values within each topic $\sum_{k=1}^{K} P(t|\beta_k)$. In comparison to term frequency counts in a collection, the probability weight of a term in a topic represents its contribution to the topic context. Even if this topic has relatively low evidence in the collection (represented by low values $\theta_{\cdot,k}$) a term can have high probability $P(t|\beta_k)$ within this topic. To not overly bias the ranks in the dictionary with very improbable topics and their words, a normalization strategy is needed. One solution is to additionally use term frequency to weight the terms within the corpus. As the final weight w_t of a term t in the dictionary, I define:

$$w_t = \log(\mathrm{tf}(t, \mathcal{V})) \sum_{k=1}^{K} P(t|\beta_k) \tag{3.2}$$

where K is the number of topics and $\mathrm{tf}(\cdot, \mathcal{V})$ the term frequency within the reference collection $\mathcal{V}$. By using log frequency the effect of high frequency terms is dampened.

Table 3.1.: Word frequency contingency table for term extraction (Rayson and Garside, 2000).

	$\mathcal{W}$	$\mathcal{V}$	Total
Frequency of t	a	b	$a+b$
Frequency of other words	$c-a$	$d-b$	$c+d-a-b$
Total	c	d	$c+d$

In a topic model usually topics with undesired content can be identified. Some topics group syntactic terms, such as stop words or foreign language terms (AlSumait et al., 2009). Other topics, although capturing coherent semantic structure, may be considered as irrelevant context for the research interest. In contrast to other keyword extraction methods which neglect interdependence of terms, the topic model approach allows to exclude such unwanted semantic clusters. Before calculating term weights, one simply has to identify those topics not representing meaningful structures and to remove them from the set of the K term-topic distributions $\beta_{1:K}$. This can be an important step for the analyst to influence the so far unsupervised dictionary creation process and a clear advantage over other methods of key term extraction.

Log-Likelihood

'Keyness' of terms not only can be calculated on basis of the collection $\mathcal{V}$ itself, but with the help of a (generic) comparison corpus $\mathcal{W}$. Occurrences of terms as events are observed in the comparison collection. Based on these observations expectations of term frequencies within the target collection can be calculated. Then, deviations of the actually observed frequencies from the expected frequencies are compared using a statistical test. For language data, the log-likelihood ratio test (Dunning, 1993) has proven to provide useful results. Rayson and Garside (2000) use this approach to calculate Log-likelihood (LL) statistics for each term by the contingency Table 3.1. Expected frequency values E_i in one corpus are calculated on the basis of observed frequencies in the other by the formulas $E_1 = c(a+b)/(c+d)$ and $E_2 = d(a+b)/(c+d)$. The LL statistic allows for conclusion of the significance of relative frequency differences between the two corpora, although thresholds for significance levels might be hard to define (ibid.). Consequently, the LL statistic can be employed as term weight w_t directly and is calculated as follows:

$$w_t = 2(a\log(a/E_1) + b\log(b/E_2)) \tag{3.3}$$

Whether the difference indicates an over- or underuse in the target corpus $\mathcal{V}$ compared to the comparison corpus $\mathcal{W}$ can be derived from the comparison of the relative frequencies of t within both corpora ($a/c < b/d \Rightarrow$ overuse in $\mathcal{V}$). The overused terms can then be sorted by their weights in decreasing order, resulting in a list of characteristic terms specific to the target corpus.

I used `deu_wikipedia_2010_100K-sentences` as comparison corpus $\mathcal{W}$—a corpus of 100,000 sentences randomly chosen from the German Wikipedia provided by the "Leipzig Corpora Collection" (Biemann et al., 2007).[4] To utilize it as comparison corpus, sentences need to be preprocessed exactly the same way as for $\mathcal{V}$, i.e. tokenization, lemmatization and lowercase reduction.

Extracting Terms

From the paradigmatic collection of the "Verfassungsschutzberichte" specific vocabulary is extracted with each of the three methods described above (TF-IDF, Topic Models and Log-Likelihood). Terms can be listed in ranks by sorting their term weights w_t in decreasing order. This results in a list of ranked words which can be cut to a certain length N. For the further process, I decide to take the first

[4]The Leipzig Corpora Collection provides language resources carefully maintained by computational linguists. Its corpora may be seen as representative of common language characteristics not specific to a certain domain or topic. Corpora containing up to one million sentences can be downloaded from http://corpora.uni-leipzig.de.

$N = 750$ terms of each list as a dictionary to build a query q for document retrieval. Cut-outs from the top and the bottom of the three extracted dictionaries are displayed in Table 3.2.

3.1.3. Retrieval with Dictionaries

Dictionaries can be employed as filters in IR systems to reduce general collections to sub-collections containing sets of documents of interest for further analysis. Using a dictionary of ranked terms for IR can be formulated as a standard VSM problem in combination with 'term boosting'. For this, dictionary terms are translated into a query q of unequally weighted key terms. Prior knowledge of unequal importance of terms is incorporated into query processing via factors based on term ranks. A simple VSM-scoring function can be computed for a document $d \in \mathcal{D}$ and a dictionary-based query q as follows:[5]

$$\text{score}_{\text{VSM}}(q, d) = \text{norm}(d) \times \sum_{t \in q} \text{tf}(t, d) \times \text{boost}(t) \qquad (3.4)$$

This baseline formula for querying a collection with a ranked dictionary only considers term frequency *tf*, term weight based on dictionary rank *boost* and a factor for document length normalization *norm*.

[5]Basic VSM scoring for IR is described in (Baeza-Yates and Ribeiro-Neto, 2011, p. 61ff). An example with 'term boosting' is implemented in Apache's famous Lucene index: http://lucene.apache.org/core/2_9_4/api/all/org/apache/lucene/search/Similarity.html.

Table 3.2.: Key terms in the reference collection of "Verfassungsschutz" reports automatically extracted with three different methods.

Rank	TF-IDF	w_t	Topic Model	w_t	Log Likelihood	w_t
1	rechtsextremistisch	282.987	deutschland	1.003	rechtsextremistisch	1580.916
2	partei	228.409	politisch	0.941	partei	1244.438
3	gruppe	203.883	partei	0.842	organisation	1128.310
4	organisation	196.795	organisation	0.686	politisch	1019.042
5	kommunistisch	196.351	deutsch	0.594	deutschland	993.258
6	mitglied	191.183	rechtsextremistisch	0.560	rechtsextremist	718.553
7	deutsch	187.280	mitglied	0.540	kommunistisch	704.539
8	deutschland	182.775	gruppe	0.460	extremistisch	664.406
9	politisch	172.092	person	0.422	terroristisch	614.421
10	extremistisch	168.843	ziel	0.392	linksextremist	596.035
11	rechtsextremist	166.631	aktivität	0.319	aktion	585.447
12	person	160.400	kampf	0.315	bestrebung	558.702
13	bundesrepublik	159.994	kommunistisch	0.295	linksextremistisch	557.763
14	terroristisch	157.004	aktion	0.294	aktivität	530.493
15	linke	156.779	insbesondere	0.286	bundesrepublik	528.302
16	linksextremist	156.195	mehren	0.285	linke	521.425
17	türkei	153.537	september	0.284	gruppe	510.109
18	gewalttat	151.343	bundesrepublik	0.265	gewalttat	493.557
...	...	...	...	...	...	...
746	prinzip	35.839	bonn	0.017	kosovo-albaner	30.112
747	rechtfertigen	35.839	besondere	0.017	partisi	30.112
748	saugen	35.839	ablehnen	0.017	provider	30.112
749	zerstören	35.839	zumindest	0.017	prozeß	30.112
750	zumindest	35.839	beziehen	0.017	strasser	30.112

Usually IR weightings also consider the Inverse Document Frequency (IDF) of a term as a relevant factor to take account of unequal contribution of terms to the expressiveness of a query. Since ranks of the dictionary already represent information about unequal importance, I skip the IDF factor. Instead, rank information from the dictionary needs to be translated into a boosting factor for the scoring function. I suggest a factor ranging between 0 and 1 for each term t

$$\text{boost}(t) = \frac{1}{\sqrt{\text{rank}(t)}} \tag{3.5}$$

which reflects that the most prominent terms in a dictionary of N terms are of high relevancy for the retrieval process while terms located nearer to the end of the list are of lesser, more equal importance.

Document length normalization addresses the problem of identifying relevant documents of all possible lengths. This is necessary because the longer the document, the higher the chance that it contains dictionary terms. Without length normalization, relevancy scores of long documents would outweigh shorter ones even if the latter ones contain a higher share of query terms. I utilize pivoted unique normalization as introduced in Singhal et al. (1996). Pivotal length normalization slightly lowers relevancy scores for shorter documents of a collection $\mathcal{D}$ and consequently lifts the score for documents after a pivotal value determined by the average document length. The normalization factor for each document is computed by:

$$\text{norm}(d) = \frac{1}{\sqrt{(1 - \text{slope}) \times \text{pivot} + \text{slope} \times |U_d|}} \tag{3.6}$$

where U_d represents the set of unique terms occurring in document d and *pivot* is the average number of unique terms over all documents of the collection $\mathcal{D}$, computed by:

$$\text{pivot} = \frac{1}{|\mathcal{D}|} \sum_{d \in \mathcal{D}} |U_d| \tag{3.7}$$

When evaluation data is available, the value for *slope* might be optimized for each collection. Lacking a gold standard for our retrieval task, I set *slope* = 0.7 which has proven to be a reasonable choice for retrieval optimization in various document collections (Singhal et al., 1996, p. 6).

Further, the *tf* factor should reflect on the importance of an individual term relative to the average frequency of unique terms within a document. Average term frequency per document is computed by:

$$\text{avgtf}(d) = \frac{1}{|U_d|} \sum_{t \in U_d} tf(t, d) \tag{3.8}$$

Moreover, log values of (average) term frequencies are used, to reflect on the fact that multiple re-occurrences of query terms in a document contribute less to its relevancy than the first occurrence of the term. Putting it all together, the final scoring formula yields a dictionary-based document ranking for the entire collection:

$$\text{score}_{\text{dict}}(q, d) = \text{norm}(d) \times \sum_{t \in q} \frac{1 + \log(\text{tf(t,d)})}{1 + \log(\text{avgtf}(d))} \times \text{boost}(t) \tag{3.9}$$

3.1.4. Contextualizing Dictionaries

The scoring function $\text{score}_{\text{dict}}$ yields useful results when looking for documents which can be described by a larger set of key terms. When it comes to more abstract research interests, however, which aim to identify certain meanings of terms or specific language use, isolated observation of terms may not be sufficient. Fortunately, the approach described above can be augmented with co-occurrence statistics from the reference collection $\mathcal{V}$ to judge on relevancy of occurrence of a single key term in our target document. This helps not only to disambiguate different actual meanings of a term, but also reflects the specific usage of terms in the reference collection.

Therefore, I compute patterns of co-occurrences (see Section 2.2.3) of the $N = 750$ terms in our dictionary with each other, resulting in an $N \times N$ matrix $\mathbf{C}$, also called Term-Term-Matrix (TTM). Co-occurrences are observed in a *sentence* window. Significance of a co-occurrence is calculated by the *Dice* statistic, a measure to compare the similarity of two sets, in our case all sentences A containing one term a and all sentences B containing another term b:

$$Dice(A, B) = \frac{2|A \cap B|}{|A| + |B|} \tag{3.10}$$

Using this measure instead of more sophisticated co-occurrence significance tests, such as Log-likelihood, is preferred in this case to achieve comparable value ranges for different corpora. The Dice statistic ranges between 0 and 1, i.e. the cases set that a and b never, or respectively, always occur together in one sentence. Although it is a rather simple metric, the Dice statistic reflects syntagmatic relations of terms in language relatively well (Bordag, 2008). This is useful for dealing with an unwanted effect, I experienced when experimenting with co-occurrence data to improve the retrieval mechanism. Co-occurrences of terms in the sentences of a reference collection may reflect characteristics in language use of the included documents. However, certain co-occurrence patterns may reflect general regularities of language not specific to a collection of a certain domain or topic (e.g. strong correlations between the occurrence of term pairs such as *parents* and *children*, or MWUs like *United States* and *Frankfurt Main* in one sentence). Applying co-occurrence data to IR scoring tends to overemphasize such common language patterns in contrast to meaningful co-occurrence of term usage specific to the reference collection. To mitigate this effect, we can apply a 'filter' to the extracted co-occurrences.

Instead of using the TTM $\mathbf{C}$ solely based on the reference collection $\mathcal{V}$, I filter the co-occurrence data by subtracting a second TTM $\mathbf{D}$, based on the previously introduced comparison corpus $\mathcal{W}$. Like in the step of LL key term extraction, the corpus consisting of 100,000 randomly chosen sentences from the German Wikipedia provided by the "Leipzig Corpora Collection" is suitable for this purpose. $\mathbf{D}$ as a second $N \times N$ matrix of co-occurrences is computed from counts in $\mathcal{W}$ and calculation of corresponding Dice statistics. Subtracting of $\mathbf{D}$ from $\mathbf{C}$ delivers a matrix $\mathbf{C}'$ reflecting the divergence of co-occurrence patterns in the reference collection compared to topic-unspecific language:

$$\mathbf{C}' = \max(\mathbf{C} - \mathbf{D}, 0) \tag{3.11}$$

Values for common combinations of terms (e.g. *Frankfurt Main*) are significantly lowered in $\mathbf{C}'$, while combinations specific to the reference collection remain largely constant. The effect of filtering co-occurrence data in the reference collection is displayed in Table 3.3. Most co-occurrence pairs found in the reference collection $\mathcal{V}$ which also exist in the filter collection $\mathcal{W}$ do not represent the desired context of the research question exclusively. Thus, leaving them out or lowering their contextual statistic measure helps to increase the precision of the retrieval process. Applying the *max* function asserts that all negative values in $\mathbf{C} - \mathbf{D}$ (representing terms co-occurring less significantly together in sentences of the reference collection than in sentences of the filter collection) are set to zero. The remaining co-occurrence pairs sharply represent contexts of interest for the retrieval process (see Table 3.4)

3.1.5. Scoring Co-Occurrences

To exploit co-occurrence statistics for IR, the scoring function in equation 3.9 has to be reformulated to incorporate a similarity measure between a co-occurrence vector profile of each term t in the dictionary and each sentence s in the to-be-scored-document d. In addition to term frequency, we extend scoring by information on contextual similarity of term usage in sentences $s \in d$:

$$\mathrm{tfsim}(t, \mathbf{C}', d) = \sum_{s \in d} \begin{cases} \mathrm{tf}(t, s) + \alpha \times \mathrm{sim}(\vec{s}, C'_{t,\cdot}), & \mathrm{tf}(t, s) > 0 \\ 0, & \mathrm{tf}(t, s) = 0 \end{cases} \tag{3.12}$$

$$\mathrm{sim}(\vec{a}, \vec{b}) = \frac{\vec{a} \cdot \vec{b}}{||\vec{a}||\,||\vec{b}||} \tag{3.13}$$

The frequency of t within a sentence (which usually equals 1) is incremented by the cosine similarity (see Eq. 3.13) between sentence

Table 3.3.: Examples of Dice statistics for term pairs of which values get drastically lowered in $\mathbf{C}'$ (see eq. 3.11), hence, contributing less to the contextualized relevancy scoring. Co-occurrence statistics from the reference collection (**C**) which are also observable in the filter collection (**D**) were ordered by significance ratio between the two collections (**D**/**C**).

a	b	C	D	D/C
verlag	auflage	0.046	0.131	2.85
million	insgesamt	0.029	0.048	1.63
demokratisch	partei	0.067	0.104	1.55
weit	verbreiten	0.101	0.155	1.53
verletzen	person	0.025	0.037	1.50
raum	deutschsprachig	0.088	0.129	1.47
jugendliche	kind	0.061	0.090	1.45
geschichte	deutsch	0.022	0.031	1.38
französisch	deutsch	0.022	0.030	1.32
scheitern	versuch	0.109	0.144	1.31
sozial	politisch	0.023	0.030	1.29
vorsitzende	mitglied	0.038	0.049	1.28
iranisch	iran	0.091	0.115	1.26
staatlich	einrichtung	0.054	0.065	1.21
sozialistisch	sozialismus	0.054	0.065	1.20
maßgeblich	beteiligen	0.076	0.088	1.15
september	oktober	0.023	0.026	1.13
million	jährlich	0.048	0.054	1.12
zeitschrift	deutsche	0.026	0.029	1.12
politisch	partei	0.056	0.061	1.08
stellen	fest	0.062	0.067	1.07
staaten	sozialistisch	0.033	0.035	1.07
ziel	erreichen	0.040	0.042	1.04
politisch	mitglied	0.027	0.027	.99
august	juli	0.045	0.045	.99
frage	stellen	0.063	0.062	.98
republik	sozialistisch	0.035	0.034	.95
verschieden	unterschiedlich	0.050	0.047	.93
november	oktober	0.027	0.025	.93

Table 3.4.: Examples of Dice statistics for co-occurrences in $\mathbf{C}'$ after filtering the co-occurrence patterns of the reference collection $\mathcal{V}$ by those from the filter collection $\mathcal{W}$. These term pairs strongly contribute to the contextualized relevancy score.

a	b	$\mathbf{C}'$
innern	bundesminister	0.851
grundordnung	freiheitlich	0.707
sicherheit	innere	0.680
hizb	allah	0.666
subkulturell	geprägt	0.577
nationaldemokrat	junge	0.526
motivieren	kriminalität	0.470
inhaftierten	hungerstreik	0.451
unbekannt	nacht	0.441
verfassungsschutz	bundesamt	0.434
sicherheitsgefährdende	ausländer	0.417
wohnung	konspirativ	0.405
nationalist	autonom	0.394
verurteilen	freiheitsstrafe	0.389
sachschaden	entstehen	0.388
unbekannt	täter	0.382
bestrebung	ausländer	0.378
extremistisch	ausländer	0.371
kurdistan	arbeiterpartei	0.365
sicherheitsgefährdende	bestrebung	0.356
orthodox	kommunist	0.324
extremistisch	bestrebung	0.319
fraktion	armee	0.317
sicherheitsgefährdend	extremistisch	0.305
rote	hilfe	0.297

vector $\vec{s}$ (sparse vector of length N indicating occurrence of dictionary terms in s) and the dictionary context vector for t out of $\mathbf{C}'$. Cosine similarity has been proven a useful measure for comparing query vectors and document vectors in the VSM model of IR (Baeza-Yates and Ribeiro-Neto, 2011, p. 76f). Here it is applied to compare usage contexts of terms in sentences from the reference collection $\mathcal{V}$ and sentences of target documents $d \in \mathcal{D}$. Adding contextual similarity to the tf measure rewards the relevancy score, if the target sentence and the reference term t share common contexts. In case dictionary terms occurring in sentences of d share no common contexts, the cosine similarity equals 0 and $tfsim$ remains equal to tf.

Because term frequency and cosine similarity differ widely in their range the influence of the similarity on the scoring needs to be controlled by a parameter α. If $\alpha = 0$, $tfsim$ replicates simple term frequency counts. Values $\alpha > 0$ yield a mixing of unigram matching and context matching for the relevancy score. Optimal values for α can be retrieved by the evaluation method (see Section 3.1.6). Finally, the context-sensitive score is computed as follows:

$$\text{score}_{\text{context}}(q, \mathbf{C}', d) = \text{norm}(d) \times \sum_{t \in q} \frac{1 + \log(\text{tfsim}(t, \mathbf{C}', d))}{1 + \log(\text{avgtf}(d))} \times \text{boost}(t) \tag{3.14}$$

3.1.6. Evaluation

Determining a large set of key terms from a reference collection and extracting its co-occurrence profiles to compose a "query" is an essential step in the proposed retrieval mechanism to meet requirements of content analysts. Due to this, standard approaches of IR evaluation (Clough and Sanderson, 2013) which focus primarily on precision in top ranks and utilization of small keyword sets as queries are hardly applicable. Test collections and procedures such as provided by the TREC data sets (Voorhees, 2005) would need serious adaptions regarding such type of retrieval task (e.g. compiling a reference collection from the relevant document set). As I also need an evaluation specific to the proposed research question on democratic demarcation, I decided to follow two approaches:

1. Generating a quasi-gold standard of *pseudo-relevant documents* to show performance improvements through the use of co-occurrence data as well as certain methods of key term extraction,

2. Judging on the overall validity manually with *precision at k* evaluation on the retrieved document set for this example study.

Average Precision on Pseudorelevant Documents

To evaluate on *precision* (share of correctly retrieved relevant documents among the top n ranks of a retrieval result) and *recall* (share of correctly retrieved relevant documents among all relevant documents of the collection) of the retrieval process a set of relevant documents has to be defined (Baeza-Yates and Ribeiro-Neto, 2011, p. 135). It is obvious that this set cannot be derived from the collection of newspaper documents investigated in this study, as it is the objective of this retrieval task to identify the relevant documents. Instead, we define a set of 'pseudo-relevant' documents as a gold standard, originating from the reference collection of the "Verfassungsschutzberichte". These annual reports were initially split into 519 pseudo-documents each containing a sequence of 30 sentences ordered by appearance within the reports (see Section 3.1.2). For the evaluation process, I split the reference collection set in two halves:

- 260 pseudo-documents with odd numbering are used for dictionary and co-occurrence extraction,

- 259 pseudo-documents with even numbering are used as gold standard of relevant documents for evaluation.

The retrieval process then is performed on a document set of 20,000 newspaper articles randomly chosen from the FAZ collection and merged with the 259 'gold standard' documents into the evaluation collection $\mathcal{E}$. To this collection $\mathcal{E}$ the process of relevancy scoring (eq. 3.14) is applied which yields a ranked order of documents. The quality of the retrieval process is better the higher the density of 'gold'-documents in the upper ranks is. This relation can be expressed in precision recall curves. Incorporating results from lower ranks of the scoring into the result set includes more relevant documents which increases recall. At the same time precision of the result set decreases, because more documents not considered as relevant are included as well. Plotted as diagram, different IR systems can be easily compared. The larger the area under the curve, the better the retrieval performance.

Figure 3.1 displays such precision recall curves for different values of α. It shows that using contextualized information ($\alpha > 0$) positively influences the retrieval result compared to simple unigram matching of dictionary terms in documents ($\alpha = 0$). Nonetheless, difference between larger influence of context information ($\alpha = 15$ vs. $\alpha = 30$) seems to be neglectable.

Retrieval quality also can be expressed in a single measure like "average precision" which computes the precision at various levels of recall (Clough and Sanderson, 2013). Figure 3.2 plots average precision for retrieval runs with the three dictionary lists and different alpha parameters. Again, it becomes evident that utilizing contextual information increases retrieval performance, as the precision increases with increasing α values. For $\alpha > 15$ precision does not increase much further. This hints to select $\alpha = 15$ as a reasonable parameter value for the retrieval task to equivalently mix information from unigram matching and context scoring of query terms in target documents.

Furthermore, average precision evaluation allows for comparison of the different term extraction methods used to create the retrieval dictionary from the reference collection. While term extraction via TF-IDF and Topic Models perform almost equal, the dictionary based on Log-likelihood outperforms the other approaches. Obviously this method is more successful in extracting meaningful key terms. This is also confirmed by Figure 3.3 which plots precision-recall curves for the three approaches.

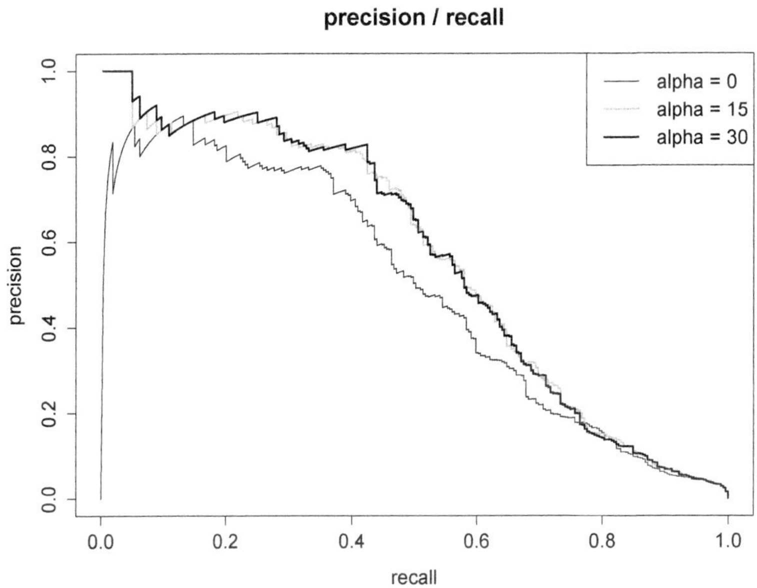

Figure 3.1.: Precision recall curves for contextualized retrieval with Log-Likelihood extracted dictionary and three different α values.

Precision at k

A second evaluation targets directly to the content relevant for the example study. Using the best performing LL dictionary for retrieval in the global newspaper collection $\mathcal{D}$ produces a ranked list of around 600,000 documents. To compare results of context-insensitive matching of dictionary terms with contextualized dictionaries, I ran retrieval twice for $\alpha = 15$ and $\alpha = 0$. For each of the top 15,000 documents per list, I evaluate how dense the relevant documents on different ranges of ranks are. The *precision at k* measure can be utilized to determine the quality of the process by manually assessing the first 10 documents downwards from the ranks 1, 101, 501, 1001, 2501, 5001, 7501, 10001, 12501, 14991 (Baeza-Yates and Ribeiro-Neto, 2011, p. 140). Documents from each rank range were read closely and marked as

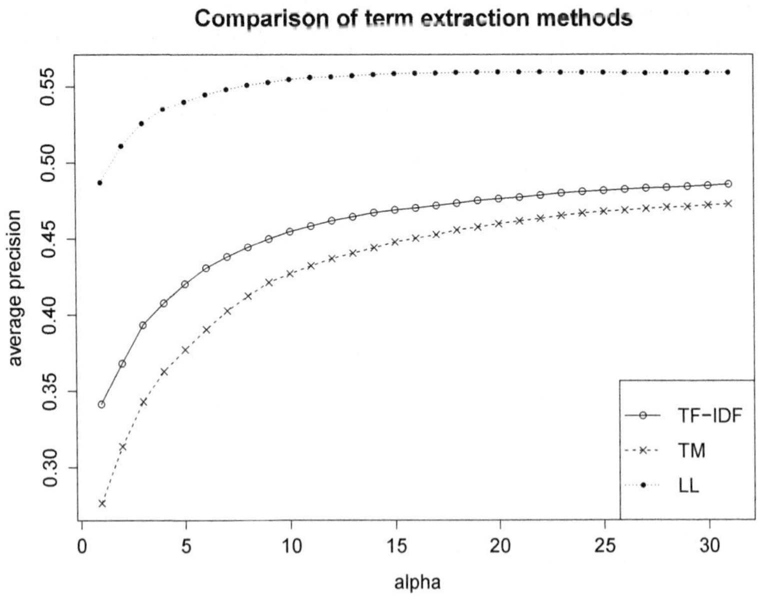

Figure 3.2.: Average retrieval precision for dictionaries based on different term extraction methods and α values.

relevant in case any part of the text expressed a statement towards democratic demarcation. This includes speech acts of exclusion or rebuttal of exclusion of (allegedly) illegitimate positions, actors or activities within the political spectrum.

The results in Table 3.5 confirm the usefulness of the contextualization approach. Density of positively evaluated results in the upper ranks is very high and decreases towards the bottom of the list. Precision in the system utilizing co-occurrence data ($\alpha = 15$) retrieves more relevant documents and remains high also in lower ranks, while it drops off in the system which solely exploits unigram matching between query and document ($\alpha = 0$). Further, since the study on democratic demarcation is targeted to domestic political contexts, I evaluated if retrieved documents were related primarily to foreign

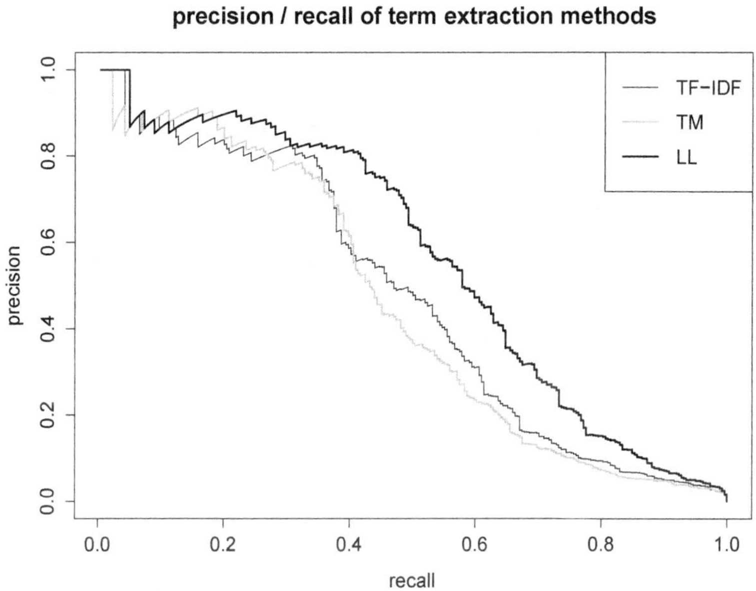

Figure 3.3.: Precision recall curve for dictionaries based on different term extraction methods ($\alpha = 15$).

or domestic affairs. Retrieval with contextualized dictionaries better captured the domestic context from the reference collection of the BfV reports, resulting in a lower share of foreign related documents.

Size of Relevant Document Set

The final retrieval to select (potentially) relevant documents for this example study from the collections of *FAZ* and *Die Zeit* is performed by extraction of a dictionary from the complete reference collection $\mathcal{V}$ of five BfV reports split into 519 pseudo-documents. Corresponding to the evaluation result, the LL approach for term extraction and a retrieval parameter $\alpha = 15$ have been used. Due to the size of the dictionary ($N = 750$ terms), almost every document of both collections gets a relevancy score greater than zero. As a matter of

Table 3.5.: Manually evaluated precision of retrieval results at increasing rank intervals. Both IR systems compared utilize the LL based dictionary.

Precision at k	$\alpha = \mathbf{0}$	$\alpha = \mathbf{15}$
1–10	10	10
101–110	9	8
501–510	7	9
1001–1010	7	9
2501–2510	8	9
5001–5010	5	5
7501–7510	4	5
10001–10010	4	3
12501–12510	2	5
14991–15000	1	4
Total	57	**67**
Foreign related	45%	**34%**

fact, documents in the lower ranks cannot be considered as relevant. The main objective now is to determine a threshold for the relevancy score. Documents below this score would be considered as not relevant. Documents above this score will be the base for the upcoming analysis.

Again, the evaluation approach of the pseudo-gold document set can help to solve this problem. It allows to compute at which rank in our relevancy ordered evaluation collection $\mathcal{E}$, consisting of *FAZ* and BfV documents, a specific recall level of gold documents from BfV reports is achieved. As desired recall level, I strive for around 80 % of all relevant documents. The corresponding rank $r_{0.8}$ can be utilized to estimate a relative proportion of relevant documents in the ranked list of the overall collection. We assume that we look for certain similarities in language use between the reference and the target collections, and that the proposed IR mechanism favors these similarities in its ranking. If this holds true, many documents from the target collection (which are per definition not part of the 'gold' set in this evaluation) should contain language characteristics similar to the reference collection, and thus, may be considered as relevant for the research question. When applying the retrieval mechanism to comparable collections (e.g. another complete archive of second newspaper), it appears to be a reasonable heuristic to consider the same proportion of the collection as (potentially) relevant as in the (randomly selected) evaluation collection $\mathcal{E}$.

For the evaluation collection $\mathcal{E}$, consisting of 20,259 documents, $r_{0.8} = 1375$ which means that 80 % of the 'gold' documents are located in roughly 7 % of the top ranked documents in the collection ($r_{0.8}/|\mathcal{E}|$). Selecting the top ranked 7 % from the entire FAZ collection ($\approx 200,000$ documents) yields a collection of 14,000 (potentially) relevant documents.[6] Selecting the top ranked 7 % from the entire *Die Zeit* retrieval yields a collection of 28,000 (potentially) relevant documents.

Filtering out Foreign Affairs

Democratic demarcation is not only expressed in the news with regard to domestic affairs. The manually conducted evaluation also showed that lots of documents were retrieved related to foreign affairs (see Table 3.5). Although the proposed IR mechanism decreases the share of documents related to foreign affairs compared to a context-insensitive retrieval, roughly one third of all manually evaluated documents fit in this category. Since this example study is concerned with democratic demarcation in the FRG, I want to filter the retrieval result for documents primarily related to domestic affairs.

This could be formulated as a complex machine learning classification task (see Section 3.3). But for the moment, there is a straightforward base line approach which yields sufficient results, too. For this, I employ two different dictionaries of location entities, either domestic or foreign related:

[6] I decided to use rounded values, because this procedure of determining a traceable threshold is an approximate heuristic.

- *Domestic affairs* (DA): a list of all German federal states and their capitals, and a list of abbreviations of the major parties in the German Bundestag;
- *Foreign affairs* (FA): a list of all United Nations (UN) registered nations and their capitals (except Germany), and a list of all cities over one million inhabitants (except German cities).

Dictionaries of these location entities can be easily compiled from Wikipedia lists which represent a valuable controlled resource for this purpose.[7] These dictionaries are employed to count occurrences of terms they consist of in the retrieved documents. Documents then are categorized by the following rules: documents

- containing at least one FA-term, *and*
- containing less than two DA-terms

are considered to be foreign-related. Evaluation of this 'naive' rule set[8] on the manually evaluated examples shows high values for precision ($P = 0.98$) and recall ($R = 0.83, F_1 = 0.91$).

Documents identified as foreign-related were removed from the retrieval set resulting in the final retrieved collection $\mathcal{D}'$.

3.1.7. Summary of Lessons Learned

As a result of the first analysis task on IR, the retrieved FAZ collection consists of 9,256 documents, the *Die Zeit* collection consists of 19,301

[7]Using a list of states registered at the UN has the advantage that it also includes states that seized to exist (e.g. Czechoslovakia or Yugoslavia).
UN nations:
http://de.wikipedia.org/wiki/Mitgliedstaaten_der_Vereinten_Nationen
Capitals:
http://de.wikipedia.org/wiki/Liste_der_Staaten_der_Erde
Large cities:
http://de.wikipedia.org/wiki/Liste_der_Millionenst%C3%A4dte
FRG states/capitals:
http://de.wikipedia.org/wiki/Land_%28Deutschland%29

[8]For more information on classification evaluation see Section 3.3.5

documents – both mainly containing articles related to domestic affairs and information relevant to the question of democratic demarcation.

Purpose of this task within the overall TM workflow was to identify relevant documents within huge topic-unspecific collections. Furthermore, it should respond to the requirements of 1) identification of relevant documents for abstract research questions, 2) focus on recall to select large sets of relevant documents for further investigation and 3) provide a heuristic solution to decide how many documents to select for further investigation. Lessons learned from approaches to this task can be summarized as follows:

- Compiling a collection of paradigmatic reference documents can be a preferable approach to describe an abstract research interest compared to standard ad-hoc retrieval (Voorhees and Harman, 2000) by a small set of keywords.
- Dictionary extraction for IR query compilation can be realized by key term extraction from the reference collection. The method of LL for key term extraction is preferred.
- Extraction of term co-occurrence statistics from the reference collection contributes to improve retrieval performance over just looking for dictionary terms neglecting any context.
- Average precision based on a pseudo-gold document set compiled from half of the reference collection can be used to automatically evaluate on retrieval performance with respect to an optimal retrieval algorithm.
- Precision at k on final retrieval results can be used to judge manually on quality of the retrieval result with respect to the research question.
- Rankings of documents from the pseudo-gold set can be employed to estimate on proportions of relevant documents in a final retrieval list, providing a heuristic for the number of documents to select.

Table 3.6.: Final data sets retrieved for the study on democratic demarcation.

Corpus	Publication	#Doc	minFrq	#Token	#Type
$\mathcal{D}'_{ZEIT}$	Die Zeit	19,301	10	11,595,578	63,720
$\mathcal{D}'_{FAZ}$	FAZ	9,256	10	2,269,493	20,990
$\mathcal{D}'$	FAZ + Zeit	28,557	15	13,857,289	53,471

- Dependent on the research question, subsequent filter processes on the retrieval results may be useful to get rid of undesired contexts for the QDA purpose, such as domestic versus foreign affairs relatedness of retrieved contents.

Future work on this task could elaborate more closely on the influence of different parameters within the workflow (e.g. altering the dictionary weighting function Eq. 3.5). Moreover, it would be interesting to integrate other sophisticated methods of term weighting and normalization strategies from elaborated ad-hoc approaches of IR to see, if they improve the retrieval quality with respect to the requirements specified.

3.2. Corpus Exploration

The process of document retrieval conducted in Section 3.1 yielded a final collection of (potentially) relevant documents for the further analysis $\mathcal{D}'$ (see Table 3.6). All methods introduced in the following subsections were conducted to explore the combined corpus $\mathcal{D}'$ containing of both publications, *Die Zeit* and *FAZ*, together. The separated inspection of corpora of the single publications is subject of analysis again for classification in Section 3.3. The corpora are preprocessed by the following procedures (see Section 2.2.2 for details on preprocessing):

- tokenization of sentences and terms,

- removal of stop words,
- merging of terms within MWUs to single tokens,[9]
- transformation of named entities to their canonical form,[10]
- lemmatization of tokens,[11]
- lowercase transformation of tokens,
- pruning of all terms below *minFrq* (see Table 3.6) from the corpus.

The pruning of terms below a minimum frequency is a useful step to keep data sizes manageable and data noise due to misspellings and rare words low. For the corpus $\mathcal{D}'$, three different DTMs were computed containing counts of types for each document, for each paragraph per document and each sentence per document separately. Identifiers for sentences, paragraphs and documents allow for selection of corresponding sub-matrices, e.g. all sentence vectors belonging to a document vector. These DTMs are the basis for the second step of unsupervised exploration of the retrieved document collection. Results are shown in this section only for the purpose of exemplary description. A comprehensive description of the interpreted findings during corpus exploration with respect to the research question on democratic demarcation is given in Chapter 4.

3.2.1. Requirements

When investigating large corpora which contain documents of several topics and from different time periods, analysts need methods to

[9]For this, a dictionary of German MWUs was applied which was compiled for utilization in the aforementioned *ePol*-project (Niekler et al., 2014).

[10]For this, a dictionary of variants of named entities assigned to their canonical form was applied. This dictionary is based on the JRC-Names resource provided by the European Commission (https://ec.europa.eu/jrc/en/language-technologies/jrc-names).

[11]For this, a lemma dictionary compiled by the project *Deutscher Wortschatz* was applied (http://wortschatz.uni-leipzig.de).

become familiar with its temporal and thematic contents without reading through all of the material. Sampling a small random subset could help to enlighten certain events and aspects in the newspaper texts. But reading selected sample documents does not give hints on distributions and shares of topics over time—they also do not contribute much to get the "big picture". Instead, one can apply a controlled process of (semi-)automatic, data-driven methods to split the entire collection into manageable segments. These segments should be defined with respect to two dimensions: time and topical structure. Each of the segments then can be described by text statistical measurements, extracted structures of meaning, corresponding graphical visualizations and representative example snippets of text. Knowledge about the overall subject can be derived by investigating and interpreting the segments, each by itself or in contrast with each other.

The procedure proposed in this section can be seen as an implementation of what Franco Moretti has labeled "distant reading" (Moretti, 2007). By combining different methods of NLP, information extraction and visualization, it strives to reveal patterns of meaning in the data. With this, not only fixed manifest contents may be identified for quantification, but also meaningful latent concepts or topics can be identified and their change over time may be tracked. This equips content analysts with an invaluable heuristic tool to grasp knowledge structures and their quantitative distribution within large data sets.

Technically, the proposed procedure may be related to the task of *ontology learning*, which is a sub-field of *ontology engineering* in information management. Ontologies formally describe types of knowledge entities of a certain domain together with their properties and relations. For example, they define a hierarchical set of key terms related to each other by hyponymy, hypernymy, synonymy or antonymy. Such structures can be learned and populated automatically from text collections to a certain extent (Cimiano, 2006). But the conceptualization of ontologies in the field of information management differs from the application requirements in QDA with respect to several aspects. Definitions of ontologies in information systems are built in a very formal way to capture characteristics of a single domain with the objective to unify knowledge application in an intersubjective manner. Knowledge representations might even be machine readable in a way that allows for logical reasoning. This is a key requirement to support business processes or knowledge bases for applications of artificial intelligence. In contrast to this, content analysts (especially in discourse analysis) are interested in knowledge patterns spread around multiple domains with rather "soft" characterizations of concepts. If longer time periods come into play they even have to deal with changes of meaning instead of fixated definitions. Moreover, especially those concepts are interesting for investigation which appear as intractable to intersubjective formal definition—so called "empty signifiers" (Nonhoff, 2007, p. 13) such as democracy, extremism, freedom or social justice which may be understood in countless manifold ways, but hardly fit into a formal ontology. We might even say that the field of information systems and the field of social science seem to represent opposing ends concerning their epistemological fundamentals—the former strives for fixation of structures to model representations of essential beings while the latter strives for *re*-construction and understanding of elusive knowledge structures shaped by discursive language evolvement over time. Luckily, this difference only is important for the application of extracted knowledge. For identification of structures and patterns both profit from a variety of data-driven NLP technologies.

For knowledge extraction, I can rely on approaches proven as useful for ontology learning, especially the idea to combine several NLP techniques to create data-driven excerpts of knowledge patterns from document collections. But instead of putting extracted information into formal conceptual containers with strict relations for my intended purpose, it is advised to provide an intuitive access to the data which allows researchers to inductively explore meaningful knowledge patterns. This intuitive access is provided by graphical display of co-occurrence networks of semantically coherent key terms in temporal and thematic sub-parts of the corpus. For generating such network graphs, I combine several technologies:

- a topic model based on the entire corpus,
- a clustering in time periods based on topic distributions,
- a co-occurrence analysis of terms per topic and time frame,
- a 'keyness' measure of significantly co-occurring terms,
- a dictionary-based sentiment measure of the key terms,
- a heuristic to identify semantic propositions based on maximal cliques in co-occurrence networks, and
- a method to extract representative example text snippets based on propositions.

The following subsections describe these methods of information extraction, pattern recognition and computation of textual statistics. Finally, information generated by the largely automatic processes is utilized as an input to render informative graphs which I call Semantically Enriched Co-occurrence Graphs (SECGs)—one for each topical cluster within a distinctive time frame. SECGs allow for visual intuitive investigation of interesting content parts within large document collections. While processes are largely unsupervised and data-driven, analysts still have to make conscious decisions in some steps in order to control parameters of processes or to make manual selections of intermediate results. This should not be seen as a flaw of the entire process chain, but as an opportunity to keep control over the analysis and to get a deeper understanding of the data and methods used.

3.2.2. Identification and Evaluation of Topics

The to-be-explored corpus $\mathcal{D}'$ contains 28,557 retrieved newspaper articles published over six decades. Figure 3.4 shows that documents are unequally distributed over time. While there are less than 200 documents per year in the beginning of the time period investigated, their number increases in the early 1960s. The smoothed long-term development shows three peaks around 1968, 1990 and 2001. We can

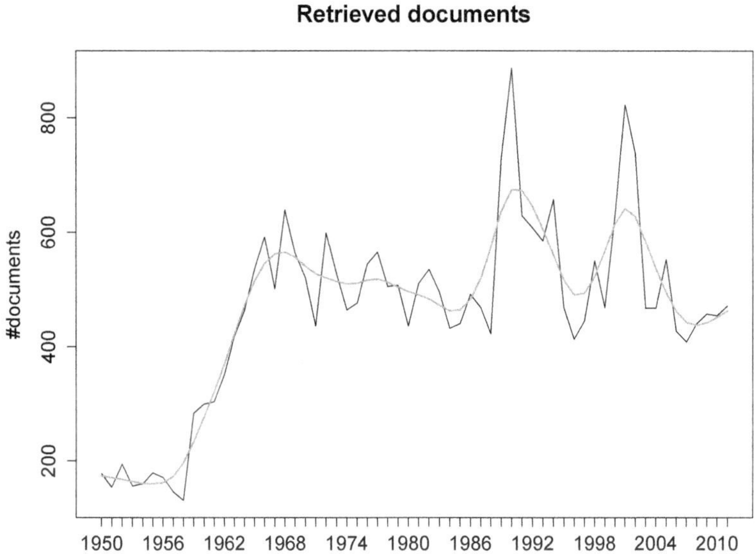

Figure 3.4.: Retrieved documents from *Die Zeit* and *FAZ* over time. The grey line represents a smoothed spline showing three peaks in long term development of the document distribution. This collection will be explored by data-driven methods in Section 3.2.

assume that certain discursive events related to democratic demarcation are responsible for these trends which can be traced by topic changes.

To support exploratory investigation of the collection $\mathcal{D}'$, topic models provide a valuable approach to cluster thematic contents. Topic models allow for investigating contents through a 'distant' perspective by inference of term distributions $\beta_{1:K}$ in K topics representing semantically coherent clusters of term usage, and inference on topic distributions $\boldsymbol{\theta}$ in documents. Topic-document distributions can be observed in single documents or in aggregated sub-collections, e.g.

documents from selected time frames. Furthermore, as documents are modeled as a mixture of topics, computed model instances allow for collection filtering on the basis of presence of inferred latent topic structures above a certain threshold. This contextual filtering is an essential step to generate thematic sub-collections on which further text statistical measures can be applied. Expressiveness of such measurements dramatically increases if a largely coherent context of the underlying collection through topic filtering can be guaranteed.

Model and Parameter Selection

For the purpose of topic identification, I rely on the standard parametric LDA model (Blei et al., 2003)—for reasons of simplicity[12] and because I prefer to keep control over the number of topics K to be inferred by the model. Besides K, parametric[13] topic models are governed by hyperparameters influencing the quality of its outcome. Hyperparameters are settings of the prior distributions in topic models. For LDA, the topic distribution per document $\boldsymbol{\theta}$ is determined by a prior α and the term distribution per topic $\boldsymbol{\beta}$ is determined by a prior η. Although it is possible to optimize these parameters automatically for model selection, selecting 'good' settings in QDA scenarios is a rather intuitive process which should be taken out carefully by analysts. Usually, in NLP developers of topic models evaluate their models in automated processes while in QDA scenarios analysts compute models with different parameter settings and judge on outcomes by manual investigation (Evans, 2014). For automatic evaluation, data sets can be divided into one part for model computation and another part of

[12] I used the performant implementations of LDA and CTM provided as packages for R by Grün and Hornik (2011).

[13] Numerically optimal choices for K can be retrieved automatically by non-parametric topic models such as HDP-LDA (Teh et al., 2006) which are reported to deliver slightly better topic qualities. But, loosing control over deliberate selection of K means giving up control over topic granularity which is in my view a relevant parameter in hands of the QDA analyst. Nonetheless, experiments with non-parametric or even time-dynamic topic models for QDA might be an interesting extension to the base line I present here.

model evaluation. The quality of the model is assessed by computing its *perplexity*, i.e. a metric based on the probability of the documents held out for evaluation. Hyperparameter settings then can also be optimized according to highest held out likelihood (Wallach et al., 2009). Although likelihood evaluation is widely used due to its pure automatic nature, Chang et al. (2009) have proven with large user studies that optimal held out likelihood does not correspond to human perception of semantic coherence of topics. My experiments with LDA and computationally optimized hyperparameters as well as with the Correlated Topic Model (CTM) (Blei and Lafferty, 2006) to generate SECG confirmed this finding. Topics of likelihood optimized models on the *FAZ* and *Die Zeit* data were less expressive and less targeted to specific semantic units than topics computed with models of some of my manual parameter selections. Numerical optimization of α values estimated higher optimal values leading to topic distributions in documents where many topics contribute a little probability mass—in other words, topics were less distinct. This diminishes the usefulness of the model for document selection as well as for identification of specific discursive event patterns over different time frames. The CTM model, although in model evaluations yielding better results in terms of likelihood of the data, inferred term distributions of which most topics were dominated by high frequent terms reducing the perceived specificity of these topics to describe a semantic coherence.

Mimno et al. (2011) responded to this circumstance by suggesting a new evaluation metric for topic models. They measure *coherence* C of a topic k by observing co-occurrences of the top N terms of each topic on a document level (ibid., p. 265):

$$C(k, V^k) = \sum_{n=2}^{N} \sum_{l=1}^{n-1} log \left(\frac{D(v_n^k, v_l^k) + 1}{D(v_l^k)} \right) \tag{3.15}$$

Hereby, $V^k = (v_1^k, \cdots, v_N^k)$ represents a list of the N terms of topic k with highest probability. $D(v, v')$ is the frequency of co-occurrence of the types v and v'. Basically, it favors models putting more probability weight on terms in one topic which actually are co-occurring in documents. Mimno et al. show that their metric is superior to log likelihood in terms of correspondence to user evaluation on the quality of topic models. Furthermore, as the purpose of this subtask is to generate co-occurrence graphs for corpus exploration, topic coherence appears to be the measure of choice for optimization of hyperparameters.

Nevertheless, numerical evaluation measures should not be the single criterion for model selection. First published empirical studies using topic models for QDA also strongly rely on judgments by the human researcher. According to Evans (2014), a conventional procedure is to compute a variety of different models with different parameters. These models then are compared by the analyst with respect to the question which one fits best to the research objective. This validation can be done in three steps:

1. investigating the top N most probable terms of each topic and check if it is possible to assign a descriptive label to them,

2. comparing measurements of semantic coherence of topics (see eq. 3.15) as an additional hint to identify overly broad or incoherent topics, and

3. evaluating whether topic distribution over time follows assumptions based on previous knowledge of the researcher (e.g. if topics on Islam and terrorist activities in the news co-occur in the 2000s, but not before 2001).

I have performed model selection by combining numeric optimization based on the topic coherence measure with steps of the manual evaluation procedure. Firstly, I decided for using $K = 100$ as a satisfying topical resolution for the collection. It is possible to judge on 100 topics manually, but the number is still high enough to capture also smaller thematic patterns which might play a role only in shorter periods of time of the overall discourse on democratic demarcation. Secondly, I computed six LDA models with different settings of α.

Each model computation was carried out with 1,000 iterations of Gibbs Sampling using the following parameters:[14]

- pruning of all types that appear less than 35 times in the corpus to reduce data size for model computation which left 30,512 types,
- $K = 100$ topics, $\eta = 10/K = 0.1$[15]
- $\alpha \in \{0.05, 0.1, 0.2, 0.3, 0.5, 1.0\}$[16]

The objective is to identify one model which yields a mixture of rather few topics with high probability allowing for more specific contextual attribution than a mixture of many broader topics. Thus, for each of the six models its mean topic coherence $(\sum_{k=1}^{K} C(k, V^k))/K$ was computed using the $N = 100$ most probable terms per topic. The results in Figure 3.5 indicate that the model with $\alpha = 0.2$ achieves highest coherence. It also shows that likelihood of the models does not correlate to their coherence measure. In the last step, a manual investigation of the topic defining terms suggested that in fact the model computed with $\alpha = 0.2$ provided the most coherent and descriptive topics for the research questions.

Performing all steps for model selection, I chose the model $K = 100, \eta = 0.1, \alpha = 0.2$ as the basis for the upcoming steps. The inferred topics of this model are displayed in Table 3.7 by their most probable terms and their distribution θ_k in the entire corpus $\mathcal{D}$.

[14]Every model took roughly 9 hours computation time using the implementation provided by Grün and Hornik (2011).

[15]For the η prior, I stuck with the default value of the topic model implementation, since I am primarily concerned with topic specificity to describe document contents governed by α.

[16]Lower α priors lead to inference of fewer, more specific topics determining document contents. For higher α priors, documents are modeled as mixtures of more evenly distributed topics.

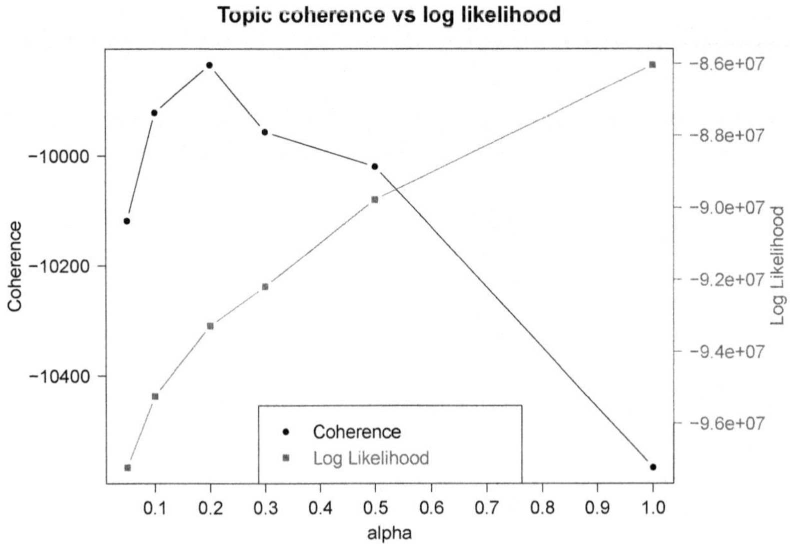

Figure 3.5.: Mean topic coherence and log likelihood of all six topic models computed with different α values. The model with $\alpha = 0.2$ achieved highest coherence.

Table 3.7.: Topics in $\mathcal{D}'$ ordered by rank_1: for each topic, the table displays ID, top eight terms, proportion within the corpus (θ_k), number of documents where it has maximum share of all topics (C_{r_1}), rank according to topic probability (r_P) and rank_1 (r_1).

ID	Top terms	θ_k	C_{r1}	r_P	r_1
71	spd partei wähler cdu wahl prozent wahlkampf fdp	0.0176	730	1	1
3	zeit glauben frage herr mensch leute jahr groß	0.0166	581	4	2
35	jahr leute haus alt tag leben stadt sitzen	0.0163	560	5	3
41	buch politisch geschichte band autor verlag darstellung beitrag	0.0143	538	12	4
68	europa europäisch gemeinsam politisch europäischen gemeinschaft national	0.0121	531	20	5
88	militärisch europa nato sowjetunion staaten bündnis westlich politisch	0.0123	521	19	6
91	fdp liberal partei genscher koalition demokrat freier westerwelle	0.0096	507	50	7
58	gewerkschaft arbeitnehmer arbeiter dgb streik organisation mitglied betrieb	0.0092	501	59	8
83	krieg international militärisch deutschland nation einsatz nato vereint	0.0094	478	55	9
32	spd schröder lafontaine partei kanzler gerd_schröder müntefering rot-grün	0.0102	475	41	10
90	ddr sed ulbricht sozialistisch honecker partei kommunistisch sozialismus	0.0105	471	39	11
51	npd republikaner rechtsradikal rechen gewalt jahr rechtsextrem neonazi	0.0089	465	62	12
59	bundesrepublik deutschen ddr wiedervereinigung deutschland anerkennung	0.0114	449	27	13
76	richter gericht urteil justiz jahr angeklagte verfahre politisch	0.0102	426	42	14
62	partei dkp kommunistisch politisch kommunist verbot öffentlich dienst	0.0095	417	53	15
54	erklären regierung französisch außenminister amerikanischen usa deutschland	0.0096	416	49	16
13	student universität hochschule schule professor schüler lehrer bildung	0.0085	413	68	17
63	polizei demonstration gewalt demonstrant aktion protest polizist student	0.0095	383	52	18
42	terrorist terrorismus anschlag raf mord terror gruppe terroristisch	0.0088	379	64	19
11	merkel angela_merkel union partei cdu kanzlerin koalition koch	0.0096	376	51	20
4	volk mensch welt leben groß kraft freiheit zeit	0.0141	375	13	21
87	spd partei sozialdemokraten brandt sozialdemokratisch wehner vogel willi_brandt	0.0105	374	38	22
50	jahr land sozial prozent milliarde arbeitslosigkeit hoch steuer	0.0111	373	29	23

10	grundgesetz verfassung land gesetz artikel bundestag bundesverfassungsgericht	0.0118	371	21	24
73	pds partei spd gysi osten linkspartei land sachsen	0.0075	371	77	25
85	kanzler regierung opposition schmidt koalition adenauer bundeskanzler groß	0.0112	370	28	26
74	ddr weste osten einheit alt ostdeutsch bundesrepublik vereinigung	0.0091	360	60	27
95	ausländer deutschland flüchtling land bundesrepublik deutschen jahr deutsche	0.0080	357	72	28
65	verfassungsschutz polizei behörde information geheimdienst wissen beamte	0.0093	355	58	29
78	deutschland adenauer deutschen zone westlich deutschlands deutsche weste	0.0098	353	46	30
20	grüne grün fischer partei grünen ökologisch jahr kernenergie	0.0081	349	71	31
29	hitler deutschen reich nationalsozialismus widerstand deutsche krieg	0.0088	346	63	32
79	frankreich französisch paris italien gaulle frankreichs italienischen franzosen	0.0083	343	70	33
14	land jahr wirtschaftlich prozent bundesrepublik wirtschaft groß industrie	0.0109	339	33	34
94	schriftsteller buch literatur jahr roman schreiben literarisch autor	0.0075	338	79	35
44	politik groß frage jahr republik kanzler denken müssen	0.0107	335	34	36
43	partei parteitag vorsitzende delegierte mitglied wahl parteivorsitzende wählen	0.0127	334	17	37
46	politisch politik gegenüber stark gewiß groß werden freilich	0.0176	324	2	38
96	türkei türkisch islam türke muslime islamisch deutschland muslimisch	0.0059	323	93	39
52	sozial gesellschaft mensch politik staat leben freiheit arbeit	0.0105	317	37	40
17	sozialismus sozialistisch revolution kommunistisch kommunist marx kapitalismus	0.0101	313	43	41
33	jahr leben werden tod freund gefängnis verhaften zeit	0.0098	307	45	42
86	iran arabisch afghanistan irak land iranisch islamisch welt	0.0066	300	83	43
12	politisch gesellschaft gesellschaftlich system sozial gruppe entwicklung form	0.0139	299	14	44
77	kirche katholisch christlich evangelisch christ bischof kirchlich gott	0.0066	298	84	45
100	frage aufgabe einzeln groß möglichkeit notwendig gebiet öffentlich	0.0171	297	3	46
48	cdu kohl union partei helmut_kohl schäuble biedenkopf politisch	0.0088	295	65	47
53	mark million geld partei jahr spende stiftung zahlen	0.0080	288	73	48
19	müssen sein können werden politik frankfurter bundesregierung zeitung	0.0143	286	11	49
80	zeitung journalist fernsehen medium rundfunk presse blatt programm	0.0075	286	76	50
6	jahr politisch freund groß halten lassen leben persönlich	0.0145	278	10	51
2	land welt afrika hilfe jahr international entwicklungsland entwicklungshilfe	0.0065	269	86	52

7	film kunst sport künstler ausstellung theater spiel bild	0.0064	269	88	53
99	mensch leben welt wissen geschichte glauben volk wahrheit	0.0134	267	16	54
39	abgeordnete parlament bundestag partei wahl fraktion mehrheit stimme	0.0101	261	44	55
57	jude jüdisch israel antisemitismus israelisch deutschland antisemitisch holocaust	0.0055	259	97	56
66	csu strauß bayer bayerisch stoiber münche franz-josef_strauß münchner	0.0062	255	92	57
16	ungarn land tschechoslowakei prag kommunistisch rumänien jugoslawien	0.0063	253	90	58
40	pole polnisch polen warschau polnischen deutschen jahr grenze	0.0053	250	98	59
47	land cdu ministerpräsident hessen nordrhein-westfalen spd landtag niedersachsen	0.0094	250	54	60
64	kritik meinung werden öffentlich frage vorwurf politisch brief	0.0155	246	8	61
93	hitler deutschen weimarer_republik republik reich reichstag deutsche weimar	0.0065	246	85	62
9	≫die jahr deutschland internet ≫wir ≫ich gut berlin	0.0097	237	48	63
67	deutschen revolution bismarck preußisch preuße deutschland könig groß	0.0068	233	82	64
92	wirtschaft sozial marktwirtschaft staat wirtschaftspolitik unternehmer ordnung	0.0084	232	69	65
84	amerika amerikanischen vereinigten staaten amerikanische usa präsident	0.0075	229	80	66
23	bonn bundesrepublik beziehung deutschen bundesregierung gespräch politisch	0.0110	227	30	67
98	frau kind jahr jugendliche jung familie mann jugend	0.0089	224	61	68
30	nation national geschichte kultur kulturell politisch deutschen europäisch	0.0093	222	57	69
81	mitglied organisation gruppe verband verein gründen jahr arbeit	0.0105	222	36	70
31	regierung land präsident jahr volk wahl million bevölkerung	0.0086	221	67	71
70	staat freiheit recht bürger demokratisch gesetz staatlich ordnung	0.0123	212	18	72
25	politisch gesellschaft öffentlich lassen bild debatte öffentlichkeit gerade	0.0114	209	26	73
89	sowjetunion moskau sowjetisch stalin sowjetischen rußland kommunistisch	0.0076	208	75	74
61	china chinesisch land japan peking jahr chinese welt	0.0053	207	99	75
72	rede wort sprechen tag beifall saal sitzen stehen	0.0115	207	24	76
45	frage lassen gewiß bundesrepublik beispiel grund scheinen gut	0.0161	203	7	77
27	unternehmen firma bank jahr geld wirtschaft markt groß	0.0079	196	74	78
55	prozent jahr zahl bevölkerung bundesrepublik million hoch groß	0.0103	193	40	79
1	vertrag staaten international verhandlung beziehung gemeinsam regierung frage	0.0107	190	35	80
82	intellektuelle denken philosophie welt theorie gesellschaft philosoph mensch	0.0075	188	78	81

36	wissenschaft institut wissenschaftler forschung professor international jahr	0.0064	181	89	82
60	partei politisch politik groß wähler programm volkspartei mitglied	0.0115	178	25	83
49	bundeswehr soldat militärisch armee general offizier truppe krieg	0.0063	177	91	84
75	lassen freilich langen rechen müssen woche bleiben gewiß	0.0162	176	6	85
24	minister amt beamte politisch ministerium staatssekretär dienst öffentlich	0.0087	174	66	86
26	berlin berliner stadt politisch berlins hauptstadt west-berlin bürgermeister	0.0065	173	87	87
8	kris regierung politisch reform land groß lage zeit	0.0155	167	9	88
34	britisch england land großbritannien regierung london britischen brite	0.0057	164	96	89
15	demokratie demokratisch politisch bürger volk system regierung parlament	0.0094	156	56	90
97	politisch ziel wichtig entwicklung aufgabe führen gemeinsam diskussion	0.0138	149	15	91
21	krieg frieden weltkrieg groß rußland deutschland spanien politik	0.0071	148	81	92
37	bundespräsident präsident amt politisch weizsäcker wahl kandidat rau	0.0059	143	95	93
69	hamburg hamburger stadt bürgermeister jahr breme bremer politisch	0.0059	142	94	94
5	politisch politik politiker entscheidung handeln frage moralisch bürger	0.0116	105	23	95
56	linke politisch link konservativ radikal mitte liberal rechen	0.0098	103	47	96
22	österreich schweiz österreichisch wien schweizer land jahr österreicher	0.0039	102	100	97
18	deutschen deutschland deutsche deutscher land deutschlands bundesrepublik	0.0116	92	22	98
38	jahr geschichte zeit groß alt bundesrepublik jahrzehnt siebziger	0.0109	66	32	99
28	tag juni november jahr oktober mai september märz	0.0109	60	31	100

Topic Model Reliability

Since the number of possible topic structures in LDA and other topic models is exponentially large, exact solutions for the models are computationally intractable (Blei, 2012, p. 81). Therefore, topic models rely on sampling-based or variational algorithms to find approximate solutions. The Gibbs sampler I used in this study, employs Markov chains as a random process to find a posterior distribution of model parameters close to the true posterior. Unfortunately, the state space of topic models consists of numerous local optima. As a consequence, the inference mechanism not only infers slightly different parameter values each time the algorithm runs for a sequence of finite sampling iterations. If the data is not separable well by the given number of topics K, solutions also may differ widely in terms of underlying latent semantics captured by the inferred topics. This can lead to low reproducibility of a model between repeated runs of the inference algorithm which may question the usefulness of the model for social science goals (Koltcov et al., 2014). To evaluate on reproducibility, Niekler (2016, p. 137f) introduces a procedure to match most similar pairs of topics from two different model inferences by cosine distance (see Eq. 3.13) between their topic-word distributions above a certain threshold t. Since most of the probability mass of a topic is concentrated at only a fraction of the vocabulary, it is suggested to only incorporate the N most probable words from each topic to calculate distances. Practically, this procedure resembles manual evaluation steps human coders apply to decide on similarity between two topics—they also look at the list of the most probable topic words and compare, how similar they are to each other. A high intersection of shared terms indicates that the same topic label could be applied to them.

For evaluating reproducibility of the previously computed model, I repeated the model inference on $\mathcal{D}'$ with the selected parameters five times. Then, I applied the matching procedure on the $N = 100$ most probable terms per topic and with a maximum distance $t = 0.3$ to find pairs between topics from all possible pairs of models. Since there are $i = 5$ models, we can compare matchings for $\binom{i}{2} = 10$ pairs. The mean number of topic pairs matched from each of the thc 10 model pairs gives a measure for the reliability of the model computation on our target collection. On average, 80.7% of the topics could be matched between several model inferences. This is a quite acceptable measure of reproducibility in the context of content analysis, particularly because the matching is successful for the most prominent topics capturing the largest share of the collection. Even when restricting the distance criterion to a threshold of $t = 0.2$, still 70,0% of the topics can be matched. If reproducibility had been insufficient due to bad separability of the investigated collection, it would have been advisable to change model parameters, at first lowering the number of topics K, or apply further measures to increase the reliability.[17]

3.2.3. Clustering of Time Periods

When exploring large document collections, it is helpful to split these collections not only thematically, but also in their temporal dimension (Dzudzek, 2013; Glasze, 2007). Identification of varying time periods allows for embedding analysis results in different historical contexts (Landwehr, 2008, p. 105). This is important because knowledge structures and semantic patterns change substantially over time by mutual influence on these contexts. Thus, gaining insights in long term developments of discourse considerably profits from observations of such changes by comparing different sub-collections split by time. Two strategies can be applied to achieve a temporal segmentation of a diachronic corpus. Time periods can be segmented manually based on text external theory-driven knowledge, e.g. legislative periods or crucial discursive events. They also can be segmented in a data-driven manner by looking for uniformity and change in language use of the corpus. For this, contents can be aggregated according to time slices to be subject of a cluster analysis.

[17]Lancichinetti et al. (2015) proposed Topic Mapping—a method to increase reproducibility by initializing topic-word assignments deterministically based on co-occurrences of words before sampling.

I apply such a data-driven clustering approach for temporal segmentation of $\mathcal{D}'$ on single years of news coverage. Such a clustering on newspaper data from longer time periods reveals clusters of mostly ongoing year spans. For the upcoming steps of analysis, this procedure helps to segment time spans for contrasting investigations. For the generation of SECGs it is useful to allow for graph representations of single thematic contents within a specific period of time, as well as for comparison of same thematic coherence across time periods.

In the previous section, we split the collection on democratic demarcation in different mixtures of topics. These topic distributions may also be utilized to identify time periods which contain similar mixtures of topics. A multitude of other measurements could also be employed to cluster time periods. For example, aggregating word counts of every document in a single year could serve as a basis for creating a *year-term-matrix* analogue to a DTM which serves well as a basis for clustering. But, using topic model probability distributions has the advantages that they 1) are independent of the number of documents over time, 2) have a fixed values range, 3) represent latent semantics, and 4) we already have computed them.

For clustering of years, we average document topic probabilities $\theta_{d,\cdot}$ from all documents published in year $y \in Y = (1950, 1951, \cdots, 2011)$ in the corpus:

$$\theta_{y,k} = \frac{1}{|\mathcal{D'}_y|} \sum_{d \in \mathcal{D'}_y} \theta_{d,k} \tag{3.16}$$

where $\mathcal{D'}_y$ is a subset of all documents from $\mathcal{D}'$ published in year y. This results in a $|Y| \times K$ matrix of topic probability distributions for each year. This matrix has to be transformed into a $|Y| \times |Y|$ distance matrix, representing dissimilarity of topic distributions between all pairs of years, which serves as the basis for a clustering algorithm. Since we deal with probability distributions, Jensen–Shannon Divergence (JSD) is a reasonable choice as distance metric for this purpose.[18] According to Endres and Schindelin (2003), the square root of JSD should be applied when using it as distance. Thus, for each pair of years we compute:

$$\mathrm{dist}(y, y') = \sqrt{\mathrm{JSD}(\theta_{y,\cdot}, \theta_{y',\cdot})} \tag{3.17}$$

$$\mathrm{JSD}(x, y) = \frac{1}{2}\mathrm{KL}(x : \frac{1}{2}(x + y)) + \frac{1}{2}\mathrm{KL}(y : \frac{1}{2}(x + y)) \tag{3.18}$$

using the Kullback-Leibler divergence $KL(x : y) = \sum_i x_i \log(\frac{x_i}{y_i})$. The distance matrix computed this way can be used as input for any clustering algorithm.

Model and Parameter Selection

Clustering algorithms can be distinguished into nonparametric and parametric approaches: the former decide on a suitable number of clusters based on the data, the latter fit to a given number of clusters k. Although nonparametric approaches appear to be attractive for identification of time periods in diachronic corpora, not all of such algorithms are suitable for clustering on text data. As language data from ongoing year spans is changing rather gradually, common nonparametric density-based clustering algorithms are hardly suitable for the problem of separating clusters of years. DBSCAN (Ester et al., 1996), for example, produces without proper tweaking one big cluster, due to the fact that vector representations of years usually fulfill the properties of density-reachability and density-connectedness in the vector-space under investigation. More suitable are parametric clustering approaches which assign data points to a previously defined number of k clusters, e.g. k-means, k-medoids or Partitioning Around Medoids (PAM). The proper selection of k then can be heuristically supported by a numerically optimal solution determined by a cluster quality index. Yet, the flexible choice of k also provides an opportunity

[18] JSD is commonly used for comparing topic model posterior probability distributions. For example, in Dinu and Lapata (2010); Niekler and Jähnichen (2012); Hall et al. (2008)

for the content analyst to control the number of clusters independent from numerical optimization. This can be a reasonable requirement because of the number of time periods for further investigation should not exceed a certain threshold—from the analyst's perspective it may seem intuitively better to investigate three or four periods within half a century rather than the numerically optimal solution of 20 or more clusters. For these reasons, I decided to use the PAM algorithm (Reynolds et al., 2006) for clustering of time periods.

The PAM algorithm clusters observations similar to the famous k-means algorithm by assigning data points to a nearest cluster center. In contrast to k-means, cluster centers are not represented by means of all assigned observations. Instead, PAM uses k medoids, i.e. cluster representative data points from the set of observations. Because no cluster means have to be calculated, PAM can run faster than k-means. But even more important, it runs with an initial 'build phase' to find the optimal medoids for initialization of the algorithm. This does not only lead to faster convergence, but also results in entirely deterministic clustering.[19]

PAM needs a previously defined number of clusters k to run. For content analysis, it is hard to define in advance how many clusters one should expect. We can certainly assume some upper boundary. For manual investigation of the to-be-generated SECGs, it would be hard to split the data into more than 10 time periods. Hence, we may employ a data-driven measurement to determine a value for $k \in \{2, \cdots, 10\}$ yielding optimal separation of the data. I decided for the Calinski-Harabasz index (Caliński and Harabasz, 1974) which is widely used as a heuristic device to determine cluster quality. For each k the clustering is done and for its result the CH-index is computed. As Figure 3.6 shows, the optimal CH-index is achieved when dividing the course of years into five clusters. Running PAM with $k = 5$ yields the time periods presented in Table 3.8.

[19] k-means in contrast may produce different clustering results, if the data is not well separable. Due to random initialization of the cluster means at the beginning, the algorithm it is not fully deterministic.

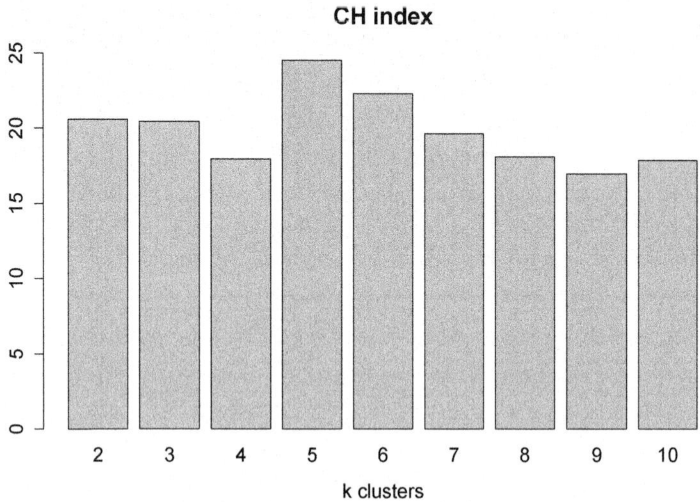

Figure 3.6.: Calinski-Harabasz index for clusterings with different k. $k = 5$ can be assumed as an optimal solution slicing the news coverage between 1950 and 2011 in five time periods.

Table 3.8.: PAM clustering on topic probabilities per year results in five ongoing year spans over time.

Cluster / years	Docs	Distribution over time
1. 1950–1956	1192	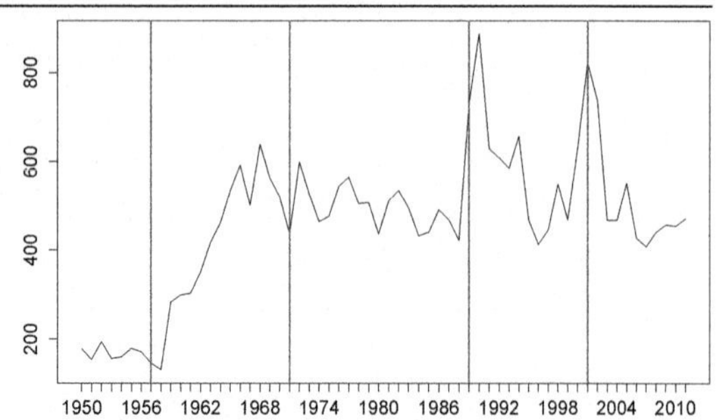
2. 1957–1970	5742	
3. 1971–1988	8852	
4. 1989–2000	7068	
5. 2001–2011	5703	

3.2.4. Selection of Topics

Not all inferred $K = 100$ topics play an important role in every cluster over time and not all highly probable topics in a single cluster are relevant for the research questions. Thus, for corpus exploration we need a deliberate selection how many and which topics to investigate further. I decide to concentrate on the $K' = 10$ most important topics for each cluster. But how can they be selected? To identify topics relevant for the research question within a certain time frame, we first need a ranking of the topics. From this ranking, we then can manually select K' topics per time frame from the top downwards. Again, manual selection should be seen as an opportunity for the analyst to control the overall process with respect to her/his research objective, rather than a deficiency in a pure data-driven process. Of course, it would also be possible to select automatically just the K' top ranked topics. But chances are high that, on the one hand, we include overly general topics which are not related directly to the research question and, on the other hand, miss important, but rather 'small' topics.

Ranking Topics

For each topic its overall proportion θ_k in the entire corpus $\mathcal{D}'$ can be computed by averaging of all topic shares $\theta_{d,k}$ of each document d:

$$\theta_k = \frac{1}{|\mathcal{D}'|} \sum_{d \in \mathcal{D}'} \theta_{d,k} \tag{3.19}$$

Accordingly, topics can be ordered by their share of the entire collection. It can be found that distribution of topics has similarities to distribution of words in general language: The most probable topics within a corpus are not necessarily the most meaningful topics.[20] The two most probable topics #71 and #46 consist of rather general terms like *partei, wahl, prozent* and *politisch, politik, groß, werden* which

[20] Characteristics of term distributions in natural language can be formally described by Zipf's law (Heyer et al., 2006, p. 87).

do not describe a single coherent theme, but account for relevant vocabulary in many documents concerned with various topics around politics. The same can be diagnosed for the other eight topics #100, #3, #35, #75 #45, #64, #8, #6 of the top ten ranked by probability (see Table 3.7).

To order topics in a more expressive manner, the *rank_1* measure can be applied. For this, we count how often a topic k is the most prominent topic within a document:

$$C_{r1}(k) = \sum_{d \in \mathcal{D}'} \begin{cases} 1, & \forall j \in \{1, \ldots, K\} \; \theta_{d,k} >= \theta_{d,j} \\ 0, & \text{otherwise.} \end{cases} \tag{3.20}$$

The normalized measure $C_{r1}(k)/|\mathcal{D}'|$ expresses the relative share of how often a topic k has been inferred as primary topic. This provides a basis for ranking all topics with respect to their significance on a document level. Topics are ordered by rank_1 in Table 3.7 as well as in Figure 3.7. The figure illustrates the effect of the re-ranking by primary topic counts on the document level. Topics with high share in the entire corpus might be distributed rather evenly over many documents without constituting a proper theme for a document by themselves. These topics are identifiable by the higher bars throughout the lower ranks of the plot.

Manual Selection

The top 25 topics of each temporal cluster ranked by rank_1 are investigated manually by judging on the 20 most probable terms in each topic. If terms seem 1) semantically coherent in a way that a single topic label could be applied to them, and 2) this semantic coherence appears relevant for answering questions on democratic demarcation or self-conception in the discourse of the FRG, they appear as candidates for further processing. Although the rank_1 metric puts more specific topics in higher ranks of a listing, it still contains topics which are describing relatively general vocabulary. But the selection process also showed that interesting topics could be

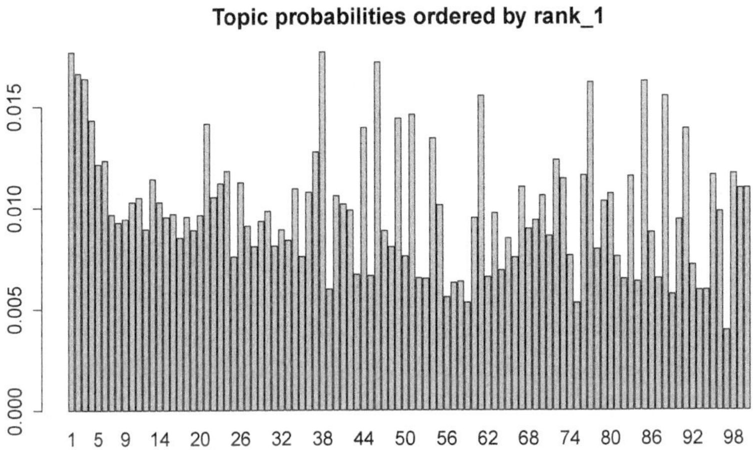

Figure 3.7.: Topic probabilities ordered by rank_1 metric. Higher bars throughout the entire rank range indicate that highly probable topics do not necessarily constitute primary document contents.

found mostly in higher ranks, while in lower ranks there were only few topic candidates for selection.

I selected the $K' = 10$ most meaningful topics for each cluster (see Table A.1). This selection also allows for a more formal evaluation of the two topic rankings just introduced. Topic rankings can be evaluated analogue to document ranking in IR (see Section 3.1.6). Computing Mean Average Precision (MAP) (Baeza-Yates and Ribeiro-Neto, 2011, p. 140) for topic ranking methods based on my manual selection assumed as 'gold standard' results in $\text{MAP}_{rank1} = 0.598$ for the rank_1 metric greatly outperforming $\text{MAP}_{prob} = 0.202$ for the ranking simply based on inferred topic probability.

For each of the K' manually selected topics per time period a SECG will be generated. This results in 50 SECGs for the exploratory analysis.

Topic Co-Occurrence

As documents are modeled as mixtures of topics, usually there are multiple topics in each document. As a first visual orientation towards the contents in each temporal cluster, we can identify co-occurrence of the manually selected topics in each cluster and visualize them as a graph network. For this, I count co-occurrence of the *two* highest ranked topics in each document using the rank_1 metric. This results in a symmetric $K' \times K'$ matrix M on which any significance measure for co-occurrence could be applied (Bordag, 2008). By using the LL metric and filtering for significant co-occurrences of any topic pair i, j above a threshold of $LL(i, j) >= 3.84$,[21] M may be transferred into a binary matrix M', where $M'_{i,j} = 1$ indicates a significant co-occurrence relation between topic i and topic j, and $M'_{i,j} = 0$ an insignificant relation. Then, M' can be used as an adjacency matrix for graph visualization. For each temporal cluster such a topic co-occurrence graph shows relevant topics and their relation (see Figure 3.8; graphs for the other four temporal clusters can be found in Chapter 4). Topics are displayed as nodes of the graph with the five most probable terms as their label. Node size indicates how often a topic has been inferred as primary topic within a document relative to the other topics in the graph.

3.2.5. Term Co-Occurrences

For constructing SECGs, we need to identify term co-occurrence patterns for each manually selected topic in each time period. The list of the most probable terms of a topic from the previously computed topic model provides a valuable basis for this. If combinations of terms co-occur significantly with each other in sentences of documents belonging to the selected topics, they are candidates for edges in the graphical visualization for corpus exploration. Co-occurrences are

[21] Rayson et al. (2004) describe this cut-off value for statistical LL tests for corpus linguistics corresponding to a significance level of $p < 0.05$.

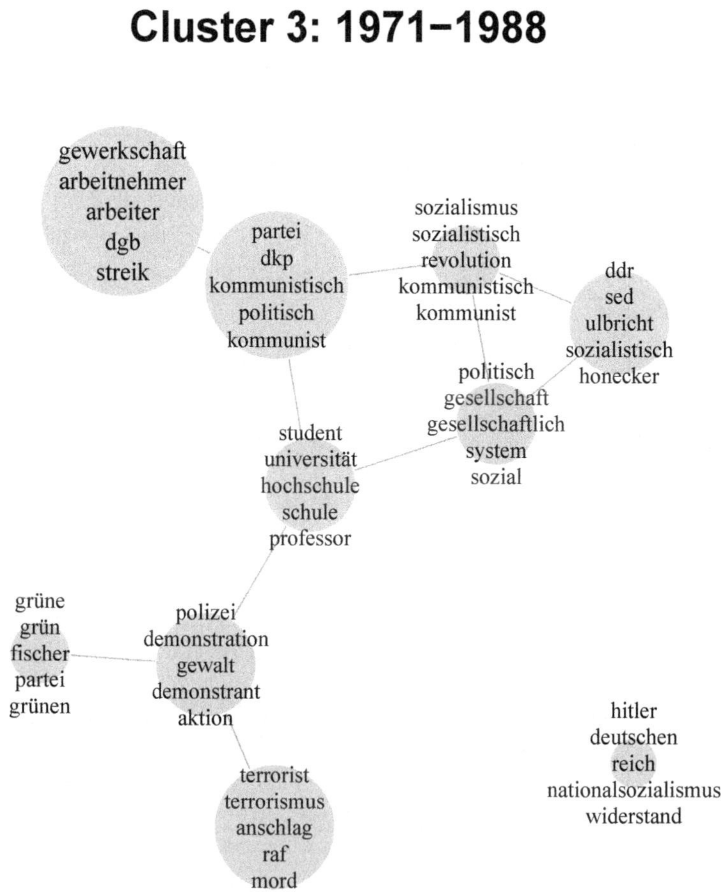

Figure 3.8.: Topic co-occurrence graph for 10 selected topics in cluster 3. Connected topics co-occur significantly as primary / secondary topic with each other in documents of that time period. Topic labels comprise of the five most probable topic terms.

extracted as follows (for a more formal description see Workflow 6 in the Appendix):

1. A set of documents $\mathcal{D}'_{c,k}$ of a time period c containing a topic share above a certain threshold $\theta_{d,k} > 0.1$ is selected. The topic mixture of the current topic model yields an average of 2.33 topics per document with a share greater than 0.1. This threshold ensures that only documents are selected, which contain topic k to a substantial share.

2. From the documents $\mathcal{D}'_{c,k}$ contained sentences $\mathcal{S}'_{c,k}$ are extracted and co-occurrence of the $N = 200$ most probable topic terms $V^k = (v_1^k, \cdots, v_N^k)$ within these sentences is counted.

3. Co-occurrence counts below a certain threshold $minC = 4$ are set to 0 to not focus on very infrequent or insignificant events.

4. Significance of co-occurrence counts $sig(a, b)$ for two terms $a \in V^k$ and $b \in V^k$ is computed using the LL measure (Bordag, 2008, p. 54f) with respect to the size of the entire sentence set $n = |\mathcal{S}'_{c,k}|$.

$$\lambda = \left[\begin{array}{l} n \log n - n_a \log n_a - n_b \log n_b + n_{ab} \log n_{ab} \\ +(n - n_a - n_b + n_{ab}) \log(n - n_a - n_b + n_{ab}) \\ +(n_a - n_{ab}) \log(n_a - n_{ab}) + (n_b - n_{ab}) \log(n_b - n_{ab}) \\ -(n - n_a) \log(n - n_a) - (n - n_b) \log(n - n_b) \end{array} \right]$$

$$sig(a, b) = \begin{cases} -2 \log \lambda, & n_{ab} < \frac{n_a n_b}{n} \\ 2 \log \lambda, & \text{otherwise} \end{cases} \tag{3.21}$$

where n_a and n_b are the number of sentences in $\mathcal{S}'_{c,k}$ containing a, or b respectively; n_{ab} is the number of sentences containing both terms.

5. Significance values below a certain threshold $minLL = 3.84$ are set to 0 to not focus on insignificant term relations.[22]

[22]For the significance thresholds, see footnote 21.

Table 3.9.: Examples of extracted co-occurrences per temporal and thematic cluster.

Term 1	Term 2	LL
Cluster 2: Topic 59		
diplomatisch	beziehung	934.745
kalten	krieg	745.370
teil	deutschlands	576.233
west	ost	507.562
anerkennung	ddr	502.969
kalt	krieg	438.752
bundesrepublik	ddr	372.925
osteuropäisch	staaten	319.468
stellen	frage	314.774
völkerrechtlichen	anerkennung	306.561
Cluster 3: Topic 62		
dienst	öffentlich	2609.087
grundordnung	demokratisch	610.448
eintreten	grundordnung	571.928
jederzeit	eintreten	514.733
verfassungsfeindlich	partei	481.145
freiheitlichen	grundordnung	479.399
jederzeit	grundordnung	418.212
freiheitlichen	demokratisch	413.246
mitgliedschaft	partei	401.283
verfassungsfeindlich	mitgliedschaft	383.501

6. Pairs of significant co-occurrences are ordered decreasingly to their LL-value.

Extracted co-occurrence pairs are the basis for the visualization of SECGs. An example for the top 10 co-occurrence pairs extracted from two topics is given in Table 3.9. In the following sections, enrichment of additional semantically insightful data on single terms participating in co-occurrence relations is described.

3.2.6. Keyness of Terms

Not all terms taking part in a significant co-occurrence relation are equally descriptive for the contents of the topic. To judge on relative importance of terms, we need to apply a statistical measure. One possible measure would be the term probability given the topic $P(t|\beta_k)$. But we do not want to weight terms globally based on the entire corpus. Instead, we want to base the judgments with respect to the topic and time period under investigation. The simplest idea would be to apply frequency counts of terms in these sub-corpora to determine their importance. But we already know, frequency alone is a bad indicator for keyness. Better measures are those which are established for key term extraction.

In Section 3.1.2, the Log-likelihood (LL) measure is described for key term extraction. As the results for document retrieval indicate its usefulness, we simply employ it once more to judge on relevancy of the terms taking part in our extracted co-occurrence relations. As a comparison collection for computing the LL measure, again the corpus $\mathcal{W}$ compiled from 100,000 randomly selected sentences from Wikipedia articles is taken (see Section 3.1.2). For every term of the $N = 200$ most probable topic terms in each SECG relative overuse to this Wikipedia corpus is computed. Table 3.10 displays examples of term keyness for two topics in two distinct time clusters..

3.2.7. Sentiments of Key Terms

Sentiments[23] expressed towards certain entities can be a valuable heuristic device to explore large document collections. Entities could be terms, concepts (lists of terms), term co-occurrence pairs, single documents or even entire topics. As terms in co-occurrence graphs can be taken as representatives of discursive signifiers within a thematic coherence, observation of sentiment terms expressed within their contexts might be a valid approach to reveal emotions to these entities in the discourse. Especially for investigating speech acts on democratic

[23]See Section 2.2.3 for some introductory notes on Sentiment Analysis in QDA.

Table 3.10.: Example key terms extracted per temporal cluster and topic.

Cluster 2: Topic 59		**Cluster 3: Topic 62**	
Term	**LL**	**Term**	**LL**
deutschen	17179.936	partei	7683.841
bundesrepublik	14244.400	dkp	6531.410
ddr	9833.421	öffentlich	4483.212
politisch	9745.186	dienst	4460.154
politik	8529.275	bewerber	3944.922
deutschland	6839.388	beamte	3803.593
wiedervereinigung	6216.722	kommunistisch	3201.241
frage	5716.529	grundgesetz	2913.200
bonn	5535.869	verfassungsfeindlich	2867.454
deutschlands	5199.870	demokratisch	2660.121

demarcation, one would expect normative or moral language towards certain actors, ideas or activities to be found in news coverage.

To enrich co-occurrence graphs with sentiment information, I compute a sentiment score for each term it consists of. For this, a rather general basic approach is used. The selected approach has the advantage of easy implementation and also allows for comparability of the results aggregated on topic level to a certain degree. For detecting sentiments, I employ the German dictionary resource SentiWS (Remus et al., 2010). SentiWS provides two lists of weighted lemmas together with their inflected forms—one list of 1,650 positive terms and one list of 1,818 negative terms. Besides category information on polarity, each term t in SentiWS is assigned with a polarity weight w_t. Positive terms are weighted on a scale between [0;1]; negative terms are weighted on a scale between [-1;0] (see examples in Table 3.11). The lists have been compiled by an automatic process which initially relies on a seed set of definitely positive or negative words (e.g. *gut, schön, richtig, ...* or *schlecht, unschön, falsch, ...*). Polarity weighting for other terms (named target terms in the following) is then performed by observing co-occurrence between these target terms and the either positive or negative seed terms in sentences of an example corpus. Co-occurrence

Table 3.11.: Examples of positive and negative terms together with their polarity weight w_t in the SentiWS dictionary (Remus et al., 2009).

Positive		**Negative**	
Term	$\mathbf{w_t}$	**Term**	$\mathbf{w_t}$
Aktivität	0.0040	Abbau	-0.058
Befreiung	0.0040	Bankrott	-0.0048
Leichtigkeit	0.1725	Belastung	-0.3711
Respekt	0.0040	Degradierung	-0.3137
Stolz	0.0797	Lüge	-0.5
beachtlich	0.0040	Niederlage	-0.3651
bewundernswert	0.0823	aggressiv	-0.4484
hochkarätig	0.0040	alarmieren	-0.0048
knuddelig	0.2086	furchtbar	-0.3042
toll	0.5066	gewaltsam	-0.0048

counts for target terms with seed list terms are judged for statistical relevance by the Pointwise Mutual Information (PMI) measure and finally aggregated to a score on semantic orientation. The approach is based on the assumption that terms of a certain semantic orientation co-occur more frequently with terms of the same orientation than of the opposite. Evaluation of this approach with human raters shows that the performance of identifying positive/negative terms correctly is "very promising ($P = 0.96, R = 0.74, F = 0.84$)" (Remus et al., 2009, p. 1170).

To infer on sentiments of each term of the N most probable topic terms $V^k = (v_1^k, \cdots, v_N^k)$ for a topic k in a specific time period, I apply the SentiWS dictionary in the following manner:

1. Analogue to extraction of co-occurrences (see Section 3.2.5), for each time cluster c a set of documents $\mathcal{D}'_{c,k}$ containing a share of topic k above a threshold $\theta_{d,k} > 0.1$ is identified.

2. For each term $v_i^k \in V^k$

   a) Extract a set $\mathcal{S}_i$ of sentences from $\mathcal{D}'_{c,k}$ which contain v_i^k

b) Count frequencies $\mathbf{n}$ of sentiment terms $t \in$ SentiWS: Set $n_t \leftarrow tf(t, \mathcal{S}_i)$, if $tf(t, \mathcal{S}_i) > 0$

c) Multiply all sentiment term frequencies $\mathbf{n}$ with their respective polarity weight $\mathbf{w}$ from SentiWS: $s_t \leftarrow w_t n_t$

d) Compute a sentiment score p_i for v_i^k by averaging over all polarity weighted SentiWS term counts $\mathbf{s}$: $p_i \leftarrow \bar{s} = \frac{1}{|\mathbf{s}|} \sum_{j=1}^{|\mathbf{s}|} s_j$

e) Compute a controversy score q_i for v_i^k by determining the variance of all polarity weighted SentiWS term counts: $q_i \leftarrow var(\mathbf{s}) = \frac{1}{|\mathbf{s}|-1} \sum_{j=1}^{|\mathbf{s}|} (s_j - \bar{s})^2$

3. An overall sentiment score $P_{c,k}$ for the entire topic in that time frame can be computed by summing up all sentiment scores $\mathbf{p}$: $P_{c,k} = \sum_{i=1}^{N} p_i$

4. An overall controversy score $Q_{c,k}$ for the entire topic in that time frame can be computed by taking the variance of all sentiment scores $\mathbf{p}$: $Q_{c,k} = \frac{1}{n-1} \sum_{i=1}^{N} (p_i - \bar{p})^2$ where $\bar{p}$ is the mean of $\mathbf{p}$.

This procedure provides a sentiment score and a controversy score for each term in one SECG. Furthermore, by computing variances of sentiment scores per term and topic, we may identify terms / topics which are highly debated. This may be assumed because we observe a broader range of positive and negative contexts for the most probable terms of a topic. Table 3.12 gives examples for highly positive and negative as well as (non-)controversial terms identified in two topics of two time periods.

3.2.8. Semantically Enriched Co-Occurrence Graphs

After having extracted various information from our to-be-explored corpus $\mathcal{D}'$ of 28,557 documents, we can now put it all together to visualize Semantically Enriched Co-occurrence Graphs (SECGs):

For each sub-collection $\mathcal{D}'_{c,k}$ selected by temporal cluster c (see Section 3.2.3) and topic k (see Section 3.2.4), we combine the extracted information as follows:

Table 3.12.: Examples of sentiment (p_i) and controversy scores (q_i) for terms per temporal cluster and topic.

Cluster 2: Topic 59		**Cluster 3: Topic 62**	
Term	p_i	**Term**	p_i
erfolg	0.1259	aktiv	0.0094
menschlich	0.1035	angestellte	0.0090
völkerrechtlichen	0.0321	gewähr	0.0029
erleichterung	0.0287	jederzeit	-0.0038
normalisierung	0.0268	sinn	-0.0067
anerkennung	0.0259	anfrage	-0.0085
drüben	0.0248	ziel	-0.0119
entspannung	0.0209	beamte	-0.0148
...	...	...	...
überwindung	-0.0141	extremist	-0.0482
recht	-0.0141	rechtfertigen	-0.0505
mauer	-0.0147	pflicht	-0.0592
offen	-0.0157	streitbar	-0.0598
teilung	-0.0169	absatz	-0.0634
endgültig	-0.0213	zugehörigkeit	-0.0743
verzicht	-0.0352	verboten	-0.0866
kalt	-0.0698	ablehnung	-0.1068
Term	q_i	**Term**	q_i
krieg	3.2601	radikal	0.7370
anerkennung	1.4999	verbieten	0.4616
erfolg	1.2228	ablehnung	0.3971
deutschen	0.6103	partei	0.2410
menschlich	0.5139	öffentlich	0.1485
bundesrepublik	0.4922	verboten	0.1358
politisch	0.3737	dienst	0.1301
politik	0.3625	pflicht	0.0806
...	...	...	...
wiederherstellung	0.0022	bundesverwaltungsgericht	0.0010
west	0.0021	gewähr	0.0008
status	0.0019	prüfen	0.0007
friedensvertrag	0.0018	absatz	0.0006
hallstein-doktrin	0.0017	frankfurter	0.0006
überwinden	0.0017	angestellte	0.0006
normalisierung	0.0015	einzelfall	0.0006
wiedervereinigen	0.0014	freiheitlich-demokratische	0.0005

1. **Graph:** Construct a co-occurrence graph $G = (V, E)$ based on extracted co-occurrence pairs (see Section 3.2.5). Vertices V are defined by terms taking part in the j most significant co-occurrence relations. Edges E are defined by existence of the co-occurrence pair relation between two terms of V. To keep the visualization clear, I set $j = 60$. This leaves aside many significant co-occurrence patterns, but helps to concentrate on the most important ones. Furthermore, disconnected sub-graphs which contain less than 3 nodes are removed from G, to not inflate the graph with many isolated term pairs. Usually, those isolated term pairs represent typical collocation patterns of general language regularities of the German language rather than specific thematic content. Removing them, puts emphasis on the giant component of the graph.

2. **Edge size:** Edges E of G are weighted by LL-significance of their co-occurrence. For visualization, the more significant the term relation, the thicker an edge will be drawn.

3. **Vertex size:** Vertices V of G are weighted by 'keyness' of their occurrence (see Section 3.2.6). For visualization, the higher the LL score of a term, the bigger the Vertex will be drawn. Vertices are labeled with the representing terms. Label sizes are also scaled along with vertex sizes to emphasize on 'keyness'.

4. **Vertex color:** Vertices V of G are colored according to their contextual sentiment (see Section 3.2.7). Vertices representing negative terms will be colored in a range from *red* $\widehat{=}$ most negative term to *grey* $\widehat{=}$ no sentiment. Vertices representing positive terms will be colored in a range from *grey* $\widehat{=}$ no sentiment to *green* $\widehat{=}$ most positive term. To translate sentiment scores into color palette values, scores are re-scaled into a value range of [0; 1].

5. **Vertex frame color:** Frames of vertices V are colored according to their controversy score (see Section 3.2.7). Controvery scores will be translated into a color range from *white* $\widehat{=}$ low controversy score to *orange* $\widehat{=}$ high controversy score. For selecting suitable color palette values, scores are re-scaled into a value range of [0; 1].

6. **Edge color:** The structure of G can be utilized to heuristically identify semantic propositions, i.e. assertions on entities within sentences. For this, one can identify maximal cliques in G of size 3 or higher. Vertex sets of these cliques represent fully connected sub-graphs of G which means that all participating terms co-occur significantly with each other in sentences of a topic and time period. These patterns reveal important meaningful language regularities, constituting central discursive assertions. Edges which are part of such a maximal clique are colored *green*. Due to vertex removal in step 1, it may happen that the clique structure is not represented any longer in G. Consequently, maximum cliques of size $>= 3$ should be identified before vertex removal such that all previously extracted co-occurrence pairs are used. Table 3.13 gives examples for extracted propositional candidates.

7. **Text examples:** In addition to global contexts represented by co-occurrence graphs, qualitative information for each SECG is provided by extracting ranked lists of 'good' text examples. For this, candidates for semantic propositions from the previous step are utilized to select sentences from $\mathcal{D}'_{c,k}$ containing all of its components. For each proposition candidate, I sampled five example sentences from $\mathcal{D}'_{c,k}$. Sets of sampled sentences are ranked according to summed LL-significance values of the co-occurrence relation it consists of.

For five temporal clusters, each with 10 manually selected topics, we can draw a SECG.[24] We get 50 SECGs supporting the content analyst by getting a quick visual overview of the most important topics during different time frames. The final SECG for the two topics/periods used throughout this section are given in Figures 3.9 and 3.10.

Further, providing good text examples together with each SECG allows for qualitative assessment of the extracted global contexts which

[24]I utilized the *igraph* package (Csardi and Nepusz, 2006) for R to generate the Graphs. Vertices are arranged on the canvas using the Fruchterman-Rheingold layout algorithm.

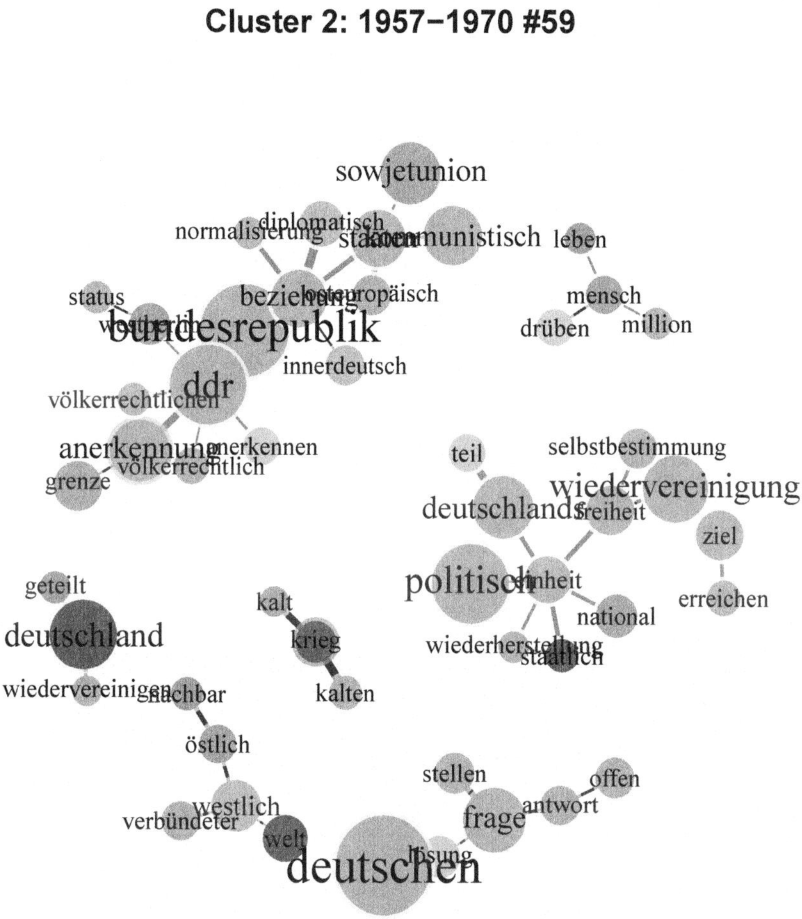

Figure 3.9.: Example of SECG (cluster 2, topic #59).

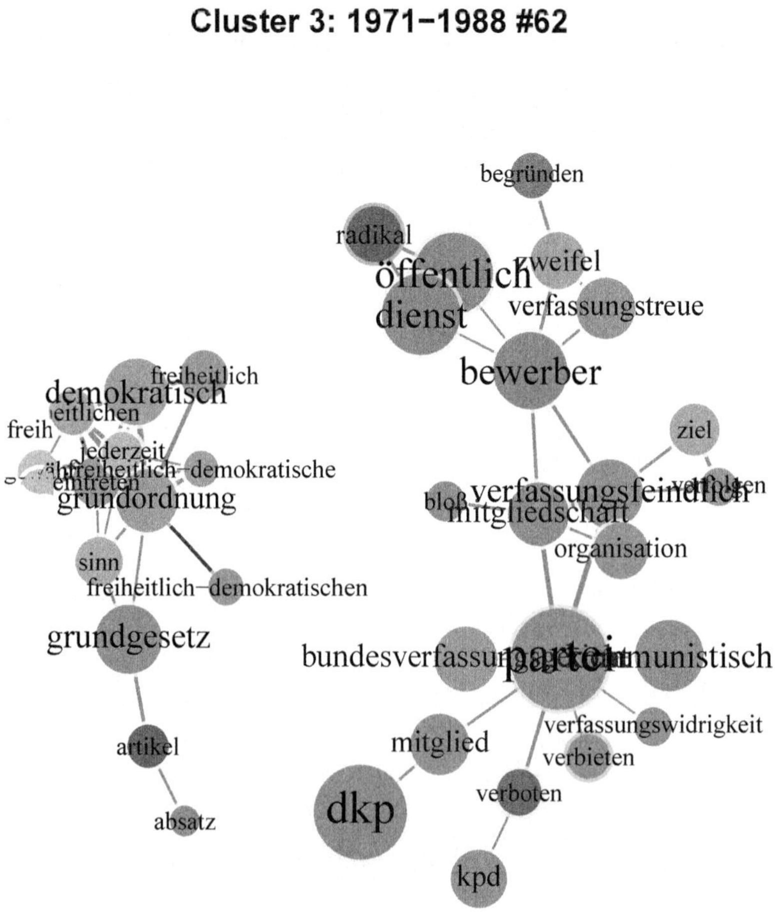

Figure 3.10.: Example of SECG (cluster 3, topic #62).

Table 3.13.: Examples for candidates of semantic propositions identified from maximum cliques in SECGs.

Cluster 2: Topic 59	**Cluster 3: Topic 62**
normalisierung, beziehung, ddr	überprüfung, erkenntnis, bedenken
wiedervereinigen, deutschlands, status	verfassungsfeinde, öffentlich, dienst
leben, mensch, million	verfassungswidrig, partei, erklären
westdeutsch, bundesrepublik, ddr	absatz, grundgesetz, artikel
hallstein-doktrin, beziehung, diplomatisch	zweifel, bewerber, begründen, jederzeit, eintreten, grundordnung
erreichen, wiedervereinigung, ziel	zugehörigkeit, partei, verfassungsfeindlich
existenz, ddr, anerkennen	extremist, öffentlich, dienst
teilung, europas, teilung deutschlands	ordnung, demokratisch, freiheitlich
anspruch, selbstbestimmung, wiedervereinigung	feststellen, bundesverfassungsgericht, verfassungswidrigkeit
teilung, europas, überwindung	kpd, dkp, verboten

is an important feature to support QDA. Table 3.14 gives examples for extracted sentences allowing for much better interpretation of semantic relational structures visualized by SECGs. In fact, text examples are selected by a notable back and forth mechanism. The data-driven process of generating SECGs reveals linguistic patterns on the global context level within a certain topic and time frame. Using such globally identified patterns to look for local contexts comprising of all of its features allows for selection of high quality examples incorporating central semantics of the topic. As vertices in G represent binary relations of co-occurrence, it is not guaranteed to find sentences or propositions containing all three or more components. But usually, at least some sentences can be retrieved, which then can be interpreted as good candidates containing sedimented discourse characteristics.

Table 3.14.: Examples of text instances containing previously identified semantic propositions (see Table 3.13).

Cluster 2: Topic 59	Cluster 3: Topic 62
"Es sei daher der Abschluß eines Vertrags zwischen allen Staaten Europas über den Gewaltverzicht nötig, ebenso 'die Normalisierung der Beziehungen zwischen allen Staaten und der DDR wie auch zwischen den beiden deutschen Staaten und zwischen West-Berlin (als besonderem politischem Raum) und der DDR'".	"Der umstrittene Extremistenbeschluß der Länderministerpräsidenten vom Januar 1972 setzt für Bewerber um ein Staatsamt weit strengere Maßstäbe: 'Gehört ein Bewerber einer Organisation an, die verfassungsfeindliche Ziele verfolgt, so begründet diese Mitgliedschaft Zweifel daran, ob er jederzeit für die freiheitliche demokratische Grundordnung eintreten wird.'"
"In der ruhigen, unablässigen Forderung der Freiheit der Selbstbestimmung, ohne Verknüpfung mit dem Anspruch der Wiedervereinigung, haben wir die Unterstützung durch unsere Verbündeten und der Weltmeinung kräftiger, rückhaltloser, eindeutiger für uns."	"'Verfassungsfeinde gehören nicht in den öffentlichen Dienst,' bekräftigte der Minister Anfang April im CSU-Organ Bayernkurier noch einmal."

3.2.9. Summary of Lessons Learned

The introduced process of generating SECGs provides an intuitive access for content analysts to explore large data collections. Knowledge structures inherent to the collection are visualized on a global context level suitable for 'distant reading'. Text snippets with high informative value based on extracted semantic structure are provided with each graph to backup interpretations from visualized display by qualitative data review. Based on the requirements initially formulated, the following insights have been obtained during this section:

- Document collections can be separated, both temporally and thematically, into small, coherent segments by using topic models. Optimal parameters for topic modeling can be obtained with the topic coherence measure (Mimno et al., 2011) alongside with qualitative evaluation of the topic results. For quality assurance, reproducibility of the model can be measured. Temporal segmentation of the data into distinctive time periods can be achieved in a data-driven manner by PAM clustering on the inferred topic proportions.

- Selection of meaningful topics from a topic model with respect to a specific research question should be done deliberately by the researcher in a manual process. Nonetheless, it can be supported by ranking topics, e.g. according to the rank_1 measure, i.e. the number of their primary occurrence in documents.
- Significant co-occurrence of topics in temporally segmented sub-collections can be visualized as network graph to reveal global thematic structures.
- Significant co-occurrence of terms in temporally and thematically segmented sub-collections can be visualized as network graph to reveal patterns of language use for content exploration. Term co-occurrence networks can be enriched by additional semantic information, such as sentiment and keyness of terms in their thematic contexts, visualized by color or size of graph vertices.
- Graph structures in co-ocurrence graphs such as maximal cliques reveal semantic fields of paradigmatically related terms which can be assumed as candidates for semantic propositions. Candidates for propositions point analysts to potentially interesting categories[25] for further investigations (see Section 3.3). Text snippets such as sentences containing these semantic propositions appear to be excellent data samples to backup interpretations from the global contexts of graphs qualitatively.

The generation of SECGs is not an entirely unsupervised process. While most parts are purely data-driven, analysts still need to decide for specific parameters at certain points. This should not be seen as a

[25]I use 'categories' here in the sense of language regularities constantly re-used over time which may give hints to sedimented discourse structures.

weakness, rather than a strength of the process. It provides analysts with opportunities to keep control over the analysis and to check for validity and compliance with their background knowledge. Retaining control in such exploratory workflows is a necessary precondition to develop confidence in the computationally produced results. To make things easier to apply, algorithms and quality measures may provide hints for best choices of parameters. But in the end, it should be the researchers decision to select

- an appropriate number of topics K for the topic model to achieve desired thematic granularity,
- a plausible α value for regulating topic distributions in documents,
- a comprehensible number of time periods, and
- a manageable number and conscious (manual) selection of topics per time period to draw graphs from.

While analysis capabilities and quality of results truly increase, given the analyst understands fundamentals of these steps, profound understanding of algorithmic details is not needed necessarily to produce useful results. Sticking to default values and data-driven optimal parameter suggestions will also lead to valuable results in most cases.

The method presented here is an exemplary application which provides a strategy tailored to the research needs and requirements for exploring the data set on democratic demarcation. Further modifications to this process could be made based on different operationalization decisions, e.g. using some other topic model instead of LDA, altering the way of how the graph vertices and edges are defined, including other text statistical measures into the visualization or choosing another layout algorithm for the graph.

As this section focused mainly on the technical realization of the presented workflow, open questions remain on the methodological aspects. From QDA perspective, researchers need to learn to integrate results from such processes into their general analysis. They need to describe steps they take comprehensibly and in a manner allowing for reproduction. Furthermore, they need to perform careful and theoretically sound interpretation of results in the light of their methodological background. Some thoughts in this direction are elaborated on in Chapter 5.

3.3. Classification for Qualitative Data Analysis

In QDA, methods of coding text operate either inductively, deductively or as a mix of both approaches, also sometimes referred to as abductive paradigm. Inductive research develops its categories from observations in the empirical data and can be supported by exploratory tools, as presented in the previous chapter. For the deductive approach, usually categories of content are derived from text external theoretical assumptions. Abductive research develops its categories from (samples of) the data and, afterwards, utilizes category systems for subsuming new data and hypothesis testing (Kelle, 1997). To support subsumptive coding of text as essential part of a QDA process, we will augment our exploratory analysis conducted in the previous section (see 3.2) by identifying concrete categorical content in the data concerned with several aspects of democratic demarcation. To prepare this step, I compose a workflow of CA utilizing supervised ML to extend manual analysis capabilities to large amounts of textual entities. The process addresses specific requirements of the social science domain and will be evaluated with example data to determine its usefulness for time series and trend analysis.

In manually conducted CA, trained persons, called coders, categorize textual entities by hand. They read through quantities of material, either the full data set under investigation or a sample randomly drawn from it, and attach a code label, if a certain entity fits into the definition of a category. Categories are defined together with example snippets in so called “code books” which try to describe a category as accurately as possible (Krippendorff, 2013). Textual entities under investigation might be from varying granularity: words, phrases, sentences, paragraphs or whole documents. In most QDA applications researchers are interested in 'propositions'—certain meaning expressed in a declarative sentence or sequence of sentences.[26] Much of this manual coding effort can be supported by computer-assisted methods to a certain extent. The most promising innovation in these analytic procedures can be expected from supervised machine learning, also referred to as classification.

Classification of text has been a broad research area in NLP for several decades. Applications range from email spam detection and genre identification to sentiment analysis. Formally, we can define the classification problem as a binary function on a set of documents $\mathcal{D}$ and a set of classes $\mathcal{C}$ in the following manner: the function $\mathcal{F} : \mathcal{D} \times \mathcal{C} \rightarrow \{0, 1\}$ assigns either 0 or 1 to a pair $[d_j, c_p]$ where $d_j \in \mathcal{D}$ and $c_p \in \mathcal{C}$. An assigned value 0 indicates that d_j does not belong to class c_p, 1 indicates it does belong to c_p (Baeza-Yates and Ribeiro-Neto, 2011, p. 283). A classification algorithm provides such a function which strives to fulfill this assignment as accurately as possible with respect to the empirical data. For this, it extracts characteristic patterns, so called features, from documents of each category in a training phase. It therewith 'learns' these pattern–class associations to build the function $\mathcal{F}$, which also may be called an instance of a classification model. With this model instance, it now is possible to assign class labels to unknown documents by observing their feature structure. Concerning the fact that the model based on training data is necessarily incomplete with regard to all existing data in a population, prediction cannot be fully exact. The quality of a model instance can be evaluated by well established quality measures such as *accuracy*, *precision*, *recall* and F_1 (Asch, 2013; Baeza-Yates and Ribeiro-Neto, 2011, p. 325) which will also be utilized throughout this study.

Although supervised text classification already has a long history in NLP, it has not been applied in QDA widely. In NLP investigation of problems in text classification usually is done by using standard

[26] For example, Teubert (2008) investigates political positions towards the European Union (EU) expressed in British Online Forums. Wiedemann (2011) investigates German parliamentary debates to identify argumentative patterns for or against data retention in telecommunication.

corpora like Reuters-21578 Text Categorization Collection (newswire texts from 1987), 20 Newsgroups data set (news group articles on sports, computers etc.) or abstracts of (bio-)medical research papers. Classes of these corpora usually are genre or topic related and rather clearly defined; classification experiments are based on label assignments to complete documents rather than snippets of documents. In real world applications of QDA such "laboratory conditions" unfortunately are seldom met. A first systematic study on applicability of ML classifiers for CA in the German context has been conducted by Scharkow (2012). Although this study states the usefulness of fully automated analysis, it also operates on rather simple genre categories of newspaper data (e.g. identifying newspaper sections such as sports, politics or culture).

Applying supervised machine learning in QDA scenarios is a challenging task. The purpose of this section is to provide a workflow to employ this technology as effective as possible within a QDA process. For this, I firstly describe requirements of that analysis task which differ from standard NLP classification scenarios in several ways. Then, I conduct experiments on real world data from a political science project on hand coded party manifestos. Base line classification accuracy of propositional categories is evaluated and compared to an extended feature set incorporating topic model data as features for 'semantic smoothing' of the data. In a third step, applicability of classification for trend identification is demonstrated. In a last step, I propose an active learning workflow to create training data for classification with low cost and high quality for the desired purpose. Thus, this section answers the questions:

- How good can automatic classification for QDA purposes be?,
- How exact has automatic classification to be to produce valid results for trend analysis? and,
- How can training data be collected effectively by active learning?

Experimental setups and the resulting best practice for applying ML in QDA scenarios are employed in the subsequent Chapter 4. The goal is to identify and investigate propositional categories on democratic demarcation in the collection $\mathcal{D}$ comprising of all *FAZ* and *Die Zeit* articles.

3.3.1. Requirements

Manual CA conducts studies on randomly drawn samples of text from certain, well-defined populations to infer on category distributions or proportions within these populations. This works well, as long as there are lots of manual coders and the number of populations where samples are drawn from is fixed and small. To investigate a category, e.g. statements expressing democratic demarcation towards (neo-)fascist ideology, in the 1950s, it would be acceptable to draw a representative random sample, hand code its content and measure code proportions. But it certainly would not be justifiable to infer on proportions in subsets of that basic population. For example, to infer on category proportions in 1951 compared to 1952 or ongoing years, we probably neither have enough hand coded data, nor do we have representative samples. To compare proportions for a time series, we would need to draw random samples of sufficient size from each time frame and manually code them. In this scenario clear advantages of (semi)automatic classification procedures come into play. A well trained classification model allows for reliable measurement of categories in varying subsets of its base population. This is because it predicts on each individual case of the entire base population whereas each case is classified independently of each other. But how reliable can machine classification be in contrast to (well-trained) human coders under circumstances of QDA?

Text classification for QDA faces several distinctive challenges in contrast to standard text classification scenarios in NLP which need to be addressed, if supervised machine learning should be applied successfully to an analysis workflow:

- **Abstract categories:** Categories of interest in QDA often are much more abstract than simple news genre labels like *sports*, *politics* or *weather*. Textual units representing desired categories are expressed in a potentially unlimited, heterogeneous variance of word sequences. In practice, the overall majority of expressions constituting a certain category is formed by only a small number of variants. Human discourse tends to use similar expressions to express similar things, which yields regular patterns in language use. This is why machine classification (as well as human understanding) of texts can be successful in the first place—the identification of patterns in language use and their mapping to categorial semantic units. Nonetheless, categories relevant in QDA studies, such as expression of democratic demarcation, economized argumentation in politics (Wiedemann et al., 2013) or ethnicized reporting in news coverage (Pollak et al., 2011) are not only identifiable by certain key words alone. In case of simple categories, the observation of the term *soccer* might be a decent indicator for a general genre category *sports*. Most QDA categories instead are constituted by complex combinations of sets of terms and even syntactic structure. Thus, employed classification algorithms should be capable of taking many different features as well as dependence of features into account.

- **Unbalanced classes:** While classes in standard evaluation corpora are mostly of comparable size[27], classes in CA contexts are highly unbalanced. Imagine again the measurement of statements against (neo-)fascist attitudes: even in a newspaper article dealing with current activities of the far right there are probably only a handful out of thirty to forty sentences expressing "demarcation" in the sense of the desired category. Odds between positive and negative examples for a desired context unit may be 1:20, 1:50 or 1:100. Classification algorithms need to be able to deal with these discrepancies.

- **Sparse training data:** Text classification for entire documents is the standard case in many NLP applications. As algorithms usually

[27]The Reuters-21578 corpus contains some very low frequent classes as well, but most studies leave them out for their experiments.

are based on vector representations of the units to be classified, document classification has a clear advantage over classification of smaller units such as paragraphs or sentences which are the 'natural' units of many CA applications. Vectors representing such units of text are much more sparse than vectors of complete documents, putting less information on features into the classification process. To address this problem, we need to engineer features representing more generalized context than just the few words contained in a single sentence or paragraph. We should also try not to 'learn' from the hand coded training data only, but in a semi-supervised classification scenario from the freely available unlabeled data of our to-be-classified corpus as well.

- **Small training data:** Standard evaluation procedures in NLP deal with scenarios where training data is abundant. In contrast to this, QDA studies investigate categories fitting a special research interest. Unfortunately, manual coding of examples is labor intense and therefore costly. For this reason, QDA studies are restricted to a limited number of training data they can generate. This situation poses different questions: Which classifier should be taken? Some classification algorithms are able to deal with small training data better than others. Can the process of generating training data be optimized by application of active learning, to get best possible results at low costs?

- **Social science goals:** Classification in the standard case tries to optimize accuracy of individual prediction for individual cases. This definitely makes sense for applications such as spam detection on emails, where we want to avoid false positives, i.e. emails deleted as spam although they are not spam. For QDA studies on large data sets, we are not so much interested in evaluating each individual case. We merely are interested in estimating proportions of categories in populations correctly (Hopkins and King, 2010). Even less restrictive, we might be interested in observing trends in the quantitative development of categories over time. In this case, even category proportions would not need to be overly exact, as long as the estimation errors for proportions in time slices of the basic population are stable. To determine the usefulness of machine classification for CA, we need to clarify at first how well it can perform with respect to conventional evaluation procedures in principle. We can expect a lowered performance compared to acceptable results of standard NLP tasks, because of the hard conditions of this task. Nonetheless, if we modify the evaluation criteria from correct individual classification towards the goal of observing proportions and trends validly and reliably, we might be able to prove the usefulness of the method for trend and time series analysis.

The following sections address these requirements and formulate practical solutions to optimize machine classification of QDA categories with respect to social science goals. For this, experiments on real world data are conducted to determine reliability and validity of the overall approach, as well as identifying best practices. Results are also compared to a method of "proportional classification", suggested by Hopkins and King (2010), which addresses some of the requirements introduced above.

Category Systems

In supervised classification three types are usually distinguished:

1. single-class: decision whether or not an item belongs into a single category (e.g. spam vs. no spam),
2. multi-class: decision to assign exactly one class label to an item from a set of three or more classes,
3. multi-label: decision whether an item belongs into one or more classes from a set of three or more classes.

The third case can be treated as a repeated application of the first case with each label separately. Hopkins and King (2010) propose a fourth type of 'proportional classification' which is not interested in labeling individual items, but in estimating correct proportions of categories within a population under investigation. For QDA purposes in social sciences, all four types of classification might be valid approaches in certain scenarios. But usually, the nature of categories of interest in QDA studies is related to the single-class / multi-label case. To clarify this, we first look at the multi-class variant more closely. Multi-class scenarios require category systems with two decisive properties:

- completeness: the set of categories needs to describe each case of the population, i.e. one label needs to be applicable meaningfully to any item,
- disjointness: categories should not be overlapping, i.e. that exactly one label of the set of categories should apply to any item of the population.

For most category systems applied in QDA studies, these conditions are not met. The property of completeness might be mitigated by introducing a special category *'irrelevant item'* to the code book which could be used to label all items which do not contain meaningful content for the study. More complex is the problem of disjointness. Categories in many QDA applications are not clearly separable. In fact, overlapping of categories in concrete items of empirical data might be of special interest for observation. These cases may represent co-occurrence of ideas, thoughts, discourses, and, hence, indicate certain argumentative strategies. Category systems could also be hierarchical, where sub-categories cannot be defined as disjoint cases, but as different perspectives on the root category which can occur conjointly in single items. For this reason, I suggest to concentrate on the single-class case for studying the applicability of machine classification for QDA. The multi-label case is treated as n cases of the single-class classification.

3.3.2. Experimental Data

In the following, several experiments are conducted to derive a reasonable workflow for the application of machine classification in QDA.

Final goal of this workflow is to infer on category proportion development over time to describe certain aspects in the discourse on democratic demarcation in Germany. But as we do not know anything about these categories yet, we have to refer to another experimental data set, to develop and evaluate an analysis strategy.

For the experiments, I rely on extracts of the data set of the *Manifesto Project Database*[28]. The Manifesto Project (MP) collects party manifestos from elections worldwide and conducts manual CA on them (Volkens et al., 2014). Each sentence of a single manifesto is annotated by trained coders with one (in rare cases also more than one) of 57 categories. Categories comprise of demands towards certain policy issues such as economics, welfare state, environment or foreign politics. The database contains frequencies of categories for each manifesto per party and election. Political scientists use this data to quantitatively compare distributions of policy issues over various dimensions (e.g. time, party, country, political spectrum).[29] It thus provides an excellent resource of high-quality 'real world' text data, which also can be used for experiments with machine classification.

For experimentation with MP data, I selected all available hand coded full-text party manifestos of the major German parties from the last elections (see Table 3.16). The total data set comprises of 44,513 manually coded sentences. To be coherent with my topic on democratic demarcation, I selected four categories out of the MP category set, which are related to the discourse on democracy or may be viewed as crucial component of it.[30] Selected categories are given by their code number, name, a short description and an example sentence in Table 3.15.

[28] https://manifestoproject.wzb.eu

[29] For methodological reflections and exemplary studies of the use of MP data in political science, see Volkens et al. (2013).

[30] The dispute on defining democracy is as old as the term itself. It is not my intention to give solid definition of democracy with my selection. It rather should be seen as a selection of democracy related categories which occur reasonably often in the data to be part of a quantitative evaluation.

Table 3.15.: Democracy related categories selected from MP data together with their number of coded sentences (n). Descriptions are cited from Werner et al. (2011), the handbook of coding instructions of the project.

Code	Name	Description	Example	n
201	Freedom and Human Rights	"Favourable mentions of importance of personal freedom and civil rights in the manifesto and other countries."	"Auch die Menschen von heute haben ein Recht auf ein gutes Leben." (FDP, 1998)	2134
202	Democracy	"Favourable mentions of democracy as the 'only game in town'."	"Mitentscheiden, mitgestalten und mitverantworten: Darauf ist Demokratie angewiesen." (SPD, 2002)	1760
301	Federalism	"Support for federalism or decentralisation of political and/or economic power."	"In der Demografiestrategie spielen die ländlichen Regionen eine große Rolle." (CDU, 2013)	632
503	Equality: Positive	"Concept of social justice and the need for fair treatment of all people."	"Deshalb wollen wir eine durchlässige Gesellschaft, in der die sozialen Blockaden aufgesprengt sind und niemand ausgeschlossen wird." (Grüne, 2009)	3577
All	Democracy Meta	Categories 201, 202, 301 and 503 are put together in one meta-category, with the aim to describe a broader picture of democratic attitude.		8103

Table 3.16.: Numbers of manually coded sentences from party manifestos of eight German parties in four elections.

Year	CDU	FDP	Grüne	LINKE	SPD	AFD	PIRAT
1998	585	1718	2292	1002	1128	0	0
2002	1379	2107	1765	880	1765	0	0
2009	2030	2319	3747	1701	2278	0	0
2013	2574	2579	5427	2472	2898	73	1794

As one can easily see, selected categories capture rather broad themes which can be expressed towards various units of discussion. Hence, realization of categories within concrete sentences of the data may be encountered in varying expressions—hard conditions for machine classifiers (and human coders as well). The size of categories is varying, as well as their coherence. A short close reading on single category sentences reveals that category 201 referencing to human rights appears much more coherent in its expressions than category 503, which contains statements towards social justice in manifold topics. Category 301 encoding federalism is rather small and often contains just references to administrative entities (federal states, municipalities or the EU), but not necessarily expresses demands for federalism explicitly. I also introduce an artificial fifth category *All*, in which I aggregate units of all other four categories. This category may be interpreted as a meta category covering a broader attitude towards democracy than just single aspects of it. For CA research this combination of codes into meta-categories is an interesting option to operationalize and measure more abstract concepts.[31]

3.3.3. Individual Classification

The selected categories represent a range of different properties of the category scheme concerning size, coherence and language variability.

[31] In quantitative studies based on MP data, index construction from aggregation of isolated category counts is a quite common approach to measure more abstract categories, e.g. right-left scales of the political spectrum (Lowe et al., 2011).

Experiments conducted in the following will examine, whether machine classification is applicable to such categories for social science purposes and under the circumstance of scarce training data.

In a first experiment, I apply supervised classification on the introduced MP data. For this, the data set of ordered sentences $\mathcal{S}$ from all party manifestos is divided in two splits:

- every odd sentence is put into a training set $\mathcal{S}_{train}$ consisting of 22,257 sentences, and
- every even sentence is put into a test set $\mathcal{S}_{test}$ consisting of 22,256 sentences.

For the experiment on individual classification, I report on decisions for algorithm selection, representation of documents as features for classification, feature selection and feature weighting, before I present base line results.

Classification algorithms: For supervised classification of textual data a variety of generative and discriminative models exists—each with its individual set of parameters to tune performance with respect to the data. For text classification Naive Bayes (NB), Decision Trees, K-nearest neighbor (kNN), Neural Networks, Maximum Entropy (MAXENT) (also known as multinomial logistic regression) or Support Vector Machines (SVM) have been widely adopted approaches (Baharudin et al., 2010).[32] Although NB performs well on many document classification tasks (e.g. spam detection), I opted it out for model selection here, because its "conditional independence assumption is violated by real-world data and perform very poorly when features are highly correlated" (ibid., p. 16). Also, Ng and Jordan (2002) have demonstrated that discriminative models for classification can be expected to outperform generative models such as NB, if training data size is large enough. Although training data in QDA scenarios usually is not abundant, we can expect enough data to learn from that discriminative classifiers appear to be the right

[32] Baharudin et al. (2010) provide a comprehensive overview on different learning algorithms and feature selection strategies for text classification.

choice. Consequently, I compare two discriminative approaches which do not assume conditional independence of features and have been reported as performing (near) state-of-the-art in many text classification applications. Approaches to compare are Maximum Entropy (Nigam et al., 1999) and SVM (Joachims, 1998). Whereas SVM is widely utilized for text classification and the baseline algorithm to beat in many ML research scenarios, MAXENT is not that common. But because of SVM having been reported to perform less optimal in situations of small training data and unbalanced classes (Forman and Cohen, 2004), I decided for comparison with MAXENT as an algorithm assumed to be more robust in this situation. For both approaches a fast and mature implementation exists in form of C++ libraries, wrapped for usage in R.[33] Decisions for feature engineering, feature selection and parameter tuning described below are based on 5-fold cross validation evaluations on the entire training set.[34]

Document representation: Documents in my experiments with MP data are single sentences $s \in \mathcal{S}$ from party manifestos, annotated with one out of five code labels. For classification, documents are transformed into feature vectors, containing potentially relevant features representing their content and class association. For this, sentences were tokenized[35] and letters transformed to lowercase beforehand. Then, the following features sets were extracted from each sentence:

- stemmed unigrams (including stopwords),
- stemmed bigrams (including stopwords),
- stemmed bigrams (with stop words removed beforehand); bigrams are not added once again, if they are already contained in the feature set from the previous step.

[33]For my experimental setup in R, I used the *maxent* package (Jurka, 2012) which wraps the MAXENT library implemented by Tsuruoka (2011), and the *e1071* package (Meyer, 2014) providing a wrapper for *libsvm* (Chang and Lin, 2011).

[34]For evaluation with k-fold cross validation see Witten et al. (2011, p. 152).

[35]For tokenization, I utilized the MAXENT tokenizer of the Apache openNLP project (https://opennlp.apache.org).

Feature selection: Performance of machine classification may be improved, both in speed and prediction accuracy, by feature selection. For this, features which do not contribute to discrimination of the classes to be predicted are removed from the feature set. Studies on feature selection repeatedly report the Chi-Square statistic as well-performing method to identify significant associations between features and class labels (Baharudin et al., 2010; Yang and Pedersen, 1997). For each feature its association with the positive and the negative class is computed by the Chi-square statistic separately. If the statistic is below a threshold of 6 for both cases, I remove the feature from the feature set.[36] A further feature pruning was applied to the extracted bigram features. Boulis and Ostendorf (2005) report that often bigrams only deliver redundant information to the classifier, compared to the observation of the unigrams they consist of. These redundant information may harm classifier performance. To overcome this issue, they propose 'Redundancy-Compensated KL' (RCKL) as a selection measure. For this, the Kullback-Leibler divergence (KL, see Eq. 3.18) between class association and unigrams/bigrams is determined. For selection, RCKL of a bigram is compared to the sum of RCKL measures of its unigram components. The goal is to remove relevant bigrams if their unigrams are also of high relevancy to distinguish between classes. Only those bigrams are kept, which add more information to the feature set, than its unigram components.

Model selection and feature weighting: For tuning SVM and MAXENT, not only feature engineering and selection is important. Finding optimal parameters for the algorithms itself is crucial, as well. For this, I performed 5-fold cross validation to infer best parameter settings (global C and C-weights per class for SVM; L1/L2 regularizers for MAXENT). Especially the C and C-weights settings were decisive

[36] Assuming degree of freedom $v = 1$ (because we distinguish two classes) a chi-square value of 6 corresponds to a significance level of $0.01 < p < 0.025$ for the association between class label and feature observation. The threshold 6 has been determined by cross validation as a valid choice to reduce insignificant features.

for SVM tuning.[37] Setting C-weights for the positive and negative class improved results of SVM classification drastically, as this parameter is supposed to mitigate the problem of SVMs with unbalanced classes. Following a heuristic, I set the weights inversely proportional to the frequency of the positive and negative class. In a last step *feature weighting* is applied to the pruned feature vectors. For this, feature counts were transformed into TF-IDF values.

Base line result: With these settings and optimization, classification for gaining base line results was conducted by training on the complete training set $\mathcal{S}_{train}$ and evaluating on the held out test set $\mathcal{S}_{test}$. For each of the selected codes of the MP data, sentences are binary classified as belonging into the category or not. Results for both classifiers are given in Table 3.17 by the conventional measures *precision*, *recall*, F_1 and *accuracy* (Witten et al., 2011, p. 163ff). We can see at the first glance that *accuracy* appears to be surprisingly high. This is an effect of the highly unbalanced classes, leaving it as a not very meaningful evaluation measure for our purpose. Comparing both algorithms we can see that SVM outperforms MAXENT in all five cases, considering the F_1 measure. While precision of MAXENT is comparable to SVM or in some cases even a little better, its recall is rather poor. Altogether, results are comparatively moderate ($F_1 < 0.5$ in four cases, $F_1 = 0.518$ in only one case for SVM). Contrasted to common ML applications which report values of $F_1 > 0.7$, these results would probably be considered unacceptable. This is clearly an effect of the very hard conditions of this classification task, described earlier (see Section 3.3.1). But firstly, we might improve the results by introducing more semantic features, and secondly, due to our changed goal of classification for trend analysis instead of individual classification, these results still might be useful.

[37]The regularization parameter C for SVMs can be seen as a penalty factor for classification errors during training. Larger C values lead to improved separation of data points of both classes by the hyperplane. But, this may also lead to overfitting to the training data. For the very sparse feature vectors of sentence classification with QDA codes, cross validation usually suggests rather small values of C as best choice.

Table 3.17.: Base line classification results: Using unigram and bigram-features, feature selection (chi-square) and feature weighting (tf-idf) yield rather mediocre classification results under the tough conditions of this task (very sparse feature vectors from single sentences $\mathcal{S}$, small amount of positive category representatives $\mathcal{S}_+$).

		SVM				MAXENT			
Code	$\mathcal{S}_+$	**P**	**R**	$\mathbf{F_1}$	**A**	**P**	**R**	$\mathbf{F_1}$	**A**
201	1083	0.359	0.556	0.436	0.930	0.336	0.373	0.354	0.933
202	903	0.350	0.592	0.440	0.938	0.430	0.348	0.385	0.954
301	326	0.457	0.331	0.384	0.984	0.242	0.196	0.216	0.979
503	1780	0.339	0.512	0.408	0.881	0.310	0.340	0.324	0.886
All	4092	0.486	0.554	0.518	0.810	0.551	0.364	0.438	0.828

3.3.4. Training Set Size and Semantic Smoothing

To approach a proper classification process for trend analysis of QDA categories, I further investigate the influence of training set sizes on the process. In a second step, the lexical feature set of uni- and bi-grams is enhanced by features generated from an unsupervised topic model process on the entire data set pushing the approach into direction of semi-supervised learning (Xiaojin Zhu, 2008). These features provide a 'semantic smoothing' on the very sparse feature vectors, improving classification quality especially for situations of small training sets.

Training set size: Baseline results in Table 3.17 suggest that training set size is significantly influencing overall performance of classification. Best results are achieved in case where all four codes are combined into the meta category 'All'. In this case, the number of positive examples $\mathcal{S}_+$ in training data is higher compared to classification of single codes, as well as the ratio of positive to negative examples is less unbalanced. However, for application of classification in QDA scenarios, generating positive training examples is very costly. Usually, the process of manual text coding involves reading through each sentence of the selected example texts for highlighting or extracting snippets fitting to categories of interest. Dependent on the prevalence of the category, coders have to read through several hundreds of documents to obtain enough positive training examples. For negative training examples, this is considerably easier, as we might assume that every sentence not labeled with a code while looking for positive sentences is irrelevant with respect to the code book, hence a negative example.

To further compare both classification algorithms under investigation and to enlighten the influence of training set sizes, I ran classification experiments on varying training set sizes. For this, I drew random samples of size $n \in \{25, 50, 100, 200, 500, 1000, 2000, 5000\}$ from the training set,[38] and evaluated classification performance on the test set. This process was repeated 10 times. Figure 3.11 plots mean values of the 10 F_1-measures for code 'All' of both, SVM and MAXENT classification. We can observe that for smaller training set sizes $n <= 1000$ MAXENT performs slightly better than SVM. At the same time, overall performance reaches values around $F_1 = 0.4$ only, if training set sizes are above 2000 examples. This appears to be a large training set at first glance, but we know already that training set sizes are highly unbalanced. As the share of positive examples on all sentences in the training set for code 'All' is about 18 %, we can expect around $2000 \times 0.18 = 360$ positive sentences in training sets of size 2000. In a real-world QDA scenario, manual coding of 360 positive example sentences for a category is absolutely manageable. Moreover, as stated above, negative examples practically come at no cost during this process. The F_1-result for code 'All' on the entire training set of size 22,256 (see Table 3.17) also makes clear that even with a lot more training examples the F_1-measure only increases up to 0.51, suggesting that generating much more training data might be inefficient.

Semantic smoothing: In Section 3.3.1, I have stated that feature vectors originating from the 'bag-of-words' model on single sentences or paragraphs are extraordinary sparse, contributing to low perform-

[38]The drawing of a random sample was repeated if there was no single positive example in the draw which may happen often for the very small training set sizes.

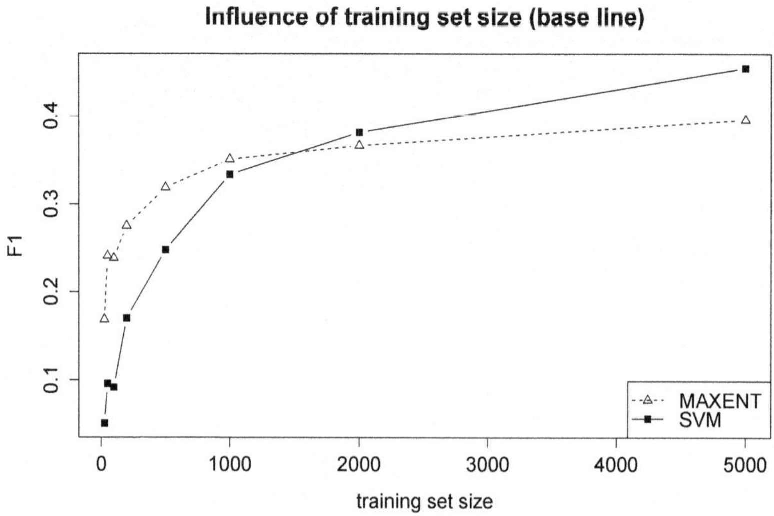

Figure 3.11.: Influence of training set size on classification performance of two classifiers, MAXENT and SVM. Classification is based on word features (uni-/ bigrams) for the meta-category *'All'*.

ance in classification processes. Based on theoretical assumptions presented in Chapter 2, I also described the importance of context and latent semantics for ML applications. To improve classification quality in sparse feature vector situations, consideration of context seems to be a valid approach. In this respect, several suggestions based on clustering semantics in unsupervised manner to extend available information for supervised learning have been made in ML literature, leading to the paradigm of semi-supervised learning (Xiaojin Zhu, 2008). For NB classification, Zhou et al. (2008) propose an approach for "semantic smoothing". They introduce a concept of 'topic signatures' to augment observations of lexical features given a class. 'Topic signatures' might be seen as a representation of latent meaning implied by word observations, which can contribute to classification by additionally taking 'topic signatures' given class into account. With their approach Zhou et al. improve generative NB classification, especially for small training data sets. For discriminative classifiers, a different, more general approach for 'semantic smoothing' needs to be obtained. Phan et al. (2011) introduce a generalized approach to generate features for supervised classification of a document collection $\mathcal{D}$ by employing LDA topic modeling on an unlabeled (universal) data set $\mathcal{W}$ (e.g. Wikipedia corpora).[39] The idea can be summarized in the following steps:

1. collect a universal data set $\mathcal{W}$ (e.g. Wikipedia articles or, if large enough, your collection under investigation),
2. compute a topic model with K topics on $\mathcal{W}$,
3. for each document $d \in \mathcal{D}$ use the topic model from step 2 to sample topic assignments θ_d for the words it contains, without updating the $\beta_{1:K}$ parameters for term distributions per topic,[40]
4. convert counts of topic assignments in d into K additional features for classification.

As an LDA topic model may be seen as an overlapping clustering of general senses or meanings, assigning new documents to these clusters enriches documents with some latent semantic information, which contributes as smoothing of its very sparse word features. I applied the framework of Phan et al. (2011) for improving the classification performance on the MP data set. As universal data set $\mathcal{W}$, I utilized the party manifestos of the MP data itself. For this, I put sequences of every 25 sentences from $\mathcal{S}$ into one pseudo-document (1st step) which serves as input collection to compute the topic model (2nd step). On this collection, a model with $K = 50$ topics was computed by

[39] An early, but less systematic realization of this idea can be found in Banerjee (2008).

[40] This proceeding is also applied for online topic modeling of document streams (Yao et al., 2009). There also, the model is initially calculated on a fixed population. Then, topics for documents from the stream are sampled on the initially computed β distribution without updating it.

1,000 iterations of Gibbs Sampling ($\alpha = 0.02, \eta = 0.002$). A short qualitative investigation of the most probable terms of each topic shows expected results: inferred topics represent semantic clusters related to various policy issues important in the last German elections. In the third step, the collection to be classified is again the set $\mathcal{S}$ of sentences from the MP data. For every sentence $s \in \mathcal{S}$, topics are assigned to all words it contains by 100 iterations of Gibbs Sampling of an LDA process initialized by the $\boldsymbol{\beta}$ parameter of the model computed in the previous step. Since sentences can be very short, results of topic assignments to words in s can be very unstable. To get more reliable results, I repeat topic inference on s 20 times. Counts of topic-word assignments in s are averaged over these 20 runs, before they are converted into 50 additional features for each sentence.

Figure 3.12 shows the average results of 10 iterations of the classification with these additional features for increasing training set sizes. For both classifiers, we observe that additional features from the topic model improve the performance up to 5 percentage points. Furthermore, improvements get lower, as training set sizes increase. If all training data available is taken into account, there is almost no performance gain of this method compared to the baseline (see Tables 3.18 and 3.17). This is due to the fact that the effect of semantic smoothing diminishes, the more training data is available to the classifier. In one case, code 301 (*federalism*) performance even considerably decreases. This is probably a consequence of the heterogeneous nature of this rather small category. Statements in favor of federalism usually come with a variety of different policy issues. Narrowing the category to certain semantic topics by topic model features improved the precision, but lowered the recall on the test set. This is an important hint towards the need for precise and coherent category definition and application during manual coding. Nonetheless, in our scenario for QDA application of ML the method of semantic smoothing provides essential improvements for the other four categories. We can expect improvements for QDA application in general, because we usually operate on small training data.

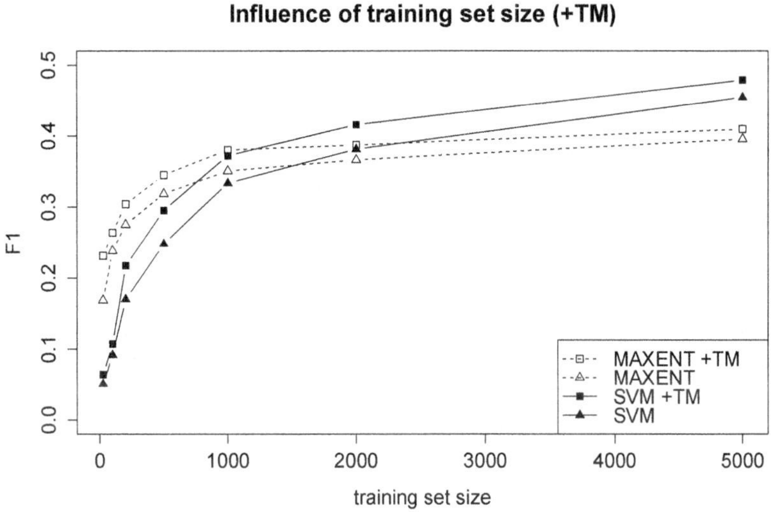

Figure 3.12.: Influence of training set size on classification performance of two classifiers, MAXENT and SVM for the meta category *'All'*. Classification is based on word features (uni-/bigrams), and additionally on features generated by topic model inference on each sentence (+TM).

Table 3.18.: Semantic smoothing classification results: features from topic modeling additionally to uni-/bigrams improve classification performance most for small training sets. If all training data available is used (this Table), performance gain compared to the base line (see Table 3.17) diminishes.

Code	S_+	P	R	F	A
201	1083	0.3567	0.5152	0.4216	0.9312
202	903	0.3791	0.5437	0.4467	0.9453
301	326	0.5145	0.1625	0.2470	0.9854
503	1780	0.3440	0.4865	0.4030	0.8847
All	4092	0.5011	0.5733	0.5348	0.8166

3.3.5. Classification for Proportion and Trend Analysis

Previous sections have shown rather mediocre results of classification performance for the content analysis scenario on the MP data set. For smaller training set sizes using an optimized SVM with unigram, bigram and topic model features, we can expect F_1-values around 0.4 to 0.5 at best. If individual classification had been the goal of our classification scenario, these results would have been rather unacceptable. Dissatisfaction with the computationally evaluated results can be somewhat mitigated by having a close look on the false positives during classification. Often these are not really false positives in the sense of not fitting the description of the category in the code book. In fact, they are often ambiguous statements which are just labeled with another label, stressing a different aspect of the manifesto sentence. Although in these cases it would make sense, multiple labels are only annotated in rare cases in the MP data set. In conclusion, for the goal of individual classification further effort would be useful to improve the category system, the annotated data set and the classification workflow (including feature engineering and feature selection).

But instead of valid individual classification, I defined valid prediction of proportions and trends in diachronic data as primary goal of the classification process in 3.3.1. For this, we investigate if the moderate individual classification performance achieved so far still might be sufficient to produce valid and reliable results towards these goals. Accordingly, we need to change our evaluation criteria. In addition to precision, recall and F_1, we assess classification performance by:

- **Root Mean-Square Deviation (RMSD)**: individual class labels assigned to documents in the test set can be counted as class proportions—the share of a class on the entire test set. Splitting the entire set into single manifestos (one document per party and election year) yields multiple measurements for each class proportion in these subsets. $RMSD = \sqrt{\frac{1}{n}\sum_{t=1}^{n}(x_{1,t} - x_{2,t})^2}$ is an established measurement to assess the deviation of predicted class proportions

$x_{1,\cdot}$ to actually observed class proportions $x_{2,\cdot}$ in a time series with n data points, i.e. proportions in single manifestos. As we compare proportion values ranging between zero and one, we may interpret RMSDs (which consequently also have a range [0, 1]) as error on the estimation missing the true proportion value of a category.

- **Pearson product-moment correlation (r)**: classification quality for trend analysis can be determined by measuring the association between predicted and actual quantities of class labels in time series. Again, we assume splits of our predicted and actual test set labels into single manifestos as two time series $x_{1,\cdot}$ and $x_{2,\cdot}$. If increase and decrease in absolute frequency of positive class labels or relative class proportion go along with each other, we expect a high Pearson product-moment correlation (Pearson's r). Significance of Pearson's r can be assessed by a statistical test.

The selected MP data contains manifestos from eight parties and four elections (see Table 3.15). For the following experiments, I treat the parties PDS and DIE LINKE as the same, as the latter has been founded as a merger of the PDS and the WASG, a second left-wing party in Germany in 2007. AFD and PIRATEN did not come up before elections in 2013. All in all, this gives us a split of the overall test set into 22 data points to determine the absolute number or the relative share of code labels in the actual data and compare them to the classifier's prediction. On these 22 test set splits, two different approaches of category proportion estimation are applied and evaluated by RMSD and Pearsons's r.

Estimating Proportions from Feature Profiles

Hopkins and King (2010) propose a method of "proportional classification" for CA, optimized for social science goals. Their method does not rely on aggregated individual classification predictions to measure category proportions in a population of documents. Instead of counting predicted labels for individual documents, they estimate proportions of categories in a test set by observing probabilities of "word stem profiles" S in the entire training set and test set. Such word stem profiles are defined as binary vectors encoding the presence or absence of unigram features in a document. For a vocabulary of size $K \leftarrow |V|$ word stems, there exist 2^K different profiles (i.e. the power set of the feature set). For each document its corresponding feature profile can be determined. In practice, because feature space is large, profiles on all features would be too numerous and mostly unique. Therefore, the procedure relies on subsets of features, e.g. $n = 1000$ repetitions of random draws of $K = 10$ features out of the entire feature set V. For a document collection $\mathcal{D}$ a multinomial distribution $P(S)$ with 2^K values, encoding probabilities of occurrence for each feature profile in the collection can be determined. Marginal probabilities of profiles $P(S)$ and probabilities of profiles given classes $P(S|\mathcal{C})$ can be observed directly in the training data. Because $P(S) = P(S|\mathcal{C})P(\mathcal{C})$ where we know already two of three terms in this equation, probabilities (i.e. proportions) of labels $P(\mathcal{C})$ in a test set can be determined by standard regression algebra[41] under the assumption that conditional probabilities of feature profiles given classes $P(S|\mathcal{C})$ in the training set and in the test set are the same.

This method provides very accurate estimates of category proportions in unknown document populations, as evaluations by Hopkins and King (2010) show. Hence, it seems reasonable to employ their approach for proportion and trend detection on the MP data as well. To evaluate the performance on the MP data set, I conduct two experiments:

1. proportion estimation in the entire test set $\mathcal{S}_{test}$,

2. proportion estimation in test set splits of single manifestos for valid trend detection.[42]

[41] To solve the regression model $\mathbf{y} = \mathbf{X}\lambda$ (without any error term) for λ we need to calculate $\lambda = (\mathbf{X}^T\mathbf{X})^{-1}\mathbf{X}^T\mathbf{y}$ (Hopkins and King, 2010, p. 236f).

[42] Hopkins and King (2010) provide the R package "readMe" as reference implementation to their paper. But because the method is rather simple and I needed slight modifications for applying it to the second experiment, I re-implemented it on my own.

Table 3.19.: Hopkins/King method of proportion and trend prediction evaluated by RMSD and Pearson' r: While error rates on the entire test set are very low, predictions for subsets of it are fairly inaccurate. Hence, trend predictions (r), although significantly positive, are not very exact either.

Code	RMSD (test set)	RMSD (splits)	r (proportions)
201	0.0041	0.1537	0.7900
202	0.0092	0.0987	0.4908
301	0.0066	0.0225	0.6049
503	0.0117	0.0723	0.7787
All	0.0116	0.2319	0.5505

Table 3.19 displays the results for these two experiments on the MP data set. They confirm that the method proposed by Hopkins and King provides valid estimations of code proportions in our test set. Estimations for the entire test set are very accurate, only producing an error around 1 percentage point for all categories classified. However, the test set represents a sample selected from the entire MP data set by the same strategy as the training set (every odd/even sentence). Hence, distributions of features may be assumed as almost identical in each of the disjoint sets. This does not hold true if we split the test set deliberately into separate manifestos of the single parties per election year. For this, averaged RMSD values are given in the third column of Table 3.19. Here, results indicate immense discrepancies between estimated and predicted proportions in four out of five categories. The method heavily over- or underestimates proportions for the codes 201, 201, 503 and 'All'. A closer look into the data reveals that overestimations seem to correlate with high relative shares of the category in certain party programs. For example, the party PDS/LINKE has a high share of sentences expressing demands for 'social equality' (code 503). As the regression model instance calculated $P(S|C)$ on the basis of the entire training set (instead of sentence only from PDS/LINKE), the higher relative share of feature profiles $P(S)$ associated with 'social equality' in PDS/LINKE manifestos yields to overestimation of

the category in their manifestos. In contrast, shares of this category in manifestos of the conservative party CDU are underestimated according to the lower share of feature profiles associated with this category compared to the entire training set of all parties. From this, we may assume that parties use their own specific vocabulary to express ideas on the same aspect of democracy in their very own words.

The crucial assumption that the association between feature profiles and class proportions $P(S|\mathcal{C})$ in the training data may as well be assumed for the test set, does not apply if the test set is a subset with a biased distribution of feature profiles. This makes the Hopkins/King model very vulnerable to altered distributions of feature profiles in sub-sets of the entire collection. To circumvent this effect, we would need to compute a new model instance $P(S|\mathcal{C})$ from subsets of the training data consistent with the splits of the test data, i.e. also split our training data by party and year. But then, training data size for each split will considerably decrease while costs for model training for time series estimation will increase drastically. All in all, the Hopkins/King model estimates proportions very accurately in situations where "among all documents in a given category, the prevalence of particular word profiles in the labeled set [... is] the same in expectation as in the population set" (ibid. p. 237). Yet, as soon as word profiles in the training set are not an (almost) identically distributed subset from word profiles of the target population, the model is unable to provide accurate estimations any longer.[43] Thus, for time series analysis, where we want to estimate category proportions in different time sliced subsets, the method becomes impractical. Consequently, correlations between predicted and actual category shares in the test set splits (column four of Table 3.19), although

[43]To further confirm this, I also conducted an experiment where I do not employ meaningful test set splits by party manifestos, but by random draws from the test set. Random draws guarantee independent and identically distributions of feature profiles in the test set splits. Results were as expected: If test set splits are random subsets from the entire test set, estimations of category proportions were rather accurate again.

Table 3.20.: Individual classification aggregation method of proportion and trend prediction evaluated by RMSD and Pearson's r: Measures evince that prediction of proportions and trends can be quite accurate ($r > 0.9$) although the corresponding F_1-measure is rather moderate.

Code	F	RMSD	r (counts)	r (proportions)
201	0.4216	0.0258	0.9593	0.9221
202	0.4467	0.0246	0.9639	0.9106
301	0.2470	0.0133	0.7504	0.5785
503	0.4030	0.0413	0.9685	0.8157
All	0.5348	0.0483	0.9836	0.9009

indeed positive and statistically significant, are not overly high that we might assume a correct time series predictions. It remains to be seen whether aggregated individual classification is able to provide us with more reliable estimations in this respect, if it is provided with good training examples.

Aggregating Individual Classification

The optimized SVM classifier with its topic model enhanced feature set (Section 3.3.4) already classified each sentence in the test set either belonging to a category or not (see Table 3.18). Having a predicted label for each sentence in the test set, error rates on proportion estimation and trend predictions on single manifestos are directly observable. Table 3.20 gives evaluation measures for supervised classification of proportions and trends for all five codes under investigation compared to the classic F_1-measure.

For the different codes classified, RMSD is not lower than 1 percentage point and not greater than 5 percentage points. Compared to the previous estimations by the model of Hopkins and King (2010), error rates for proportion estimations on the entire test set are noticeably higher. Still, error rates are not unacceptably high.[44] Nevertheless, as the share of sentences of a certain code in the test set is very unbalanced, deviations of some percentage points indicate significant over- or underestimation in absolute numbers. For example, category 201 has only a share of 4.86 percent in the entire test set. An RMSD of 0.025 indicates an average over- or underestimation around 2.5 percentage points, or 50 percent in absolute numbers of sentences classified as belonging to category 201. We can conclude that on the one hand, estimations of proportions are rather stable and do not deviate heavily from the global perspective on the entire data set investigated. On the other hand, we need to be careful by assessing on exact numbers of proportion quantities as small numbers of deviations on proportions may entail significant over- or underestimation in absolute numbers of classified analysis units.

Evaluation on trend correlation is more promising. Instead of exact estimation of proportions, we judge the quality of the classification process only by its ability to predict increases or decreases of quantities in time series correctly. Correlation coefficients for absolute counts are very high: $r > 0.95$ for four out of five codes. If correlation is based on estimated proportions instead of absolute counts we still obtain very high correlations ($r > 0.9$ in three cases). Judging trend prediction on relative proportions is preferable, because correlation between absolute counts and predictions is not only determined by the quality of the classifier, but by the size of the test set splits as well. If there are more sentences in a split, it may be assumed that chances are higher for more sentences to be classified positively.

As noticed earlier, category 301 (federalism) appears to be problematic due to the very small number of training examples and heterogeneity of its content. Except for this category, trend correlation of individual classification significantly outperforms correlation based on proportional classification with the Hopkins/King approach by large extent. In contrast to the latter, the SVM model is able to generalize

[44]Hopkins and King (2010) state that in comparison to survey analysis with random sampling on a national level, RMSDs up to four percentage points are not considered as unusual (p. 241).

its information learned from the training set, to predict proportions in arbitrary test sets reliably well—a finding that also has been reported by Hillard et al. (2008). The fact that for trends on relative proportions we may obtain correlations of $r > 0.9$, although the F_1-measure with values around 0.4 is moderate only, is an important extension of that finding. It shows that even with small F_1-values, we are able to predict trends in diachronic data correctly.

The connection between conventional evaluation measures for text classification (F-measure, precision, recall) and the two newly introduced evaluation criteria can be investigated further experimentally. Figure 3.13 plots the correlation coefficient r and RMSD in dependency of different levels of precision and recall from classification of the code 'All'. Varying precision/recall ratios are introduced artificially by varying the threshold of probability values, in which case to assume a positive code label. The SVM classifier can provide a probability value for each predicted instance $s \in \mathcal{S}_{test}$.[45] Usually, if the probability $P(+|s)$ of a positive label given s is higher than threshold $t = 0.5$, the classifier attaches the label to the instance. By changing this probability threshold t within a $(0, 1)$ interval, lower values for t increase recall while decreasing precision. Higher t values have the opposite effect. The interesting observation from this experimental setup is that the correlation coefficient r as well as RMSD reach very good result levels over a wide range of t. From this, we may infer that classification errors of the supervised SVM approach do not lead to arbitrary false predictions of trends. Even if the ratios between precision and recall change drastically, estimation of trend correlations remain stable. At the same time, we observe optimal r and RMSD measures, in case

[45] Actually, the SVM classifier infers a separating hyperplane in the feature space based on the training data which allows for deciding whether an unlabeled data instance lies inside or outside of the region of the positive class. This is indicated by the classifiers output of the margin to the hyperplane, i.e. 0 indicates values located exactly on the hyperplane, values above 0 indicating the positive class and values below 0 the negative class. Margin values can be transformed to probability values by applying the method of Platt scaling (Platt, 2000). Scaled data instances located near the hyperplane with margins around 0 correspond to probability values around 0.5 for positive labels.

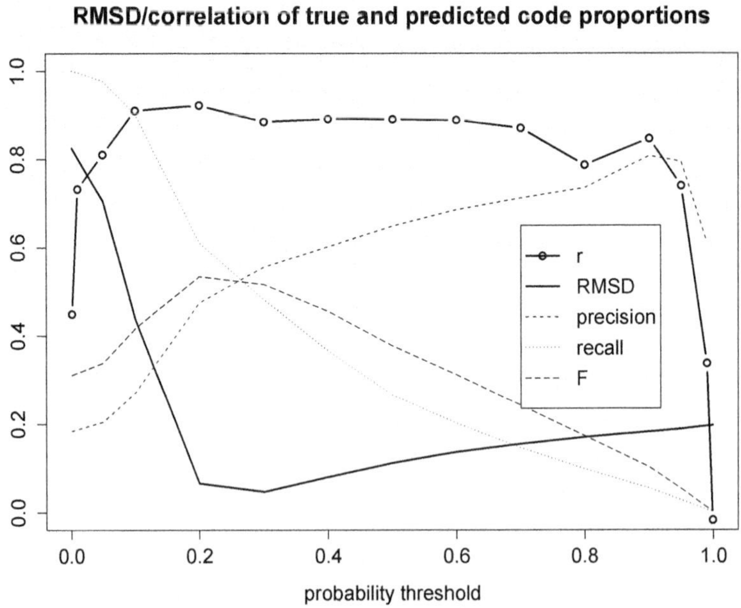

Figure 3.13.: RMSD and correlation dependent on different levels of precision and recall.

the F_1-measure is highest. Thus, optimizing a classification process with respect to the F_1-measure clearly is a worthwhile strategy to obtain valid results for trend and proportion analysis. Nonetheless, we do not need to push it into regions of $F_1 = 0.7$ or higher to get acceptable results for our QDA purposes.

To visualize the classification performance for trend detection, Table 3.21 displays classifier predictions and true values for absolute counts and relative proportions of the investigated codes for the five major German parties during the last four elections. These plots confirm visually the numeric evaluations of high correlations between automatic retrieved and actual (manually labeled) category quantities. The classifier tends to label more instances as positive for a code than there are actually in the test set.[46] In a last step, we want to investigate how to collect good training data for automatic CA efficiently.

3.3.6. Active Learning

Experiments to evaluate classification performance have been conducted on the entire training set so far. This includes between 326 (code 301) and 4092 (code 'All') positive training sentences per code (see Table 3.17). Collecting several hundreds or even thousands of positive training examples for CA is very costly. Analysts need to read through many documents and code positive analysis units for each category manually. To support this work, I introduce in the final step of our classification experiments a workflow for the efficient production of training data with high quality for trend analysis.

For efficient training data collection we can employ the active learning paradigm: "The key hypothesis is that if the learning algorithm is allowed to choose the data from which it learns [...] it will perform better with less training" (Settles, 2010). The basic idea is to start with a little training set $\mathcal{S}$ based on manual reading and coding. This initial training set is then augmented by new instances, which are suggested by supervised classification of the set of unlabeled analysis units $\mathcal{U}$. Suggestions, so called *queries* of the active learning algorithm, have to be evaluated by an *oracle*, e.g. a human annotator, who accepts or rejects them as a positive example for the category of interest. After evaluation of suggested queries, supervised classification is performed once again on the training set extended by the newly reviewed examples.

Active learning scenarios might be distinguished into stream-based and pool-based (ibid.). In the stream-based scenario, the algorithm

[46] A short manual investigation of the false positives reveals that retrieved sentences are often not really bad examples for the category of interest, if judged by the code book. Again, this is a hint to carefully craft categories and apply code books during codification. Beyond classifying unlabeled data, this process also might be utilized to improve the quality of the already labeled training data by revising alleged 'false positives' on held out training data.

Table 3.21.: Left column: Estimates and true values for counts of coded sentences in manifestos of the five major German parties (1 = CDU, 2 = FDP, 3 = Grüne, 4 = PDS/LINKE, 5 = SPD). Right column: Estimated against true proportions.

Code	Absolute Counts	Proportions
201	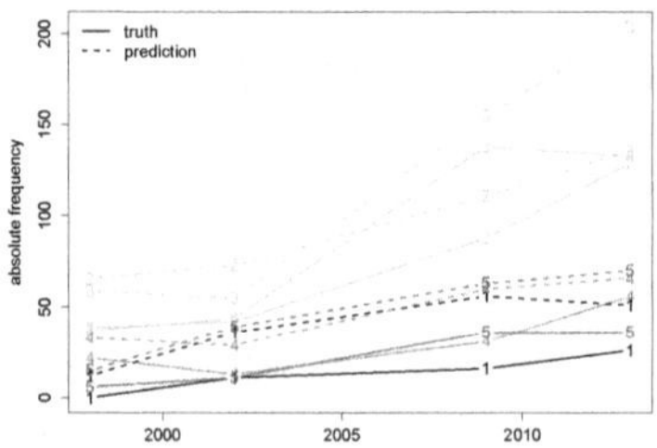	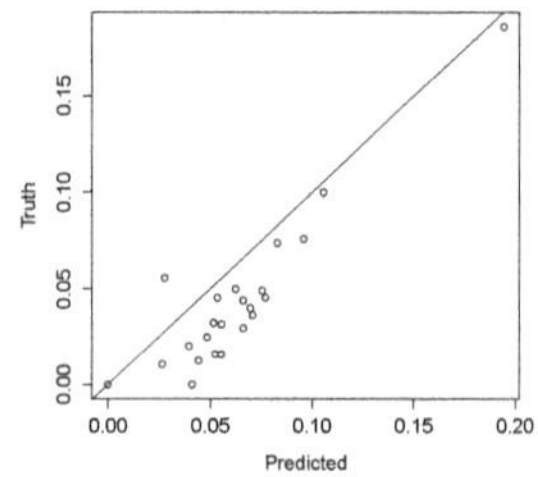
202	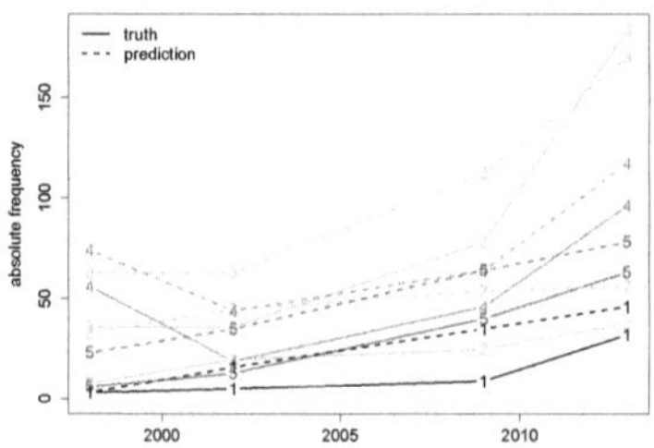	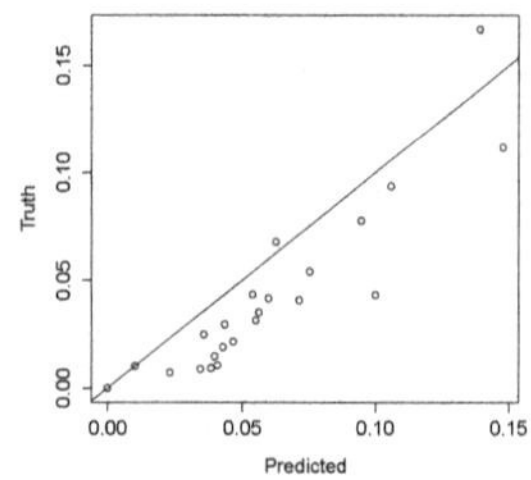
503	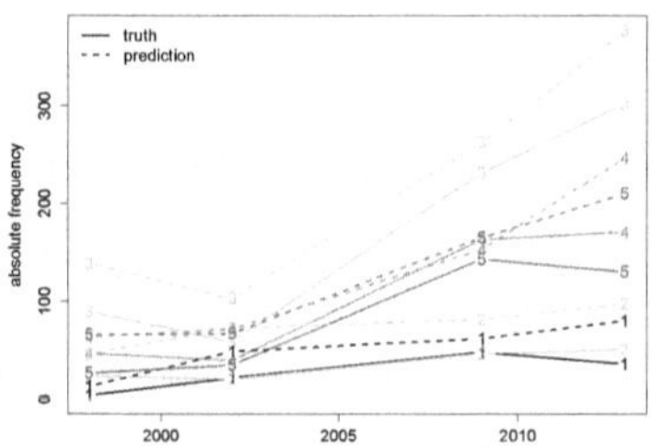	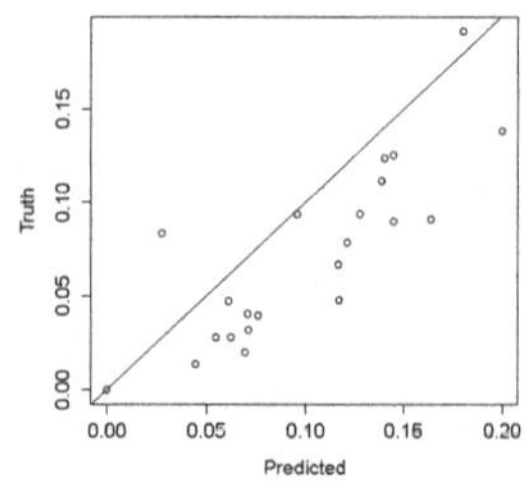
All	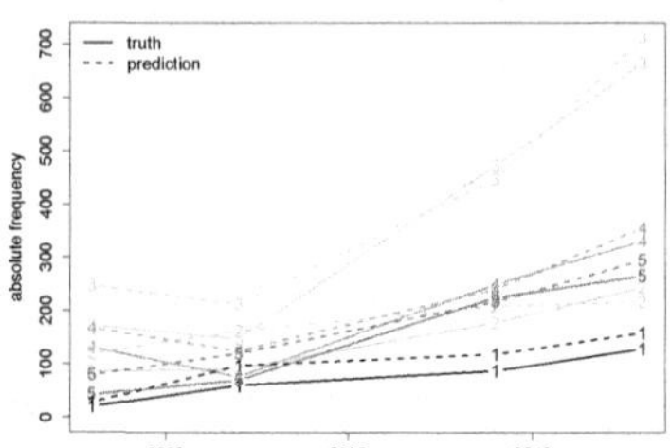	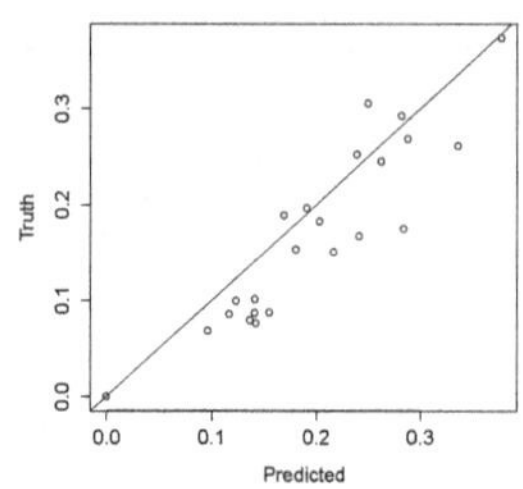

Workflow 1: Pool-based batch-mode active learning

Input:
Initial set $\mathcal{S}$ of manually labeled sentences
Set $\mathcal{U}$ of unlabeled sentences
Query selection strategy q
Batch size n
number of maximum iterations $iMax$
Output:
$n \times i$ new high quality training examples

$i \leftarrow 0$
while $i < iMax$ **do**
    $i \leftarrow i + 1$
    Train model on $\mathcal{S}$
    Apply model on $\mathcal{U}$
    Rank sentences in $\mathcal{U}$ by strategy q
    Manually label top n sentences
    Move labeled sentences from $\mathcal{U}$ to $\mathcal{S}$

decides for every unlabeled data instance in $\mathcal{U}$ individually whether it should be presented as a query to the oracle. For this, it employs some kind of 'informativeness measure' on the data instance to reveal, if it lies in a region of uncertainty of the feature space. In the pool-based scenario, the algorithm first ranks all unlabeled data instances in $\mathcal{U}$ according to their informativeness, and then selects the best matching data instances for querying the oracle. Pool-based query selection appears to be much more common among application scenarios (Settles, 2010, p. 12). It can further be distinguished into serial and batch-mode active learning (ibid. p. 35). In the former only one query is evaluated per iteration, while in the latter a set of n best matching queries is selected for evaluation, before a new iteration is started (see Workflow 1). This strategy is advisable, if costs for training the classifier are high or multiple annotators should evaluate on queries in parallel. Hence, the pool-based batch-mode scenario of active learning is perfect for our application to develop an efficient training data generation workflow for QDA classification.

As 'informativeness measure' to select queries from unlabeled sentences $u \in \mathcal{U}$, I simply decide for the positive category probability the SVM can provide when predicting a label for u based on the current training set $\mathcal{S}$. As probability suggests, the region of uncertainty lies around values of $P(+|u) = 0.5$. The active learning process for our task is then influenced by three parameters mainly:

1. *Query selection strategy:* how should queries be selected from the pool of unlabeled data, to a) minimize evaluation efforts of the oracle, and b) maximize classifier performance with respect to valid trend prediction?

2. *Size of the initial training set:* how many training examples should be collected before starting active learning to guarantee the goal of valid trend prediction in time series data?

3. *Probability threshold:* a threshold on the classifier's output of the probability for assigning a positive label to a data instance may influence the pool-size where queries can be selected from. Above which probability threshold a data instance should be considered as query candidate during an active learning iteration?

In the following experiments, I simulate the active learning procedure to investigate the influence of query selection strategies as well as initial training set sizes and probability thresholds for the process. For each category to classify, I initiate the learning process with a random selection of $a = 100$ positive training sentences and the same amount of random negative examples. In every following iteration the $n = 200$ best sentences, according to a certain selection strategy, together with their true labels are added to the training set. Adding the true labels mimics the oracle decision of query evaluation usually done by human annotators. During every iteration step, acceptance rate (number of evaluated queries as positive), F_1-measure of 5-fold cross-validation on the training set, F_1-measure on the test set and Pearson's correlation

r on the test set splits of single manifestos are calculated, to judge on the improvement while learning. Evaluation measures are plotted in Figure 3.14. Additionally, F_1 and r from previous experiments on $\mathcal{S}_{test}$ utilizing the entire training set $\mathcal{S}_{train}$ (see Table 3.18) are given as reference values—both are drawn into the plots as horizontal lines. They allow to visualize how evaluation criteria approach results of optimal training data situations very early during the active learning process with small training data sizes already.

Query selection strategy: Three query selection strategies are tested and compared. During each iteration of active learning, sentences from the so far unlabeled data set $\mathcal{U}$ are selected by

1. *Certainty:* highest probability of belonging into the positive category
2. *Uncertainty:* proximity to the decision boundary $t = 0.5$ of the probability belonging into the positive category,
3. *Random:* sampling from all sentences above a probability threshold $t = 0.3$ in $\mathcal{U}$.

Figure 3.14 displays the progress of learning with the three different query selection strategies on the code 'All' during 10 iterations. Main evaluation criterion for the strategies is, how the selected training examples perform on predicting trends in the test set correctly (dotted black line). Visually we can determine that relying on the most certain examples for active learning does not improve the classification towards the goal of trend prediction very well. Although the acceptance rate of queries (solid circled line) is highest compared to the two other strategies, examples selected provide rather redundant information to the classifier instead of learning new, so far ambiguous information. Relying on uncertain examples instead (strategy 2) slightly lowers the acceptance rate, but improves trend correlation. We need one more iteration, to collect 400 or more positive training examples (marked by the vertical red line). But these training examples certainly describe better the decision boundary between the positive and the negative

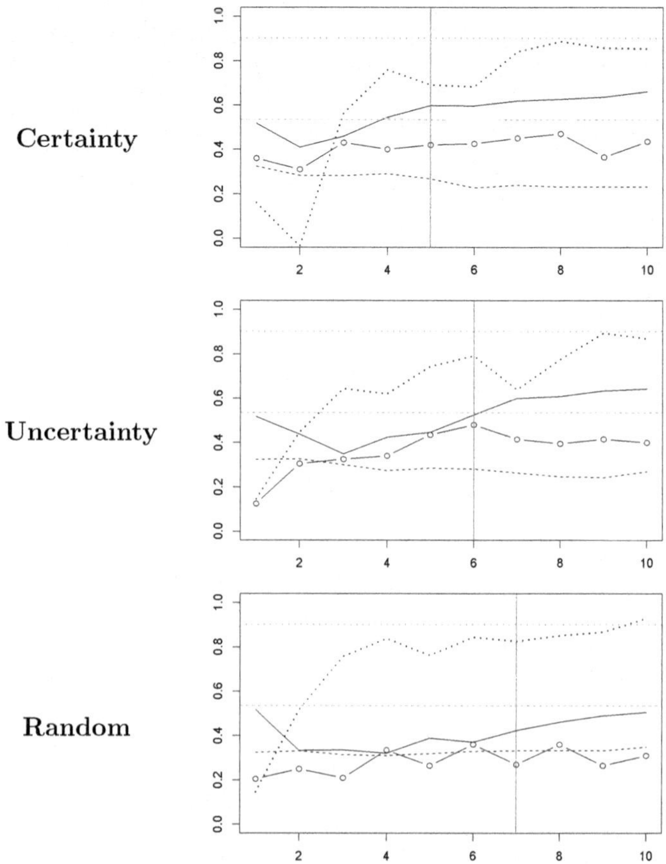

Figure 3.14.: Performance of query selection strategies by ongoing iterations of active learning (x-Axis): F_1 on the test set (dashed black line), F_1 of 5-fold cross validation on the current training set (solid black line), acceptance rate of queries (solid, circled line) and Pearson's correlation r between predicted and true label quantities on test set splits (dotted black line). Green horizontal lines indicate F_1 and r as reference, when the entire sets $\mathcal{S}_{train}$ and $\mathcal{S}_{test}$ are used. The vertical red line marks the iteration, when 400 or more positive training examples are collected.

class of the category 'All'. Nevertheless, just ranking and selecting queries by uncertainty also includes redundant examples centered around the decision boundary. Homogeneity of the iteratively learned training set is also suggested by high rates of F_1-measures (solid black line) for 5-fold cross validation on the learned training set. After four to six iterations, their value exceeds the reference value for the F_1-measure on the entire sets $\mathcal{S}_{train}$ and $\mathcal{S}_{test}$ from previous experiments (horizontal dashed green line).

Redundancy and undesired homogeneity of the learned training set are mitigated only by the third strategy of randomly selecting queries $u \in \mathcal{U}$ with a positive class probability of $P(+|u) >= 0.3$. For all strategies we can observe, when collecting training data long enough, reference values for trend correlation (i.e. using the entire training data set) are reached (dotted green line). At the same time, F_1-measures on the entire test set $\mathcal{S}_{test}$ (dashed black line) remain with values between 0.3 and 0.4 significantly below the reference value. Again, this is a strong indication for the fact that we do not need overly accurate individual classification, to perform valid trend prediction.

We also would like to know how many positive examples we need to collect, until we can expect a valid estimation on proportions and trends in the data. Unfortunately, this is hard to answer in general. There are some approaches of defining "stopping criteria" for active learning processes (Vlachos, 2008),[47] based on the idea that the process should stop, if no queries could be identified in the unlabeled pool that would add significantly more information to the classifier than it already contains. However, these approaches seem to be rather impractical for CA purposes. Because of language variety, we still can

[47] Vlachos (2008) suggests to use certainty measures of classifiers on an unlabeled held out data set to define a stopping criterion. For SVMs certainty can be defined as averaged absolute margins of classified instances to the separating hyperplane. Average margins of instances in held out data should increase during active learning iterations up to a certain point due to rising certainty based on more training examples. If there are no longer examples in the pool of unlabeled training data which provide new information to the SVM, classifier certainty on held out data is supposed to decrease.

find new informative examples after many iterations. Settles (2010) also states: "the real stopping criterion for practical applications is based on economic or other external factors, which likely come well before an intrinsic learner-decided threshold" (p. 44).[48] At the same time, our classifier might be able to predict trends correctly, based on the information learned at a much earlier point of the process. To keep the effort manageable, I will provide a rule-of-thumb as stopping criterion based on the training set size of positive training examples, as well as the number of learning iterations. Hopkins and King (2010) suggest to collect not more than 500 training examples to get accurate estimations of category proportions. Since we are interested in measuring certain code book categories realized in sentences in our data, we should instead concentrate on the number of positive examples of a category than on the whole set of annotated examples, positive and negative altogether.[49] During experimentation, I observed that collecting around 400 positive examples was sufficient in all cases, to provide reliable estimates of trends and proportions in the MP data. This is also a manageable number of examples to collect. Hence, I decided for 400 examples as a reference goal in the active learning process.

Measuring trend correlations at a point when 400 or more positive training examples have been collected allows for strategy and parameter comparison beyond visual display of the learning curves. As results of this simulation heavily depend on random initialization of training examples—in case of query selection strategy 3 also on random selection of active learning queries—the procedure is repeated 10 times for every code. Results of the 10 runs are averaged and

[48]In an experiment I conducted on the MP data set, average margins of the SVM started to decline after the 14th or 15th iteration of evaluating batches of $n = 200$ newly selected training examples. This suggests, we would need to evaluate around 3,000 example sentences for a single category until reaching the numerically advised stopping criterion. For the most applications, this appears to be too much of an effort.

[49]As mentioned earlier, during manual annotation of sentences / paragraphs, negative examples come in large numbers at low cost. At the same time, they do not contribute much to understand and define the category of interest.

Table 3.22.: Comparison of averaged 10 runs of three query selection strategies for active learning. Trend correlation as Pearson's r on the test set as well as improvements of the best strategy (random) over the other two are given. * ($p < 0.05$) and ** ($p < 0.01$) indicate statistical significance of the improvements.

Code	r (cert.)	r (uncert.)	r (rnd)	vs. cert.	vs. uncert.
201	0.8060	0.8954	**0.9108**	**13.0%	1.7%
202	0.7558	0.8927	**0.9025**	*19.4%	1.1%
503	0.6376	0.7182	**0.7422**	**16.4%	3.3%
All	0.6576	0.8058	**0.8340**	**26.8%	3.5%

evaluated by a statistical t-test to determine statistical significance of differences between the strategies. Table 3.22 displays average trend correlations and the improvement of the best strategy against the others in percent. We can observe that the random selection strategy (rnd) yields classification models which predict label quantities correlating highly in trends with the actual data already after few iterations. Although collecting positive examples quicker, the other two strategies need more iterations to collect a training set which contains sufficient good and varying examples to predict trends validly. This finding is consistent with experiments in the active learning literature on standard NLP corpora (Settles, 2010, p. 35).

Initial training set size and probability threshold: After having identified the random query selection strategy as preferred for active learning towards trend prediction, we shortly have a look on two further parameters of the process. Firstly, does the size of the initial manually labeled training set have an influence on the efficiency of the learning process? Should we start with larger or smaller quantities of training examples to provide sufficient information at the beginning of the process or to avoid selection bias of analysts? Secondly, we want to select a suitable threshold value t for the probability of a positive label as the basis for the pool of potential queries during each active learning iteration. Choosing a small threshold might

Table 3.23.: Comparison of averaged 10 runs of different initial training set sizes a and probability thresholds t for query pool selection. Initial training set sizes seem not to have a clear influence on the process. For probability thresholds there is a tendency to lower thresholds for better results. Yet, improvements are not statistically significant. $\bar{I}_{400}$ gives the average number of active learning iterations per test scenario to reach the goal of 400 positive training examples.

Code	initial training size (a)			probability threshold (t)			
	200	**100**	**50**	**0.2**	**0.3**	**0.4**	**0.5**
201	0.9070	**0.9108**	0.8717	**0.9232**	0.9108	0.8751	0.8882
202	0.8339	0.9025	**0.9042**	**0.9056**	0.9025	0.8966	0.8635
503	**0.7773**	0.7422	0.7431	**0.7556**	0.7422	0.7366	0.7287
All	0.8037	0.8340	**0.8359**	0.8212	**0.8340**	0.8088	0.7915
$\bar{I}_{400}$	6.75	7.72	7.82	9.25	7.72	6.67	5.92

produce more valid results for trend prediction, as a bigger variety of training examples has the chance to be selected from the pool. On the other hand, a too small threshold increases the number of iterations $\bar{I}_{400}$ necessary to collect the targeted goal of 400 positive training examples, since there are more queries from ranges of lower probability which actually belong into the negative class. Table 3.23 displays experimental results for variations of initial training set sizes $a \in \{50, 100, 200\}$ and probability thresholds $t \in \{0.2, 0.3, 0.4, 0.5\}$. Differences between the results of 10 averaged runs are statistically insignificant, indicating that influences of initial training set sizes and thresholds are not especially decisive for the overall process. Nonetheless, evaluation suggests that there is a tendency towards smaller probability thresholds. From this experiment we can infer that decisions on initial training set sizes and thresholds may be taken pragmatically. If there are many good examples for a category which are easy to collect, it seems to be maintainable to start with a bigger training set. If a category is expressed in fairly coherent language without much variety (codes 201 and 202), it seems absolutely valid, to just collect a few examples to initiate the process. For probability thresholds, we can weigh between an acceptable number of batch iterations $\bar{I}_{400}$ (tendency towards higher thresholds) and a better quality (tendency towards lower thresholds). With respect to this trade-off, selecting $t = 0.3$ appears to be a reasonable default choice.

3.3.7. Summary of Lessons Learned

The section on text classification addressed a wide range of research issues from NLP in the light of their application for QDA. Conducted experiments identified reasonable solutions for this purpose. Applying supervised machine learning to the process of 'coding', i.e. assigning semantic categories to (snippets of) texts, allows for efficient inspection of very large data sets. Qualitative categories become quantifiable through observation of their distribution in large document populations. To effectively execute this, special requirements and circumstances for the application of machine classification have to be taken into consideration. For this, the previous sections suggested solutions for optimization and integration of these aspects into a text classification workflow which allows content analysts to determine category quantities in large text collections reliably and validly. Methods of classification model selection, feature engineering for semantic smoothing and active learning have been combined to create a workflow optimized for trend and proportion estimation in the data. Evaluations during single steps of the entire chain have contributed to some valuable experiences for the overall process:

- SVMs provide a suitable data classification model in CA scenarios of small and sparse training data.
- Sparse training data can be augmented in a semi-supervised classification scenario by features inferred from unsupervised topic models to improve classification quality.
- If machine classification is mainly targeted towards estimation on category proportions and trends in diachronic corpora instead of

classifying individual documents, already moderate performance on precision and recall of the classifier provides sufficient quality.

- Collection of training data in CA studies is expensive. It can be supported efficiently by processes of active learning, where analysts start with a small set of manually collected training data and iteratively augment this set by evaluating on examples suggested by a machine classifier.
- Selection of training examples for active learning randomly from a pool of data instances above a certain probability threshold for the positive category provides the best strategy to obtain a training set which validly identifies trends in time series data.
- Collecting around 400 training examples for a certain category or repeating active learning for at least eight iterations provides sufficient information to the classifier to estimate trends highly correlating with the actual data (Pearson's $r > 0.9$ for well-defined categories can be expected).

The workflow of classification for QDA was developed in this section on the basis of the MP data set as a kind of gold standard. It is applied in the next chapter together with the results of corpus exploration (see Section 3.2) to investigate on the discourse of democratic demarcation in Germany. For this, time series of several content analytic categories are computed and inspected in the document collection retrieved by the earlier IR process (see Section 3.1).

4. Exemplary Study: Democratic Demarcation in Germany

The Text Mining (TM) workflows presented in the previous chapter provided a variety of results which will be combined in the following to a comprehensive study on democratic demarcation in Germany. The purpose of this chapter is to present an example of how findings from the introduced set of TM applications on large text collections contribute to investigations of abstract political and social science questions. Consequently, the character of this chapter differs from the previous ones with respect to the disciplinary perspective I take to describe the applied methods and results. First, I briefly introduce research questions, hypotheses and aspects of underlying political theory (Section 4.1). Then, I describe findings of the exploratory investigation of the data via Semantically Enriched Co-occurrence Graphs (SECGs) (Section 4.2). In a third step, I conduct a supervised analysis of content analytic categories with machine classification (Section 4.3) to allow for hypothesis testing on important aspects of the discursive formation of democracy in Germany. Finally, important findings are summarized along with an outlook to further analysis in Section 4.4.

4.1. Democratic Demarcation

After the experience of the rise of the national-socialist movement during times of the Weimar Republic, paving the way for World War II, the constitution of the Federal Republic of Germany (FRG) was conceptualized as a *'Wehrhafte Demokratie'*, also known as 'Streitbare Demokratie' (fortified democracy). Several legal and organizational institutions should deal with consequences of one paradox of democracy: that liberal and democratic orders cannot guarantee the conditions of their persistence by democratic rules alone.[1] Politicians in the early FRG along with historians and political scientists point to the experience of the Weimar Republic as an example where the unrestricted guarantee of fundamental rights to all political actors within the political spectrum led to strengthening of undemocratic parties and politicians during times of economic depression. Instead of defending democratic constitutional rights against attempts to abolish them, political actors of the early 1930s surrendered the first German parliamentary democracy to the Nazis (Jaschke, 2007, p. 62).

To prevent a similar development in the new democratic system, legal and organizational institutions of the 'Wehrhafte Demokratie' were introduced during the early phase of the FRG. In this arrangement, the German constitution allows, among other things, for bans of political parties or associations if they act hostile to the constitution. Special intelligence services on federal and state level, the 'Bundesamt' (BfV) and the 'Landesämter für Verfassungsschutz' are commissioned to observe political actors who are considered suspicious to hostile acts against the liberal democratic order–*Freiheitlich-demokratische Grundordnung* (FdGO). Some more lawful regulations exist such as restricting fundamental rights for enemies of the constitutional order or the prohibition to alter specific parts of the constitution in their legal essence (Jaschke, 2007, p. 19ff). These institutional aspects of the political arrangements of democratic demarcation in the 'Wehrhafte Demokratie' are referenced by discursive formations of language observable in media. In accordance with Foucauldian approaches to discourse analysis Lemke and Stulpe (2015) argue that such discursive patterns can be conceived as representatives for social reality which not only reflect but also evince power in interpersonal or societal relationships. Hence, I strive for their systematic investiga-

[1] Political theorists have argued about several paradoxes of democracy. Lee (2001) points to conflicts between norms of equality and democracy. Mouffe (2009) argues about the conflict between two democratic principles, the rule of law and popular sovereignty.

tion to gain insight into the state of the fortified democracy and its demarcation strategies.

Against this background, political debates on democratic demarcation are influential especially within the German public discourse. It is expressed in popular slogans such as 'Keine Freiheit für die Feinde der Freiheit' (no freedom for enemies of the freedom) and also in specific terms or concepts expressing a normative demarcation between the democratic center and a deviant, non-democratic outer. For example, to mark distinctions between the new liberal political order to the defeated Nazi-regime on the one hand, and the establishing socialist republic in the Eastern German zone of occupation on the other hand, the concept of 'totalitarianism' became popular during the early post-war period (Arendt, 1998; Žižek, 2011). Since the 1970s, vocabulary on 'extremism' was introduced by political scientists and security authorities as an instantiation to demarcate democratic from non-democratic phenomena, and steadily prevailed in political discourses (Oppenhäuser, 2011).

The thin line between two opposing goals becomes apparent: Measurements of the 'Wehrhafte Demokratie' shall be applied against enemies of the democracy to stabilize its fundamentals. At the same time, unjustified restriction of democratic participation of political actors has to be avoided as it would undermine the fundamentals of liberal democracy itself. In political theory, Laclau and Mouffe (2001) provided a useful conceptualization of 'radical democracy' to approach this problem. For their theory, they adopt Carl Schmitt's concept of *the political* as the clear distinction between the 'friend' and the 'enemy'. Drawing this distinction is a vital element of the political, but it may be realized in distinguished ways. Enemies are constituted by an *antagonistic* relation implying undemocratic, potentially violent conflict resolution procedures. Within democratic regimes in contrast, relations of hostility between actors need to be transformed into relations of adversary, so called *agonistic* relations that allow for conflict resolution based on a set of rules accepted by all participants. In political discourses of the public sphere, demarcation of boundaries is centered around generally defined concepts identified by a certain terminology. So called *empty signifiers*, often high value terms (Niehr, 2014) like 'democracy', 'freedom', 'diversity' on the one hand, and stigma terms (ibid.) such as 'extremism', 'fascism' or 'fundamentalism' on the other hand, are put into relations of equivalency or difference with each other by participants of the discourse, and thus, constitute a discursive network, in which antagonistic spheres of the political are constructed. Hence, not only negative demarcation needs to be expressed. At the same time, an offer for positive formation of identity has to be made, e.g. by expressing equivalency between the idea of democracy and (more specific) concepts what it consists of—namely human rights, freedom of speech, et cetera.[2]

Societal negotiations on what belongs into each sphere—the democratic inside versus the to-be-excluded outside—is conceptualized as a fight for hegemony between discourse participants, which can be analyzed systematically (Nonhoff, 2008). For example, the chaining of the signifiers *public health care—social equality—socialism—totalitarianism* as equivalent terms in the US-American discourse might represent an attempt to achieve hegemony and exclude a certain liberal[3] policy as illegitimate position. Buck (2011) describes conceptualizations of 'extremism' and its counterparts 'Freiheitlich-demokratische Grundordnung' and 'Leitkultur' in the German public discourse as a hegemonic strategy to exclude a variety of non-conform actors: Neonazis, left-wing activists, Marxist foreign groups or even Islamic migrants as a whole. Such manually conducted discourse studies already have provided valuable insights into formation of the political spheres for nowadays discourses. They show that the societal definitions of insiders and outsiders of the democratic system rely on conceptualizations of the political spectrum and specifics of the

[2]Discursive formations towards European identity as an important aspect of democracy are also subject to investigation by a large scale text analysis in the project *eIdentity*. Kantner (2014) studies more than 100,000 newspaper articles in six languages for a comparative study in the field of transnational security policy.

[3]'Liberal' as opposed to 'conservative' in the US-American sense of the term, which can be translated to left-wing in a European conceptualization of the political spectrum.

hegemonic antagonism. In European democracies a very common conceptualization of ideologies and corresponding actors employs a one-dimensional scale between a left and a right outer pole. This political left-right scale originated from the seating order in the French parliament after the revolution in 1789 (Link, 2006, p. 419). The 'extremism model' common in German political science distinguishes five segments on that scale (Stöss, 2005, p. 18): Around the *democratic center* it identifies a range of left-wing and right-wing *radical* positions. The democratic center together with the ranges of radical positions form the constitutional spectrum. Distinguished from this spectrum, the model identifies left-wing and right-wing *extremist* positions outside of the constitutional order. Consequently, once certain actors or ideologies are considered as located outside of the constitutional spectrum by hegemonic positions in the political discourse, the application of coercive measures such as bans of parties, protests etc. appears legitimate to defend the democratic order.

In a linguistic study Ebling, Scharloth et al. (2014) recently have examined the vocabulary of alleged 'extreme' actors in German politics. While they do not pay much attention to debates in political theory on democratic demarcation by using such categories rather affirmative, they still provide valuable insight to the fact that certain language regularities can be observed to identify positions of *the self* and *the other* in the political spectrum. The study presented here will examine the complementary side to some extent. We dot not look at the language of 'outer poles' of the spectrum, but on how 'the center' discursively produces them. With the help of TM, we try to figure out, how intense discursive disputes for hegemony on defining the 'right' political antagonism were fought in Germany over time. By investigating mainstream quality newspapers, we mainly look at this dispute from the perspective from within the center of the political spectrum. We try to identify which ideas and their corresponding actors were discursively located within the unconstitutional range of the spectrum and around which topics this takes place. Complementary, we have a look at the self-description of democratic identity as the 'antagonistic other'.

Analogue to the applications introduced in Chapter 3, I split the analysis into three distinct steps:

1. *Document selection:* From a large collection of documents (the complete corpus of the newspaper *Die Zeit* and a representative sample of the *FAZ*), we retrieved potentially relevant documents by a contextualized dictionary (Section 3.1). This dictionary was built data-driven on the basis of five reports of the German BfV. The "Verfassungsschutz" departments of the German executive power can be interpreted as institutionalization of the 'extremism model' itself. Their mission is to observe actors who might be a threat to the liberal democratic order of the state. For this, they are allowed to employ intelligence measures, e.g. wiretapping of suspects, intrusion of associations with secret informants or public accusations on the alleged threat of certain actors. These measures may violate fundamental democratic rights of the suspects.[4] Because of their character as institutionalized fortified democracy, the annual reports of the BfV provide an excellent source of specific language use expressing democratic demarcation. Five of them (1969, 1979, 1989, 1998, 2009) form as paradigmatic documents the basis for the dictionary which feeds the retrieval process.

2. *Corpus exploration:* Around 29,000 documents identified as relevant for the research question are explored visually by Semantically Enriched Co-occurrence Graphs (SECGs), generated by a process described in Section 3.2. The graphs provide insight into time clusters and topical structures of the retrieved collection and, hence, allow for inductive analysis of the material. With the help of these graphs we can explore important themes, actors and developments of the German democracy during distinct temporal phases in a data-driven manner.

[4] The annual reports of the BfV, for example, certainly negatively influence the chance of political actors to participate in the free and equal democratic dispute on opinions. Scholarly critics such as Jürgen Seifert consequently have blamed them as "Hoheitliche Verrufserklärung" (sovereign disrepute) (Kohlstruck, 2012).

3. *Category classification:* By having explored the range of topics on democratic demarcation over time, we are able to identify categories of interest which seem to play an important role in the data. For a more deductive approach, we define categories representing a certain content of interest, e.g. demarcation from left-wing or right-wing policies and reference to coercive measures of the fortified democracy. With a supervised classification process, we observe these categories in the entire base population of documents to infer on category proportions, trends and co-occurrence of categories. This supports the identification of discursive strategies in debates on German democracy in a long-term view.

The integrated analysis of newspaper articles with the applications presented in Chapter 3 will enlighten how democratic demarcation has been discursively performed in Germany over the past six decades. When did dispute on exclusion of certain actors take place intensively? Which actors, positions or activities have been described as illegitimate? How intensively is the discourse referring to countermeasures of the 'fortified democracy'? And, as a result, does changing volatility of the discourse indicate for changing stability of the German democratic system? The investigation of the data is guided by the following hypothesis:

1. Societal experience of the defeat of the NS-regime and the establishing socialist regime in East Germany heavily influences debates on democratic identity and demarcation in the FRG.

2. Focal points of exclusion towards left-wing or right-wing ideologies and actors change over time.

3. Newspapers from different parts of the political spectrum emphasize different focal points of democratic demarcation at certain points of time.

4. Newspapers from different parts of the political spectrum report on trends similarly in the long term.

5. Fortified democracy is a substantial aspect of German democratic identity.

6. Discursive patterns and strategies to exclude left-wing or right-wing positions from the democratic center differ from each other.

4.2. Exploration

To reveal temporal and thematic structures in a document collection of around 29,000 newspaper articles from more than 60 years of recent history, I introduced a workflow in Chapter 3.2 to generate SECGs. These graphs present meaningful clusters of terms co-occurring in sentences of documents of a certain topic and time frame. Size and color of the nodes of the graph indicate significance, sentiment and controversy of terms in its specific topical and temporal context. Altogether, the graphs allow for identification of important contents contained in the collection, which can be described along with the theoretical background of democratic demarcation introduced above. Fundamental within the discursive dispute striving for hegemony to define the antagonistic difference between democracy and its enemies are the concepts of self-identity and attribution of properties to the supposed non-democratic other. Both can be studied from SECGs, as we are able to identify many topical patterns expressing either identity formation or 'othering' of actors and ideologies (potentially) to be excluded from the legitimate sphere of the political. The topic model underlying the co-occurrence graphs also provides measurements which allow for evaluation on importance of topics within a specific time frame.[5] By evaluating on importance, description of the collection contents can be restricted to the major topics during a certain time frame. Accounting for this, I do not only concentrate on qualitatively meaningful topics within the discourse on democratic demarcation,

[5] As intuitive measurement there is the probability of the topic itself aggregated from documents of a certain time frame. But, for the topic co-occurrence graphs presented here, I utilized the *rank_1* measure counting how often a topic occurs as most probable topic in a document.

but in extension of manual QDA also take their quantitative relevancy into account.

As an overview on topics within a single time frame, we look on *topic co-occurrence graphs* introduced in Section 3.2.4. The topic co-occurrence graph for cluster 3 has already been given (see Figure 3.8). The remaining four are given in Figure 4.1. These graphs provide an overview of the major relevant topics in each cluster of time. From the overview provided by the topic co-occurrence graphs, I drill down to the SECGs which provide deeper insights into contents of each single topic in that time frame. Since there are 50 SECGs, I do not present them all in this chapter. A selection of the most important graphs for each cluster is given in the Appendix. Descriptions of the topics are mainly based on the visualized representation of its content in combination with a close reading of a small number of topic representative documents[6], extracted example sentences based on semantic propositions[7] and my prior knowledge as political scientist. Furthermore, descriptions are presented along the antagonistic formation of democratic identity within the community of legitimate political actors, and in contrast to the attribution of illegitimate threats to democracy by perceived outsiders of the constitutional spectrum. As reference, topic numbers for each SECG according to Table A.1 are given. Further, selected exemplary sentences based on semantic propositions from SECGs are quoted to augment brief topic descriptions with empirical examples illustrating extracted patterns more qualitatively.

4.2.1. Democratic Demarcation from 1950–1956

This very early stage, the constitutional phase of the democracy in Western Germany, is characterized by the emerging antagonism

[6] Topic representative documents from a time period are selected by their high topic share.

[7] In Section 3.2.8 candidates for semantic propositions per time cluster and topic were identified by maximal cliques in in SECGs providing semantic fields of closely related terms. Example sentences to each SECG are selected, if containing all terms of a proposition.

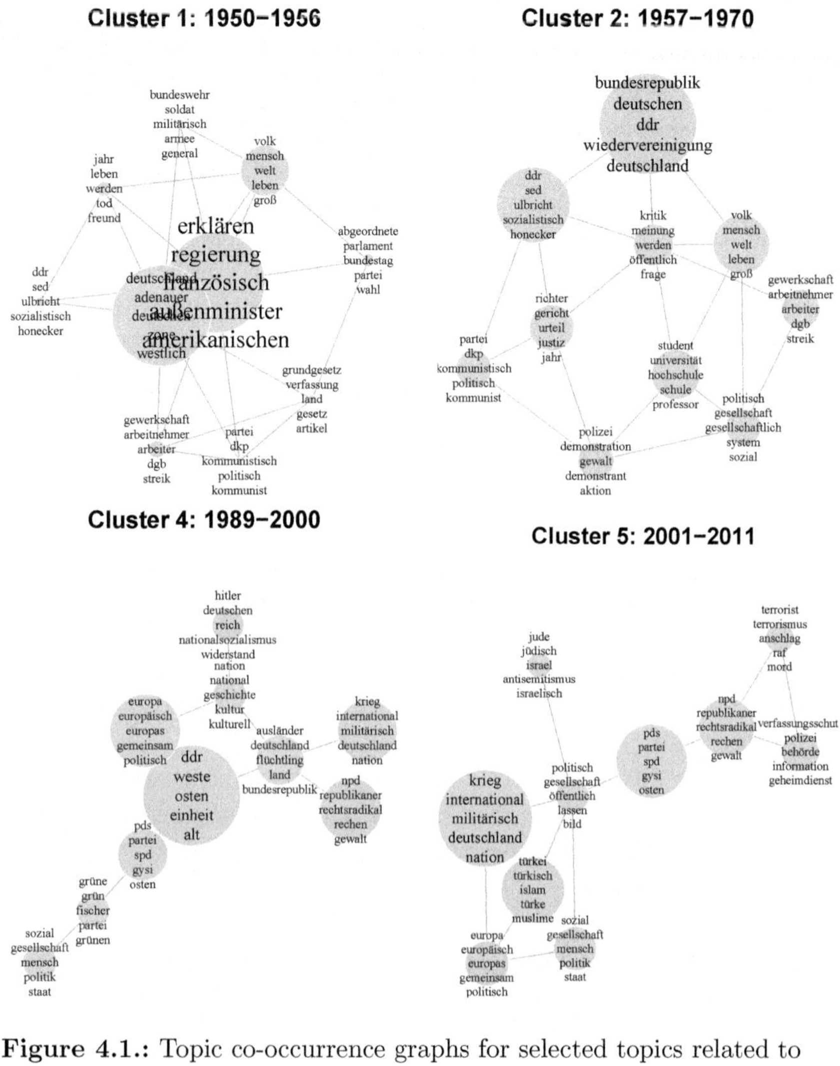

Figure 4.1.: Topic co-occurrence graphs for selected topics related to democratic demarcation in temporal clusters 1, 2, 4 and 5. Connected topics co-occur significantly as primary / secondary topic with each other in documents of the given time period. Node size indicates how often a topic has been observed as primary topic in a document of the time frame.

between the East and West, or respectively the political systems representing these hemispheres. The overall distribution of documents over time (see Table 3.8) suggests that there is a constant, but comparably small amount of documents related to democratic demarcation in this time frame. After the defeat of the national-socialist movement, the Western allies moved on to integrate the FRG into their system of international security, while the Eastern German part, the GDR, oriented itself towards the Soviet regime in the USSR. Within this conflict, the beginning of the cold war, and a widespread unwillingness of the German society and Western allies alike to face barbarities of the 'Third Reich', there was an implicit, but unspoken demarcation towards right-wing political movements. The constitutional court banned the Sozialistische Reichspartei (SRP) in 1952, because of their continuation of the program of the Nationalsozialistische Deutsche Arbeiterpartei (NSDAP). Notably, this first ban of a political party in Germany is not reflected in a broad discourse identifiable in the newspaper data. Probably there was a rather large consent within the political elite that starting a democratic system in Germany from scratch should not be influenced negatively by too openly acting successors of Hitler's politics. Instead of intense dispute on demarcation to the right, we can observe an overarching debate on questions of the new German democratic identity, including demarcation to the Eastern communist regimes. The FRG is conceptualized as a Western-oriented state, tied to establish close relations to France and the USA primarily. The graph for topic #54 signals the Schuman-Plan, the predecessor of the European Coal and Steel Community, the status of the Saarland and the Korean war as issues defining Germany's new role in the Western Bloc. Topic #4 encompasses moral and ethic vocabulary accompanying these developments for a German future with their new partners. It consists of terms describing ideals such as freedom, humanity or political, social and economic responsibility with very positive sentiments:

> "Die echte Freiheit des Menschen muß nicht zuletzt darin bestehen, daß in einem Leben, das zu einem großen Teil aus notwendigen Schablonisierungen besteht, doch Räume bleiben, in denen der einzelne

> zur Entfaltung kommt, in der das Persönliche sein Recht behält, gewiß in Rücksicht und Verantwortung, aber doch auch in Freiheit." (*Die Zeit*, 08/13/1953)

Additionally, debates on the ideological level are accompanied by intense disputes on institutions such as the electoral system (topic #39) and the constitutional order (topic #10).

Efforts defining a new democratic self-identity are contrasted by topics relating to conceived threats of the new order. In topic #78 documents report primarily negative on developments in the Eastern German zone controlled by the Soviets. The idea of reunification is discussed conjointly with political demands and conditions towards the Eastern German authorities. Communist ideology is not only an issue in the new neighbor state, it also is perceived as a threat to the German workforce relations. Consequently, the most severe intervention into political participation took part in 1956 when the constitutional court banned the Kommunistische Partei Deutschlands (KPD). The graph for topic #62 shows lots of legal vocabulary to justify the ban of the KPD as an anti-constitutional party and its role as an enemy of democracy:

> "Die Bundesregierung hat an das Bundesverfassungsgericht den Antrag gestellt, die Kommunistische Partei Deutschlands als verfassungswidrig zu erklären, sie mit allen ihren Teilorganisationen aufzulösen, die Schaffung von Tarn- und Ersatzorganisationen zu verbieten und das Vermögen der Partei und ihrer Teilorganisationen zugunsten des Bundes zu gemeinnützigen Zwecken einzuziehen." (*Die Zeit*, 12/02/1954)

Not only parties, but also the workers unions and their umbrella organizations are subject and object in a discussion on the influence of communist ideology and their role as political actors (topic #58).

4.2.2. Democratic Demarcation from 1957–1970

Distribution of documents during the second phase is characterized by a large increase on documents related to democratic demarcation during the 1960s with a peak in 1968. Debates on political identity during the second phase are dominated by the issue of reunification with the Eastern part. The GDR takes the role as a contrast to define the perception of the own development goals. The goal of reunification is bound to the demand for self-determination and freedom for all German people. Thus, the question of international recognition of the GDR and the normalization of the relations to its authorities is a heavily debated one, which implies the factual acceptance of two German nation states (topic #59). Besides these issues on foreign relations, democracy in the first phase of the FRG has been a project of political elites and occupying powers mainly. During the second phase we can identify certain topics indicating a growing democratic consciousness from below. Topics #4 and #12 reflect on identity formation processes of Germany as a modern, open society guaranteeing personal freedom, political pluralism and democracy in manifold aspects of society. At the same time, this development of pluralization of political opinions did not seem to be approved by all actors alike:

> "Durch die in ihnen zum Ausdruck kommende Demokratisierungstendenz sieht er deshalb die Freiheit gefährdet, weil mit der Demokratisierung sozialer Institutionen, unter anderem der Hochschulen, nach den Prinzipien der politischen Verfassung jede Unterscheidung von politischem und unpolitischem Raum wegfalle, alle gesellschaftlichen Bereiche politisiert würden und damit einem freiheitsgefährdenden Totalitätsdenken gehuldigt werde." (*Die Zeit*, 11/07/1969)

Topics #64 and #12 indicate disputes on an emerging criticism to certain aspects of the German post-war society. Expressions used in these topics contain peculiarly negative sentiments. Actors of this political change originated from the young generation, students at universities mainly, which loudly demanded for autonomy of their educational institutions and the (left-wing oriented) politicization of the students (Topic #13). But not only students, also left-wing oriented professors backed up demands for societal change, for example along the approach of critical theory. Formation of student organizations as part of the *Außerparlamentarische Opposition* lead to street protests demanding peace in Vietnam and the democratization of all parts of society, while also discussing the need for violence to fundamentally change ingrained societal structures (Topic #63). Security authorities and the justice system reacted repressively to this development. While protests often went along with violence and arrests by the police, Topics #76 and #62 signal measurements of the judicial system against communist activities (e.g. trials because of treason), the role of communist actors within the public service and the ban of successor organizations of the KPD:

> "Die Vierte Strafkammer des Düsseldorfer Landgerichtes hat am Dienstag die beiden sowjetzonalen Funktionäre der Einheitsgewerkschaft FDGB, den 36jährigen Benz und den 66jährigen Moritz, wegen Staatsgefährdung zu acht Monaten Gefängnis ohne Bewährung beziehungsweise sechs Monaten mit Bewährung verurteilt." (*FAZ*, 12/18/1963)

Interests of workers unions within the political system seem to be split-up (topic #58): blue collar workers (*Arbeiter*), organized in the DGB consist of an exceptionally negative sentiment. White collar workers (*Angestellte*) organized in the DAG relate to a largely positive sentiment in the data. Both groups intensely fought for the right strategies to influence politics:

> "Unter dem Motto 'Angestellte für sich – Arbeiter für sich – Selbständige für sich – und der Staat für uns alle' wirft die DAG dem DGB vor, daß die große Einheitsgewerkschaft der Bundesrepublik auch auf sozialpolitischem Gebiet 'den großen Eintopf' ansteuere." (*Die Zeit*, 06/07/1968)

Nevertheless, the question whether or not unions should be a political organization also utilizing strike as means of politics plays a minor role compared to the previous phase. Instead, topics like co-determination of unions in corporations and labor disputes for wage increases or reduction of working time prevail over debates on the political system.

4.2.3. Democratic Demarcation from 1971–1988

Document distribution in the 1970s and 1980s suggests a stabilization of the number of documents related to democratic demarcation on a high level. During this phase, hegemonic democratic identity of

Germany further consolidates in a two-fold manner. On the one hand, we can observe integration of actors into the inner circle of legitimate participants of democracy which were formerly reputed suspicious. Workers unions further split up into smaller organizations of special interest groups and mainly restrict themselves to industrial work relations instead of being political actors:

> "Es kann kein Zweifel daran bestehen, daß die meisten Spitzenfunktionäre im Deutschen Gewerkschaftsbund (DGB) und seinen 17 Einzelgewerkschaften den politischen Streik – und damit auch den Generalstreik – als Mittel der gewerkschaftlichen Interessenvertretung ablehnen." (*Die Zeit*, 05/20/1983)

Influences of radical groups in the workforce only play a minor role (Topic #58). On the other hand, there is a concentration on discursive activity to exclude newly emerging inhomogeneous actors and ideologies from the left side of the political spectrum. Interestingly, for the first time we can identify a large affirmative topic towards Marxist ideology in the data. Topic #17 refers to the relation between the social democrats (SPD) and socialist or communist ideas by referring to concepts such as Marxist analysis, revolution or class. Within the struggle for discursive hegemony to define the constitutional democratic antagonism, this left-wing inspired discourse spreads to other fields. Topic #12 shows an ongoing dispute on the political system and its relation to the social and economic order with strong reference to the academic field and the education system. Again, critics of a liberal development play a major role demanding defense of the FdGO:

> "Aber auch die Lehrer, die Eltern und die Schüler werden ernsthaft prüfen müssen, ob sie den Frontalangriff gegen unser freiheitliches politisches und ökonomisches System hinnehmen und auf Dauer gegen ein autoritäres, scheindemokratisches System eintauschen wollen." (*FAZ*, 04/02/1973)

Debates are focusing on potentials and conditions for societal change and development. They also incorporate issues posed by emerging new social movements.

An influential contribution to the formation of democratic identity through demarcation resulted from terrorist activities of small radicalizing groups in the aftermath of 1968. Topic #42 describes activities of the terrorist group Rote Armee Fraktion (RAF), injuring and killing people in various attacks. Under the impression of terror on the one hand, and the discursive and societal swing to the left on the other hand, we can observe severe backlashes to the liberal order in the FRG. Topic #62 reveals an intense debate on the requirement of employees in the public sector to confirm to the liberal democratic order (FdGO):

> "Der SPD-Parteitag hat am Kernsatz des Ministerpräsidenten-Beschlusses vom Januar 1972 gegen Radikale im öffentlichen Dienst festgehalten: Beamter soll in der Bundesrepublik nur werden oder bleiben dürfen, wer 'die Gewähr dafür bietet, daß er jederzeit für die freiheitliche demokratische Grundordnung im Sinne des Grundgesetzes eintritt'." (*Die Zeit*, 04/20/1973)

This discussion led to regulations that hundreds of thousands of employees and applicants to public service were screened by the domestic intelligence service (BfV). Suspects were not employed or removed from their positions. Suspicious were not only members of the former KPD or the newly founded Deutsche Kommunistische Partei (DKP), but also activists within the new social movements. Topic #63 on public protests and demonstrations incorporates references to autonomous groups, squat movements and anti-nuclear protests together with the question on violence as means of politics versus demands for non-violent resistance. Prevalence of references to the police and their repressive means indicate a heated environment for the new social movements to bring their positions into the public sphere. From these non-parliamentary movements a new political party began to shape. The (Grüne) Alternative Liste (AL), or DIE GRÜNEN (the Green party) later on, realized its first electoral successes in the 1980s (topic #20). During their early phase, they acted as melting pot for various political currents (environmentalists as well was radical left-wing and some right-wing actors), resulting in ongoing disputes between 'fundamentalists' and 'realists'. In the beginning the established parties in the German parliamentary system, especially from the conservative side of the spectrum, reacted with strategies of exclusion and marginalization. Democratic demarcation towards the right-wing side of the spectrum plays an increased role in third phase as well. Topic #29 reveals an intensified debate on the NSDAP dictatorship and resistance against it:

> "Nicht allein der 20. Juli, das Attentat auf Hitler, sondern überhaupt jeder Widerstand gegen die Nazis kann für die Jugend viel bedeuten, aber besonders soll er eine Mahnung sein und zum Nachdenken veranlassen." (*Die Zeit*, 07/28/1978)

4.2.4. Democratic Demarcation from 1989–2000

Distribution of documents during this fourth phase peaks around 1990 to its highest point of the entire time frame in this study, then steadily declines during the mid of the nineties, before it rises again to a high peak at the end of the century. The two peaks can be clearly associated with two developments: the downfall of the socialist regimes in the Eastern bloc on the one hand, and the rise of right-wing extremist movements in Germany on the other hand. From 1989 onward, we observe a major shift within discourses related to democratic identity as well as to demarcation due to the incident of the fall of the wall and the reunification of GDR and FRG. The socialist regimes as counter-model to the liberal democratic Western bloc largely failed economically as well as in fulfilling their ideological promise of approaching truly liberated societies by overcoming pressure of capitalist imperatives. In Germany societal search for democratic identity after 1990 is shaped by unity and overcoming of gaps between the Eastern and the Western part (topic #74). National identity becomes a heated topic in German public discourse after reunification debating concepts such as nation, people (Volk), language, culture and national feeling (topic #30). Overly positive affirmation of these concepts for identity are contrasted by an increased debate on German history of World War II and resulting responsibilities (topic #29):

> "Weil eine bis in die Mentalitätsbildung hineinreichende Auseinandersetzung mit der NS Periode im Osten Deutschlands nur oberflächlich,

> im Westen erst mit erheblicher Verzögerung stattgefunden hat, besteht heute die Bereitschaft, mit größerer Energie nachzuholen, was nach 1945 versäumt worden ist." (*Die Zeit*, 05/13/1994)

Economically, the reunited FRG needs to deal with the legacy of the failed 'real existing socialism', especially with rising unemployment rates and poverty in the Eastern part, resulting in controversies on social justice, equality and the proper relation between market and politics (topic #52). On the supranational level, the EU becomes a major player for identity formation as well as for economic development (topic #68). Debates concentrate on institutional arrangements of the EU, such as a common currency or common foreign and security policy, but also on conflicts such as loss of national sovereignty or expansion versus deepening of the confederation.

In 1998 the German government changes from a liberal-conservative coalition to a coalition between social democrats and the Green party. The latter, formerly considered as suspicious to the liberal democratic order, finally became completely accepted as legitimate within the constitutional spectrum and pushed aspects of its agenda into the center of the political, e.g. environmental protection and phasing out nuclear energy (topic #20). While the Green party became largely accepted, three other topics indicate new frontiers of demarcation towards left-wing political, right-wing political and foreign influences. Topic #73 deals with the Partei des Demokratischen Sozialismus (PDS), successor of the former State party Sozialistische Einheitspartei Deutschlands (SED) in the GDR which became a political player mainly in the Eastern part of reunited Germany. As representative of the former socialist regime, the new left-wing party quickly became object to discursive exclusion by the established parties of the FRG. Attempted approaching between PDS, SPD or Greens in the Eastern federal states were disapproved by a range of political actors:

> "Etwas anderes aber ist das Verhältnis zur PDS als Partei: Sich auf eine Zusammenarbeit mit den Erben der SED einzulassen, sich vielleicht gar bei politischen Entscheidungen von ihr abhängig zu machen – das muß auch künftig für die SPD ein Tabu bleiben." (*Die Zeit*, 11/04/1994)

At the same time, due to intensified international crises, many people migrated to Germany seeking for asylum at the beginning of the decade and German society started to realize that millions of formerly foreign 'guest workers' were now permanent residents. Topic #95 shows related debates on the change of the constitutional right to asylum, the question whether Germany de facto is an immigration country, double citizenship and integration of migrants. This debate is heavily linked to the debate on German identity, resulting in attempts to define 'Germanness'. Right-wing extremists strongly took over this debate in their interest, gaining ground mainly in the new federal states of the East (topic #51):

> "Rechtsextremistisch motivierte Gewalttaten gefährdeten in einem zunehmenden Maße Demokratie und Rechtsstaat, verängstigten und verunsicherten die Menschen und minderten das Ansehen Deutschlands im Ausland." (*FAZ*, 08/29/2000)

The public discourse negatively reports on neonazis, xenophobia, right-wing oriented youth and series of violent attacks against refugee centers and migrant people. The opportunity to legally ban parties of this nationalist current—namely Deutsche Volksunion (DVU), Nationaldemokratische Partei Deutschlands (NPD) and Die Republikaner (REP)—is debated intensely.

4.2.5. Democratic Demarcation from 2001–2011

During the fifths and last phase of this study's time range, document distribution on democratic demarcation drops after 2002 to its average level. Democratic identity formation seems to be mainly influenced by international developments and foreign policy relations. Since there was already a topic on the new German role in international politics including military interventions, e.g. in Kosovo, in the previous time cluster, we observe an increased discussion on the German role in international relations (topic #83). Issues discussed are a permanent seat in the UN Security Council, the relation between USA and FRG, explicitly concerning the war in Iraq and the military as means of politics to counteract international terrorism. The EU and its initiatives for a common currency and common foreign and security policy provide new sources for identity (topic #68) and answers to challenges of globalization (topic #52). The effect of globalization and neoliberalism on conditions to achieve societal goals concerning freedom, social justice and security are of special interest:

> "Sie griffen die Idee der sozialen Gerechtigkeit frontal an und behaupteten, die Aufgabe des Staates bestehe einzig und allein darin, Sicherheit und Freiheit zu garantieren." (*FAZ*, 05/21/2007)

At the same time, the political center reflects itself in debates on civic and political culture discussing concepts like mainstream middle class, moral elites and the myth of the generation of 1968 (topic #25).

On the other side, democratic demarcation is oriented mainly against the ongoing threat of right-wing extremists and newly occurring issues with the Islamic religion. Demarcation towards the right-wing side is concerned mainly with neo-Nazi groups who act violently against migrants and political opponents (topic #51). In this context, a ban of the party NPD which became elected into parliaments of Saxony and Mecklenburg-Western Pomerania is debated intensively. The topic on Islam is two-fold. On the one hand there is a strong demarcation against Islamist terror started to be seen as a severe threat after the 9/11 attacks in 2001 in the United States (topic #42). On the other hand, a debate on the relation between German autochthonous identity and Muslim migrant influences can be found. Topic #96 shows general debates on the relation between Germans and Turks, Muslims and Christs, religion and secularism as well as specific issues such as religious education, gender relations and the 'Kopftuchstreit' (headscarf-controversy). One may assume that many discourse participants perceive Muslim migrant people as a threat to their national identity. Discourses on gender roles in Islamic milieus or the special responsibility of Germany towards Israel and the fight against antisemitism (topic #57) might be employed as a vehicle to strengthen racist, ethnic sources of German identity against migrant identities. Demarcation against left-wing oriented politics seems not to play a vital role any longer, as the discourse on the PDS shows trends towards acceptance within the constitutional spectrum—especially after its fusion with the West German party formation Wahlalternative Arbeit und Soziale Gerechtigkeit (WASG) to the new party 'Die Linke' in 2007 (topic #73). Interestingly, for the first time in the data set there is a significant share of documents relating directly to the main state actor of democratic demarcation, the 'Verfassungsschutz' (BfV) and other intelligence services (topic #65). Their role is discussed both, affirmatively as institutions to guarantee protection of the democratic liberal order, and critically as a threat to even this liberal order due to violation of fundamental rights and support of undemocratic actors by their operation:

> "An der Spitze des THS stand Tino Brandt, der vom Verfassungsschutz als V-Mann geführt wurde und dafür im Laufe mehrerer Jahre bis zu 200 000 Deutsche Mark eingenommen und zum Teil in den Ausbau rechtsextremistischer Aktivitäten gesteckt haben soll." (*Die Zeit*, 08/15/2002)

4.3. Classification of Demarcation Statements

In the previous section, I inductively explored topics on democratic demarcation within five distinct phases of time and observed that demarcation towards left-wing ideologies and actors played the major role during Germany's first decades. After 1990 demarcation towards far right-wing activities became more salient, extended to demarcation towards Islamic issues ranging from national identity to terrorist threats at the beginning of the new century.

We now systematically operationalize these findings as a deductive measurement approach by defining content categories on democratic demarcation and identity formation. These categories will be assigned to expressions in the textual data. Observation of categories in our corpus allows for identification of proportions and trends to quantitatively determine on the development of democracy related discourse patterns. In a first step, I introduce the category system to measure developments and give example texts. Secondly, a training set for these categories is annotated manually and extended by an active learning workflow (see Section 3.3.6). In a final step, this extended training set is utilized to classify categories in both, articles of the *FAZ* and *Die Zeit* separately, to judge on trends, correlations and co-occurrence of statements on democratic demarcation.

4.3.1. Category System

In Section 4.1, I have introduced the one-dimensional political scale between left and right as a basic theoretical conceptualization of relating political actors and ideologies to each other. Although this left-right scale may be seen as a gross simplification from a political science perspective, it is widely used in academics and majorly referenced outside of theoretical contexts by public political discourses. Hence, for analyzing development of democratic demarcation, I also stick to this model of the political spectrum.

Left and right are rather blurry concepts of the political. They are useful to juxtapose certain actors or ideologies, but their concrete or associated meaning may change over time. Generally speaking, the political left-right scale can be conceptualized along the ideal of universal equality. Left-wing ideologies advocate for universal equality of all human beings, while right-wing ideologies negate such equality (Bobbio, 1994). Politics of both directions consequently follow these premises, either by striving for collectively binding decisions which favor equal participation of all members of society universally, or by concentrating on the promotion of particular groups, usually associated with the ruling authorities by certain identity constructs. In this conceptualization, the idea of the center appears as the appropriate, sensible balance between the two extremes: radical equality versus radical inequality. Political theorists of normative democracy theory affirm this political center as source for stability and fair balance of all interests (Backes, 2006) while largely neglecting the relative character of these concepts. It is apparent that assumptions of what is considered as discriminating or supporting equality, i.e., rather right or left, drastically changes over time or between societies when it comes to specific politics.[8] Consequently, affirmation of the center of the political spectrum as a matter of principle can lead to naive affirmation of the status quo resulting in political inertia.

In general, statements on self-identity are expressed by protagonists of a specific position in rather positive language while separating it from the 'other' use negative sentiment expressions. Hence, normative view points of discursive actors located in the political mainstream affirm their centrist position as something positive, while considering positions towards the extremes as rather negative, not to say dangerous (Prüwer, 2011). Such positioning is performed by discursive actors in specific speech acts. These speech acts make a perfect basis of data to investigate democratic self-perception of a wide range of participants in the public discourse together with their attempts to exclude certain actors or positions as a threat for the center of the spectrum. Speech acts of democratic demarcation usually need to be performed in two ways. On the one hand, there are speech acts fostering democratic identity and measurements to defend it against its enemies. Complementary, there are speech acts excluding certain actors or positions directly.

In the following, I investigate such speech acts operationalized as five categories within the data: 1) demarcation towards left-wing politics, 2) demarcation towards right-wing politics, 3) demarcation towards left- and right-wing politics alike, 4) reference to fortified democracy, and 5) reference to (centrist) democratic identity.[9] Categories have to be identified on sentence level as context unit for annotation. Statements should relate to interior politics and contain an implicit or explicit normative statement, either approval or rejection, to be annotated. Negations are treated the same way as

[8] As examples may serve women's suffrage being introduced at the beginning of the 20th century, or contrary views on the necessity of a universal health-care system in Europe and the USA.

[9] From the previous section, we have learned that demarcation towards Islam starts to play an increased role in the last time phase. As this type of demarcation does not fit well into the left-right scale and only occurs at the end of the study period, I left it out for the category system.

non-negated statements because they, although rejecting it, reference to the same concept. Consequently, I assume them also as a valid unit to measure presence of the targeted discursive formation. The five categories are defined as follows:

1. *Right-wing demarcation*: This category encompasses sentences expressing demarcation against or a demand for exclusion of right-wing political actors or ideologies from the legitimate political spectrum. This includes normative negative statements on the historical national socialism and its consequences, contemporary phenomena of right-wing extremism or rejection of racism and antisemitism. It does not include statements which merely mention actors who are labeled as right-wing extremists in other contexts, if no explicit harsh critique or demand for exclusion is present.

2. *Left-wing demarcation*: This category encompasses sentences expressing demarcation against or a demand for exclusion of left-wing political actors or ideologies from the legitimate political spectrum. This includes normative negative statements on the socialist or communist ideology, the regimes in the Eastern bloc and contemporary phenomena of left-wing extremism or direct associations of left-wing actors with violence and undemocratic behavior.

3. *Left- and right-wing demarcation*: This category encompasses sentences expressing demarcation against or a demand for exclusion of left-wing and right-wing political actors or ideologies alike. This can be implicit by referring to demarcation using terms such as totalitarianism or extremism to characterize actors not further specified. It can also be explicit by mentioning or equating negative properties of left- and right-wing phenomena in the same context.

4. *Fortified democracy*: This category encompasses sentences referring to the concept of 'Wehrhafte Demokratie' or expressing the need to defend the public liberal order. It also applies to general statements on measurements of the fortified democracy, e.g. ban of political parties or exclusion of alleged enemies of the constitution from the

public service sector, which are not explicitly targeted to a specific left- or right-wing actor.

5. *Democratic identity*: This category encompasses sentences expressing positive values as sources of democratic identity. This might be a positive reference to democracy as political system itself, as well as reference to specific aspects it consists of, e.g., human rights, freedom or civil society.

Table 4.1 gives three example sentences per category. The next section describes how this category system is utilized within an active learning workflow.

Table 4.1.: Example sentences for five content analytic categories.

Category	Example sentences
Right-wing	• Wer jetzt mit ihr um die Wette laufen wollte, dem würde bald die Luft ausgehen, Rechtsextremistische Phrasen gelingen immer noch am besten den Rechtsextremen. • Aber in einem Milieu, das Rassisten, antisemitische 'Arier' und sonstige gewalttätige Rechtsradikale in nach wie vor beträchtlicher Zahl hervorbringt, finden sich genug Einzeltäter, die sich zur Nachahmung aufstacheln lassen. • Insbesondere an den Universitäten war und ist man mit dem Wort Faschismus und einem Vergleich mit dem Nationalsozialismus schnell bei der Hand, wenn es gilt, gegen 'die Rechten' zu Felde zu ziehen.
Left-wing	• Gegenüber linksextremen Gruppierungen, die jenen Anstrich der Seriosität, um die sich die DKP so sehr bemüht, nicht haben, darf es vielleicht gesagt werden: Das Verbot muß sein. • Den Freunden der Freiheit und des Pluralismus in Deutschland ist naturgemäß mit jenen Kommunisten viel besser gedient, die keinen Hund hinter dem Ofen hervorlocken, also den drei moskautreuen Parteien SED, DKP und SEW. • Inzwischen ist die Fernhaltung von Kommunisten vom öffentlichen Dienst obsolet; es gibt die PDS, die SED-Nachfolger, als Kommunisten im Verfassungsbogen [...].

Left- and right-wing	• Sie sollen jedoch im 21. Jahrhundert nicht so totalitär ausfallen wie im zwanzigsten, sondern eine 'Pluralität der Eigentümer und Wettbewerb der Wirtschaftseinheiten' zulassen. • Es gibt seit dem Sonntag keinen Grund mehr, irgendeiner extremistischen Richtung politische oder strafrechtliche Rabatte zu geben. • Es ist genug geschehen, um auch dem Arglosen zu zeigen, daß die Extremisten links und rechts einander brauchen und sich dabei voranhelfen.
Fortified democracy	• Wenn das Mittel des Verbots verfassungswidriger Parteien zum Schutz der freiheitlichen demokratischen Grundordnung nicht zu einer Theaterwaffe werden soll, dann muß hier Ernst gemacht werden mit dem Satz des geltenden Rechts, daß auch Nachfolge-Organisationen verbotener Parteien zu verbieten sind. • Diese bestehe in dem Grundsatz, daß Verfassungsfeinde nichts im öffentlichen Dienst zu suchen hätten. • Der Gedanke der Verfassungsväter von der 'wehrhaften Demokratie' wird an der linken Front mehr und mehr preisgegeben.
Democratic identity	• Zwar einigte man sich auf Grundsätze wie Demokratie, Pluralismus und Menschenrechte. • Toleranz ist eng verbunden mit so modernen Konzepten wie Demokratie, Freiheit, Menschenrechte und der Herrschaft der Gesetze; diese ergänzen einander. • Doch in einer parlamentarischen Demokratie geht es immer so.

4.3.2. Supervised Active Learning of Categories

As introduced in Section 3.3, we can apply supervised machine classification in an active learning setting to reliably and validly identify trends and proportions in diachronic collections. For this, I manually coded a sample of documents with the categories introduced in the previous section. It is important to note, how this sample was drawn to guarantee a good initial training set for the active learning process. To get proper examples for each category from each phase of time and of a broad range of themes, I utilized the lists of documents from each

Table 4.2.: Active learning of five categories: The table shows set sizes of manually coded sentences ($\mathcal{M}_c^+$), how many iterations of the active learning process were taken (i), sizes of the positive $\mathcal{T}_c^+$ and negative $\mathcal{T}_c^-$ training set, and how this final training set evaluates in 10-fold cross validation (F_1).

Category	$\mathcal{M}_c^+$	**i**	$\mathcal{T}_c^+$	$\mathcal{T}_c^-$	$\mathbf{F_1}$
Right-wing	400	6	725	3358	0.686
Left-wing	334	6	532	6132	0.527
Left- and right-wing	210	7	384	3889	0.542
Fortified democracy	203	8	348	3421	0.517
Democratic identity	150	6	418	4046	0.545

temporal and topical cluster the 50 SECGs base on. Documents per temporal/topic cluster can be ranked in decreasing order according to the proportional share of the topic they contain. From each of the resulting 50 lists, I read the five most prominent documents to evaluate, if they contain sentences relevant for the category system. If so, I annotated all sentences I considered as relevant for any specific category.[10] As the description of the SECGs already suggested, there are some topics containing numerous examples for representatives of the annotation categories. And there are others, containing only little or no reference to democratic demarcation or democratic identity in the sense of the code definitions. By reading through 250 articles, I annotated 1,252 sentences as positive examples for either one of the five categories.[11] Table 4.2 gives the size of the manually annotated sentences $\mathcal{M}_c^+$ for each category c.

To asses the quality of my manual annotations, I re-evaluated 100 example sentences from the training data for each of the five

[10]For annotation of sentences and the active learning process, I utilized the infrastructure 'Leipzig Corpus Miner' (Niekler et al., 2014).

[11]To get an idea on time consumption for this step: It took me about three work days to read through all 250 articles and annotate them.

Table 4.3.: Number of sentences $\mathcal{S}_c$ per category c positively classified in the complete corpora of *FAZ* and *Die Zeit*. $\mathcal{D}_c$ indicates corresponding document frequencies.

Category	$\mathcal{S}_c^{FAZ}$	$\mathcal{D}_c^{FAZ}$	$\mathcal{S}_c^{ZEIT}$	$\mathcal{D}_c^{ZEIT}$
Right-wing	14120	7467	77866	30987
Left-wing	10930	7418	23949	15015
Left- and right-wing	6825	5444	17165	13394
Fortified democracy	7223	5897	23244	17903
Democratic identity	6470	5268	25242	17264

categories.[12] Based on these two codings of sentences, intra-rater reliability can be calculated (Krippendorff, 2013). Table 4.4 gives the results for simple code agreements (Holsti index), Cohen's κ, and Krippendorff's α. The values indicate that categories could be annotated pretty reliably, since the last two measures show chance corrected agreements around 0.75 and higher.[13]

With the five initial sets of annotated sentences, I started the active learning process for binary classification of each category on the democratic demarcation collection $\mathcal{D}'$.[14] Each iteration of the process extracted 200 new unlabeled sentences from $\mathcal{D}'$ as potentially positive examples. For each sentence suggested by the learning process, I approved or rejected the classifiers decision for a category.[15] In 6 to 8 runs i for each category c, this produced training sets $\mathcal{T}_c^+$ of around

[12] There was a time period of three months between the initial annotation of training data and its re-evaluation to ensure that intra-rater results are not distorted by memorizing just recently annotated examples.

[13] I relied on re-evaluation by myself, because I had no resources for training a second coder when conducting this analysis step. Of course, measuring inter-rater reliability would be preferred above the intra-rater reliability as it expressed inter-subjective agreement.

[14] $\mathcal{D}'$ is the set of around 29,000 documents retrieved from the complete newspaper population $\mathcal{D}$ (see Section 3.1).

[15] Evaluating on 200 sentences for a single category took about 30-45 minutes. Hence, 33 iterations of active learning for all five categories together needed another 2-3 work days.

Table 4.4.: Intra-rater reliability of categories evaluated by Holsti-index, Cohen's κ and Krippendorff's α.

Category	Holsti-Index	Cohen's κ	Krippendorff's α
Right-wing	93%	0.831	0.832
Left-wing	90%	0.742	0.741
Left- and right-wing	90%	0.752	0.753
Fortified democracy	92%	0.813	0.813
Democratic identity	89%	0.740	0.741

400 positive examples and a much larger set of negative examples $\mathcal{T}_c^-$,[16] enough to get acceptable quality measures F_1 between 0.5 and 0.7 for 10-fold cross validation on the final training sets.

As shown in Section 3.3.6, when using around 400 positive training examples from six or more iterations of active learning, we can expect reliable and valid estimation of trends and proportions in our data, even if the F_1-quality achieved moderate results only. The final training data sets were used to classify sentences for each category in the complete document set $\mathcal{D}$ of all *FAZ* and *Die Zeit* articles. Table 4.3 shows sizes of positively classified sentences $\mathcal{S}_c^{FAZ}$ and $\mathcal{S}_c^{ZEIT}$ per category c for each newspaper separately, and together with their corresponding document frequencies $\mathcal{D}_c$.

The set of sentences annotated per machine classification can now be utilized for content analytic evaluations exactly the same way, as if annotated by hand. Results on such investigations are presented in the following section.

4.3.3. Category Trends and Co-Occurrences

Supervised classification identified around 200,000 sentences in the corpus of both publications fitting into one of the investigated categories.

[16] Again, it is important to note that through manual revision of suggested examples during active learning, also negative examples are of high value for classification performance. In contrast to single runs of classification, the process allows for correction of falsely learned features.

We can assume that individual classification of these sentences may be inaccurate in a reasonable number of cases. But, as our classification process is targeted towards trend analysis in a long time series to infer on category development, we only need to assume that proportions of positively classified sentences in time slices are sufficiently accurate and do not fluctuate arbitrarily over time. Experiments in Section 3.3 have proven that we can assume valid estimation of trends using (semi-)automatic classification in an active learning scenario providing a sufficient number of training examples. Sentence sets resulting from individual classification can be evaluated further qualitatively by including findings from the exploratory analysis, external research literature and close reading of result samples.[17]

To quantitatively evaluate on trends in the data, we need to respect different document lengths of the two publications *FAZ* and *Die Zeit* and the fact that categories might be expressed in varying intensity within single documents. For example, a long report on right-wing extremism in Saxony from the 1990s containing various statements on demarcation towards far-right attitudes may be better captured as a single discourse artifact. For this, I transform sentence category counts to document counts by just factoring if a document either contains at least one sentence of a given category or not. Document frequencies $|\mathcal{D}_c|$ per category are given in Table 4.3 for each publication separately. By comparing sentence and document frequencies, we can actually observe that the average number of positively classified sentences per document ($|\mathcal{S}_c|/|\mathcal{D}_c|$) is highest for the category right-wing demarcation, while all other categories appear to be represented less dense in single articles.

[17]Due to the NLP focus of this work, I waived a systematic manual evaluation step, which definitely would be recommendable for a more detailed political science study. An exploratory look into the sets of positively classified sentences revealed that sentences mainly fit the desired contexts, e.g. statements on communism or right-wing actors, although in some cases lacking an explicit normative demand for demarcation.

Comparing Categories

We now evaluate on the developments of the categories over time by plotting their relative document frequencies aggregated per month. I normalize to relative frequencies because numbers of articles published per month continuously increased during the studied time range which could lead to false trend assumptions or invalid time series peaks. As time resolution of observations on a monthly basis is rather high, resulting in many data points and high variance, I used spline smoothing to plot time series for better visualization of trends in the data.[18] Raw time series data without smoothing is plotted in light-grey behind the smoothed thick lines. Figure 4.2 compares all five categories in both publications, *FAZ* and *Die Zeit*, together. Categories left- and right-wing demarcation are grouped as well as fortified democracy and democratic identity to visualize any parallels.

From the first plot, we can observe that demarcation towards left- and right-wing politics follows different trends over time. While in the first phase (1950–56) the number of documents containing demarcation categories is decreasing, frequencies for both, left and right-wing, significantly increase towards the end of the second phase (1957–1970). Peaks in demarcation from right-wing politics appear around 1965 and 1969, during the first half of the 1990s, and a smaller one around 2004 in the last phase. Peaks in demarcation from left-wing politics appear as well around 1965 and 1968, the 1976/77, and around 1990. After German reunification, demarcation towards the far-left seems to steadily become less salient with only little peaks around 1994 and 1998 shortly interrupting the decreasing trend. Demarcation towards the far-right is contained in the data to a higher proportional share than towards the far-left almost over the entire time range. Only around 1976/77 left-wing demarcation outweighs right-wing demarcation. Nonetheless, we need to be careful with such a direct comparison as in this plot frequencies from both

[18]For this, the function *smooth.spline* of the R base package was utilized, which fits a cubic smoothing spline analogue to the function described in Chambers and Hastie (1992).

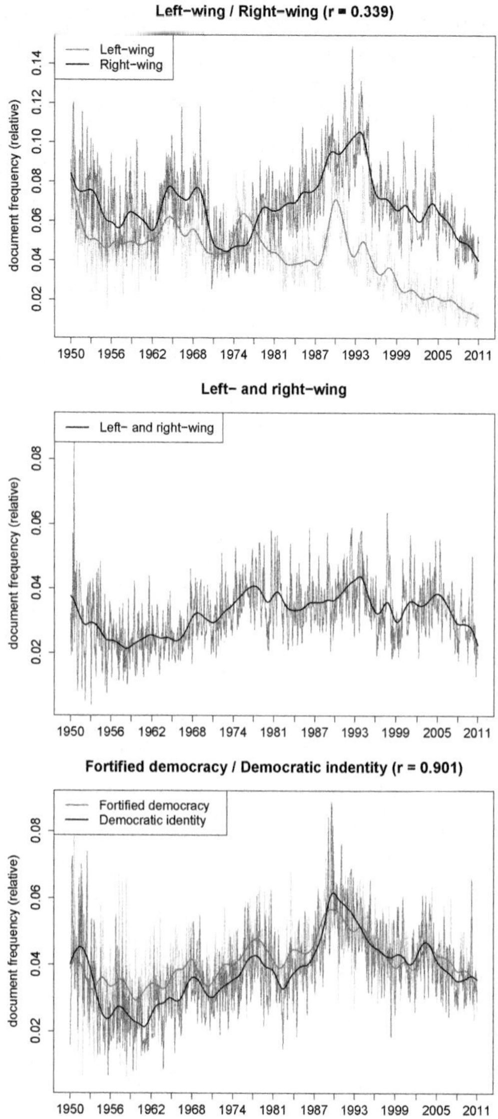

Figure 4.2.: Monthly aggregated, relative frequencies of documents containing expressions of democratic demarcation in both publications, *FAZ* and *Die Zeit*, together. A spline-smoothed line ($spar = 0.5$) is plotted to visualize trends.

newspapers are aggregated. In fact, until 1991 demarcation to the far-left dominates in articles of the *FAZ* (see Appendix).

Demarcation towards *left- and right-wing politics* alike is analyzed as an extra category. The idea behind is that statements expressing demarcation from both political orientations can be operationalized as discursive instantiation of totalitarianism/extremism theory. Normative democracy theory demands 'equidistance' for any legitimate democratic standpoint to the (supposed) extremes at both ends of the political spectrum (Jesse, 2004). In practice, the idea of equidistance often is utilized as a specific discursive strategy, either as demarcating speech act from a center position of the political spectrum to consolidate the democratic self-perception, or as a diversionary tactic from a politically oriented standpoint to direct attention to specific issues fitting own political interests.[19] Statements about 'extremists from left and right' or 'radicals of any kind' in the latter intent may obfuscate major differences of ideological backgrounds of the opposite political current, resulting in a rather unpolitized form of dispute.[20] Trend analysis on this category of equidistant demarcation shows high levels in the first phase of the FRG, a high peak in the second half of the 1970s, the beginning 1990s and 2004. A qualitative look into the sentences extracted from these time ranges will have to reveal what caused the rising of this category.

The third plot in Figure 4.2 shows relative document frequencies of the categories fortified democracy and democratic identity together. We can observe an almost parallel coherent course of the trend lines,

[19]Not only in practiced discourse, but also as theoretical conception 'equidistance' is problematic, since it narrows the legitimate space around the center of the political spectrum to a minimum while at the same time neglecting fundamental differences of left- and right-wing ideology. Schubert (2011) points to actual compatibility between left-wing premises and democracy concerning the ideal of equality in political and social participation. Proponents of 'equidistance' instead warn of a normative overstraining of democracy through public demands for too much equality, or too much participation respectively (ibid., p. 108).

[20]In a sharpened form, elitist political dispute may simply distinguish between order and incidents of disruption to this order resulting in a post-democratic state of the political (Feustel, 2011; Tiqqun, 2007).

suggesting that both categories measure a similar aspect of the discourse on democratic demarcation. While fortified democracy stresses legal measurements against supposed enemies of the democracy, it can be seen as a negative definition of democracy. Its positive counterpart is operationalized in the category of democratic identity, stressing values such as human rights, freedom etc. In combination, they form a complete self-perception of democracy in Germany. The category trends show highest peaks in the early years of the FRG and around 1990 overlapping with the constitutional phase and the reunification with the Eastern part.

Comparing Publications

In Table 4.5 comparison of category frequencies between the two publications *FAZ* and *Die Zeit* is given. We can see that proportions and trends in both largely agree on demarcation towards the far-left, while there is significant deviation on right-wing demarcation and the other three categories. Overall, *Die Zeit* is much more concerned on right-wing extremism and also more often references to democratic identity or fortified democracy. This is probably due to its character as a weekly newspaper concentrated on longer reports related to societal issues instead of short daily news-wire content. Moreover, the liberal orientation of this paper seems to influence attention towards the far-right which appears to be rather neglected by the conservative *FAZ* during the early 1960s and 1980s.

Correlation and Co-Occurrence of Categories

In the last sections, I have described trends of measured categories to reveal periods of their temporal significance and evaluate on differences in coverage of the two analyzed newspapers. For further insight from a distant view, measuring correlation between trends and their co-occurrence may reveal even more complex patterns. For this, I compute correlation coefficients between selected category pairs in both newspapers separately. Results displayed in Table 4.6 indi-

Table 4.5.: Comparison between *FAZ* and *Die Zeit* for relative monthly frequencies of documents containing five categories. Spline-smoothed lines ($spar = 0.5$) are plotted to visualize trends.

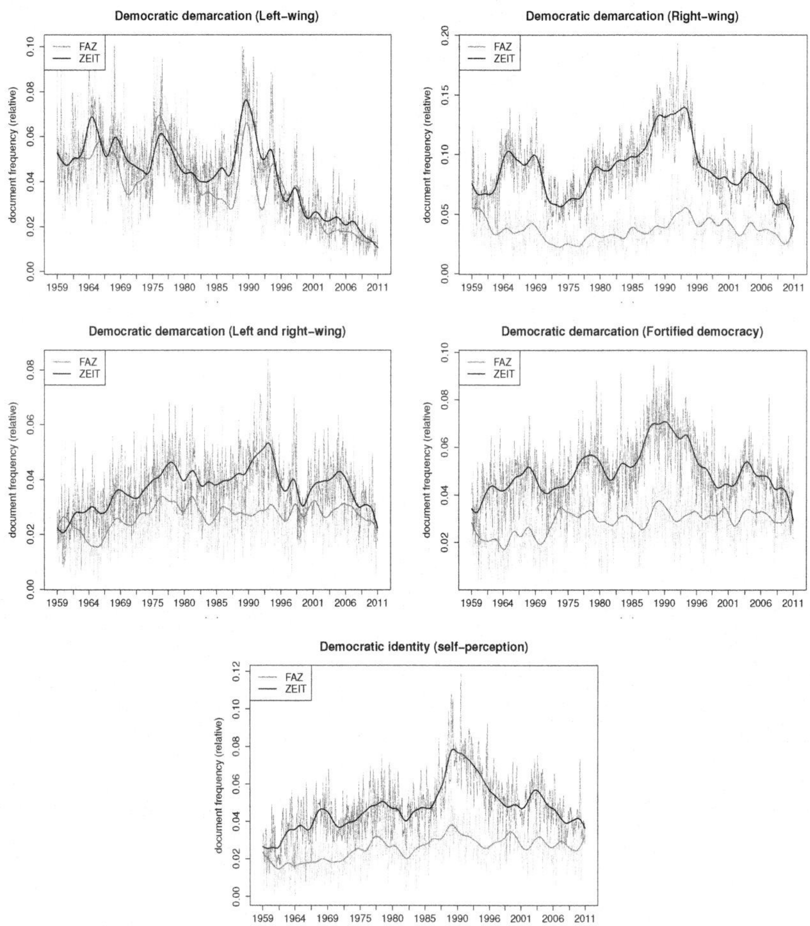

Table 4.6.: Correlations between categories in *FAZ* and *Die Zeit*, based on (smoothed) monthly aggregated relative frequencies (* $p < 0.01$).

Category 1	**Category 2**	r_{FAZ}	r_{ZEIT}
Democratic identity	Fortified democracy	* 0.818	* 0.903
Fortified democracy	Left-wing	* -0.195	* 0.223
Fortified democracy	Right-wing	-0.056	* 0.832
Fortified democracy	Left- and right-wing	* 0.607	* 0.839
Democratic identity	Left-wing	* -0.243	* 0.106
Democratic identity	Right-wing	* 0.133	* 0.790
Democratic identity	Left- and right-wing	* 0.590	* 0.850
Left- and right-wing	Left-wing	* -0.143	0.0650
Left- and right-wing	Right-wing	-0.020	* 0.637

cate interesting significant differences between categories of political orientations and newspapers.

As the plot in Figure 4.2 already suggests, we observe a very high correlation between democratic identity and fortified democracy in *FAZ* and *Die Zeit* ($r > 0.8$), supporting the assumption that both categories depict two sides of the same coin. Remarkably, we observe large differences in correlations between both publications comparing trends of fortified democracy with categories of ostracized politics. Reference to legal measurements to defend democracy is only low correlated with reference to left-wing demarcation in *Die Zeit*, even negatively correlated in the *FAZ*. In contrast, demarcation to the far-right is uncorrelated in the *FAZ*, while highly correlated in *Die Zeit*. Reference to exclusion of both 'extremes' alike correlates with fortified democracy high in both publications. These findings are mirrored with the category of democratic identity correlated to the three exclusion categories.

How can these findings be interpreted? It appears that there is no strong dependency between left-wing demarcation and reference to fortified democracy, suggesting that in times of intense dispute against far-left politics, measurements of fortified democracy are not discussed with equal intensity. This allows for the interpretation that demarcation towards the far-left largely resides on a level of *moral* speech acts. In contrast, at least to be observed in *Die Zeit*, we observe increases and decreases in references to fortified democracy and right-wing demarcation with comparable levels of intensity over time. This suggests that debates against the far-right do not only rest on a moral level, but are accompanied by demands for *legal* intervention. Remarkably, while this demand for legal measures cannot be observed for exclusion of right-wing politics in the *FAZ*, both publications seem to go with this demand when it comes to the equidistant exclusion of left- and right-wing politics alike.

From these findings, we may derive an important conceptual assumption towards future refinement of the categories of democratic demarcation. A speech act to demarcate against certain actors from the legitimate field of politics may be two-sided: Firstly, there is a negative moral statement on an actor or ideology putting it in an equivalence relation with a signifier denoting legitimate exclusion from the political sphere, e.g. by reference to its 'extreme' or 'totalitarian' nature. Secondly, there is a clear demand for exclusion by legal means of fortified democracy. Apparently, this second step less often applies to far-left politics.

While right-wing demarcation and fortified democracy go along, for left-wing demarcation we may derive a distinct discourse strategy. Correlating reference to equidistant left and right-wing demarcation alike with left-wing demarcation only yields little or no connection. Equidistant demarcation and right-wing demarcation instead correlate, at least in *Die Zeit*. One possible interpretation is that discourse on right-wing demarcation frequently is accompanied by pointing to issues on the left side of the political spectrum as well, or to general extremist threats to democracy as a whole. This hypothesis can to be investigated further by switching from the hitherto observed macro-level of trends to category observation within documents.

Up to this point, we have observed correlation of categories only on an aggregated distant level of trends. Our analysis gets more specific,

Table 4.7.: Heatmap of co-occurrence of categories left- and right-wing (LRW-D), left-wing (LW-D) and right-wing demarcation (RW-D), fortified democracy (FO-D) and democratic identity (ID) per time cluster. The darker a square, the more significant two categories appear together in documents (Dice measure). Co-occurrence of one category with itself indicates its relative proportion to all others.

Period	Die Zeit	FAZ
1950–1956	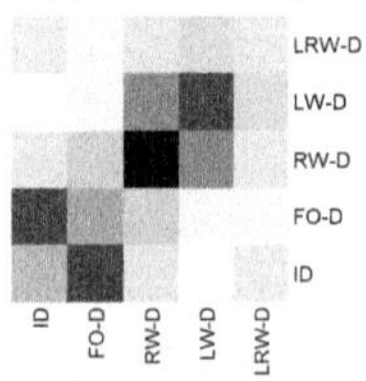	
1957–1970	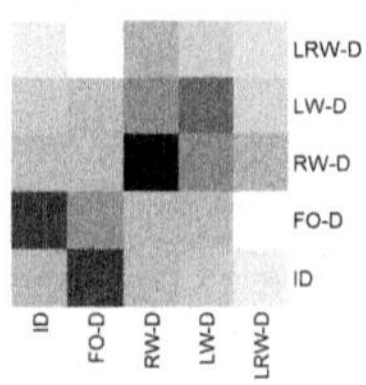	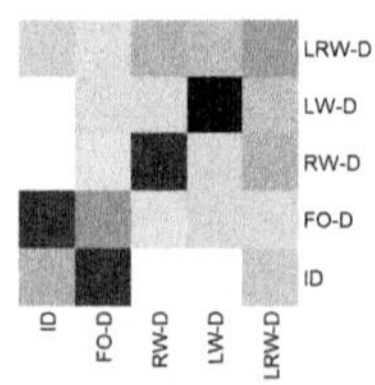
1971–1988	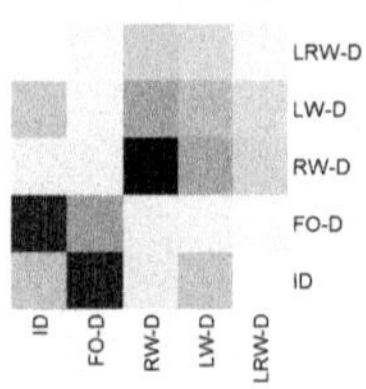	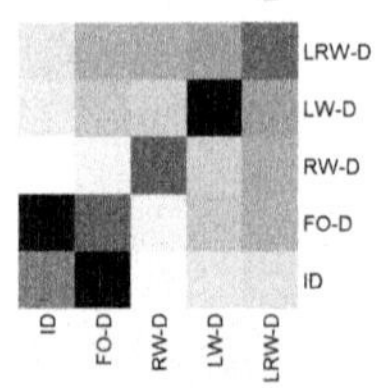
1989–2000	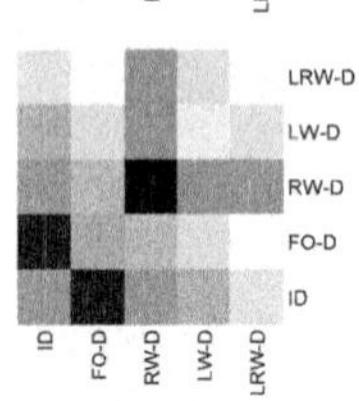	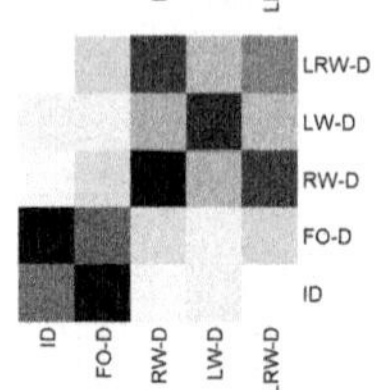
2001–2011	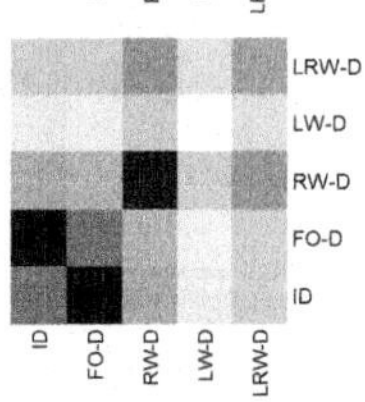	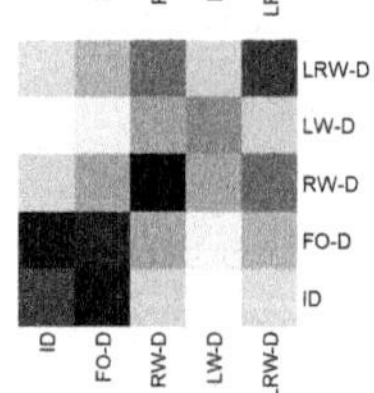

if we look directly into the documents to observe co-occurrence of categories. Co-occurrence cannot only be visualized as graph as we did already for words in sentences before, but also with the help of heatmaps. The heatmaps in Table 4.7 indicate levels of co-occurrence of two categories by color. Statistical significance of co-occurrence is determined by the Dice coefficient (see Eq. 3.10). The more often two categories appear together in one document with respect to frequency of their single occurrence, the higher the Dice coefficient gets. This value is then transformed into a color value to color squares of a quadratic map. The darker a square in the map gets, the more likely the co-occurrence of the two categories represented by row and column is. The diagonal from top right to bottom left of each heatmap is colored according to its relative proportion on the set of all categories identified in one temporal cluster.

With such heatmaps, significance of category co-occurrence can now be compared in a single temporal cluster per publication, or between temporal clusters and publications. The following conclusions from comparing map patterns can be highlighted:

- As trend correlation already has suggested, fortified democracy (FO-D) and democratic identity (ID) significantly co-occur with each other in documents stable in all periods and both newspapers. Relative proportion of both categories is higher in the *FAZ* than in *Die Zeit* and has its highest share from 2001 onward.

- In *Die Zeit* the category of right-wing demarcation (RW-D) occours with highest proportion in all periods of time. The *FAZ* in contrast puts most attention to left-wing demarcation (LW-D) in the second an third period, before the focus of awareness also switches to RW-D from 1989 onward.

- While LW-D proportions decrease over time, there is an increasing proportion of statements of demarcation from left- and right-wing politics alike (LRW-D). In both publications LRW-D occurs more often together with RW-D, but not with LW-D.

- FO-D co-occurs in *Die Zeit* more often with RW-D than with LW-D in the first, the fourth and the fifth period. In the second and third period, it appears with LW-D and RW-D in almost equal proportion while in the *FAZ* FO-D and LW-D co-occur more frequently during these periods.

Looking at category co-occurrence on the document level confirms some findings of the trend correlation. Moreover, it allows for more fine-grained inspection of the classification results, e.g. by partitioning in time periods.

In extension of category co-occurrence, we can even look closer by conditioning on their joint occurrence. Defining A and B as sets of documents containing one category and another to compare, we can express their occurrence in terms of probabilities, $P(A) = |A|/n$ and $P(B) = |B|/n$, where n is the size of the entire set of documents containing a positively classified sentence of any category. Co-occurrence then measures the joint probability $P(A, B) = |A \cap B|/n$, which very much resembles the Dice coefficient. But instead of just looking at joint probability, we now want to evaluate on conditional probabilities $P(A|B) = P(A, B)/P(B)$ and $P(B|A) = P(A, B)/P(A)$. Due to different marginal probabilities of each category, the co-occurrence matrix containing conditional probabilities no longer is symmetric. From it, we now can infer on the likelihood of observing, for example, expression of left-wing demarcation in case of having observed right-wing demarcation before, and vice versa. In Table 4.8 such probabilities are plotted as directed graph. Vertex sizes indicate the proportion of the category on all categories. In these graphs, I skipped the category *democratic identity* to reduce their complexity.

This display complements findings from the heatmap by revealing different patterns of category use in the corpora. Interesting cases are those, where conditional probabilities between two categories exhibit a larger difference in their edge direction, and differences between LW-D and R-WD conditioned on the other categories. For instance, in *Die Zeit* during all times $P(\text{LW-D}|\text{RW-D}) > P(\text{RW-D}|\text{LW-D})$, which means it is much more likely that if we observe RW-D, we also observe

Table 4.8.: Graphs displaying conditional probabilities of categories in documents. Arrow direction from A to B indicates $P(B|A)$. Vertex size indicates the share of a category relative to all categories in the time period and publication.

<table>
<tr><th>Period</th><th>Die Zeit</th><th>FAZ</th></tr>
<tr><td>1957–1970</td><td>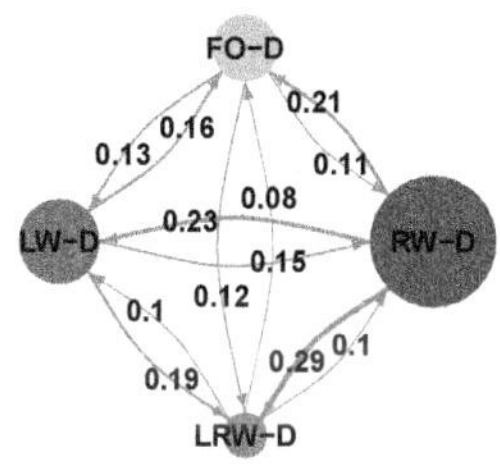
</td><td>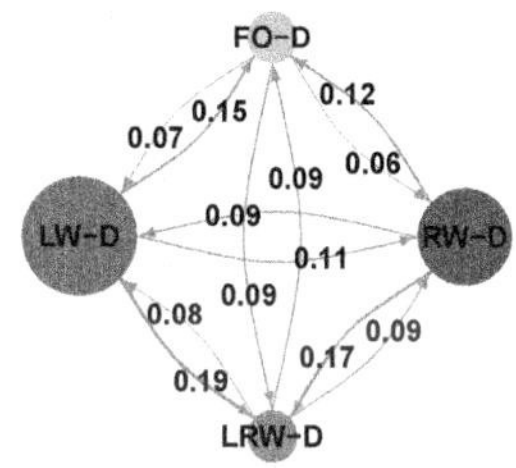
</td></tr>
<tr><td>1971–1988</td><td>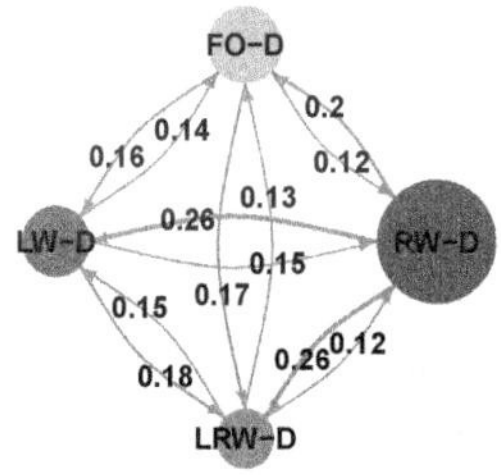
</td><td>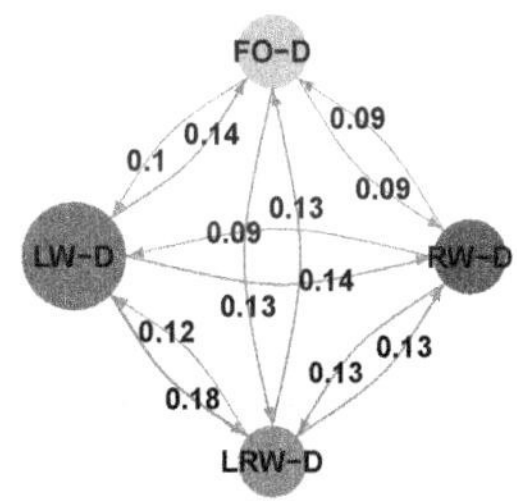
</td></tr>
<tr><td>1989–2000</td><td>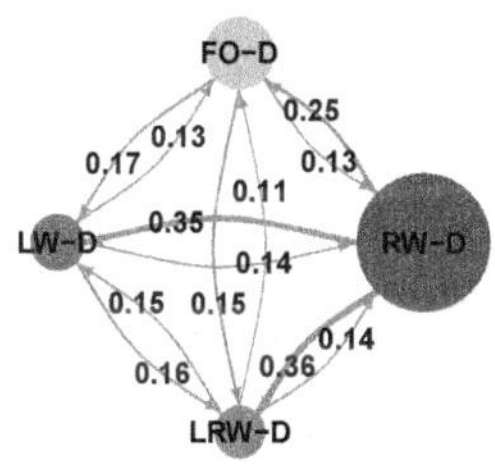
</td><td>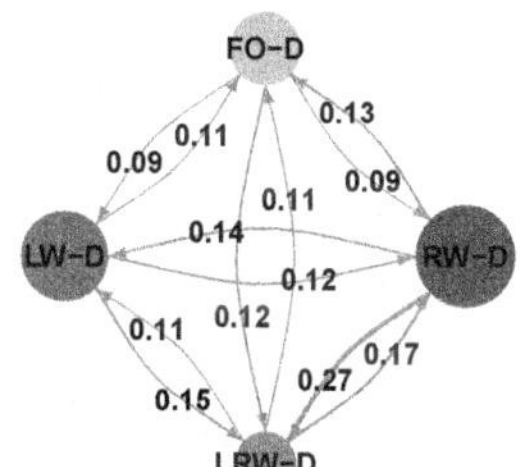
</td></tr>
<tr><td>2001–2011</td><td>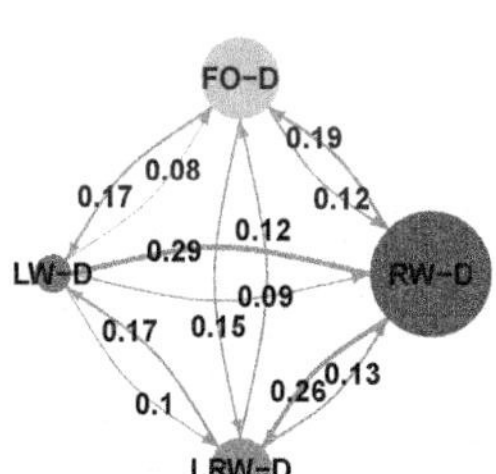
</td><td>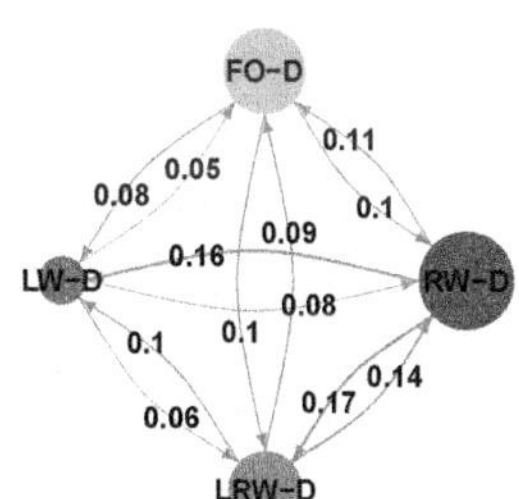
</td></tr>
</table>

L-WD, than the other way around. In contrast, in the *FAZ* from 1957–1988 occurrence of RW-D is more likely if we observed LW-D before than the other way around. At the same time, the relative proportion of LW-D is dominating over RW-D in this publication. It may be interpreted that the dominating category of demarcation more likely triggers speech acts also pointing to the opposite demarcation category. The same is mirrored for $P(\text{LRW-D}|\text{RW-D}) > P(\text{LRW-D}|\text{LW-D})$: In documents containing RW-D, it is more likely that LRW-D occurs than in documents containing LW-D during all times in *Die Zeit* and after 1989 in the *FAZ*. Reference to fortified democracy is more likely in documents where we observe RW-D than in those containing LW-D, $P(\text{FO-D}|\text{RW-D}) > P(\text{FO-D}|\text{LW-D})$, except from the two periods in the *FAZ* with LW-D dominating over RW-D.

Additional to the general description of these observations, which conclusions can be drawn from these findings? Generally, we may interpret this as an effort in discursive production of 'equidistance' from the political fringes. The larger the difference between the shares of left-wing demarcation and right-wing demarcation becomes, the more likely it gets that while referencing to the larger of both categories, we also observe a reference to the smaller category or to both, left- and right-wing demarcation alike. I would suspect, this is due to discursive strategies of actors within the constitutional center of the spectrum which lean either to the left or right side. In their ambition to retain equidistance to the major political threat from their perspective, they put weight on (allegedly neglected) threats for democracy to contrast current mainstream focuses. Specifically, we observe a change in discourse patterns related to left-wing demarcation after German reunification until nowadays. We do not only find a focus shift from left-wing demarcation to right-wing demarcation. Moreover, we can infer on a shift in the discursive strategy to demarcate against far-left politics. As the Soviet counter-model disappeared in the early 1990s, the political far-left no longer was addressee of measurements of fortified democracy to the same extent. Discursive strategies of political antagonists, especially from the conservative side of the political spectrum, less often relied on demands for legal actions against their political enemies. At the same time, we observe an increase of statements of demarcation against left- and right-wing politics alike co-occurring with statements on right-wing demarcation. From this, I conclude that in contexts of right-wing extremism speech acts more often morally point to the far-left side of the spectrum or to all extremists alike as severe issues for German democracy. This can be seen as a hint for increased relevancy of the extremism model and its demand for equidistance underlying the political discourse. As far-left wing politics has lost some of its threatening character for representative democracy, political opponents of leftist ideas not longer demand for legal exclusion, but discredit their opponents by putting them discursively on an equivalent level with neo-fascist or right-wing extremist threats to democracy.

4.4. Conclusions and Further Analyses

In this chapter, I have introduced basic theoretical thoughts on the concept of democratic demarcation. Subsequently, I have described contents of selected relevant documents by exploring them with the help of visualizations as SECGs showing co-occurrence of topics and topic defining terms in single time periods. Many important issues of contemporary history in the political debate on state and conditions of democracy in Germany could be revealed by these exploratory descriptions. The rather qualitative insights were backed up by automatically extracted sets of representative sentences containing important semantic propositions derived from co-occurrence patterns in single SECGs. Qualitative findings were further extended by a quantitative approach of machine classification to determine on the development of content categories expressing statements on democratic demarcation. These quantitative measures of categories exhibited interesting differences in discourse developments of perceived societal threats for democracy from the far-left or the far-right. Moreover, it allowed for interpretation of shifts in discourse strategies of demarcation from left- or right-wing politics. While in recent history, demarcation from the far-right is disputed along with legal measurements of fortified democracy, demarcation from the far-left is expressed largely without that reference. Instead, we can observe an increase of speech acts equating it to the threat of the far-right side or by referencing to an unspecific conception of 'extremism' as a whole.

The quantified view on categories of democratic demarcation revealed such shifts in discursive patterns and strategies. Ideally, the interpretation of this data should be supported by a qualitative analysis. For this, sentences of each category identified by classification can be selected and filtered by meta-data, e.g. their publication origin and time. Selected and filtered sentences further can be clustered by their specific content features in a separate unsupervised machine learning process.[21] Investigation of these clusters is helpful to explore underlying discursive events of a category in a very efficient manner. For example, we can answer questions such as: *What is the reason for the increase of right-wing demarcation statements during 2004 and 2005 in Die Zeit?* Clustering of around 1,000 sentences from these years by lexical features (uni-/bi-grams) and topic features showed that in these years there is an intense debate on growing scenes of neo-Nazis and right-wing extremism in Germany, resulting in electoral successes of the party NPD which entered two federal parliaments. At the same time, there is an intense debate on history of the Third Reich and politics of commemoration. A further exploration of such clustered sentences from interesting time frames, e.g. peaks in category trends, would help to improve the understanding of discourse processes and contents allowing for inference on development of scopes and limits of democracy.

For the hypotheses guiding this exemplary study introduced in Section 4.1, some important insights could be generated by the TM supported analysis of large newspaper corpora. In fact, exploration of

[21]Clustering can be done analogue to the process of clustering years to identify time periods presented in Section 3.2.3. But, instead of aggregating topical features of documents from a whole year, topic proportions of single documents can be utilized together with lexical features extracted from single sentences to reveal clusters of contextually similar sentences.

the retrieved sub-collection of relevant documents contained strong reference to national-socialism and socialist regimes of the Eastern bloc, largely framing disputes on democratic demarcation. By conceptualization of the political spectrum as a one-dimensional left-right scale we could observe strong demarcation against far-left politics during the first decades of the FRG, but largely diminishing after 1990. Right-wing demarcation interestingly did not emerge as a very prominent topic on its own before the second half of the sixties, then almost vanished, before it occurred again in the eighties and has been dominating the dispute after the German reunification. We also saw differences between the more conservative *FAZ* and the more liberal *Die Zeit*, although long-term trends between the two publications correlate to a large extent—nonetheless, correlation is much higher on left-wing than on right-wing demarcation. Further, we saw that reference to fortified democracy as a special version of German democracy conception is tightly coupled to positive references to democratic identity. Yet, both categories are more frequently used in contexts of right-wing demarcation than in demarcation towards far-left politics. This is true especially after German reunification, where we observed that left-wing demarcation itself only plays a minor role, but right-wing demarcation is increasingly accompanied by pointing to problematic issues of leftist or generally 'extreme' positions alike. In conclusion, the integrated interplay of qualitative and quantitative information extracted from the large amount of hundreds of thousands of newspaper documents allowed us a deep and insightful analysis, giving answers to a complex, abstract research question which we would have been unable to generate otherwise.

5. V-TM – A Methodological Framework for Social Science

Chapter 3 has introduced a selection of Text Mining (TM) procedures and integrated them into a complex workflow to analyze large quantities of textual data for social science purposes. In Chapter 4 this workflow has been applied to a corpus of two newspapers to answer a political science question on the development of democratic discourses in Germany. In this final chapter, I extend the workflow to a general methodological framework describing requirements, high-level design and evaluation strategies to support Qualitative Data Analysis (QDA) with the help of TM.

The method framework is drafted in analogy to concepts from the field of Software Engineering (SE) or, more specific, to Requirements Engineering (RE). In (business-oriented) computer science RE is a well-established field of research. It is defined as "a coordinated set of activities for exploring, evaluating, documenting, consolidating, revising and adapting the objectives, capabilities, qualities, constraints and assumptions that the system-to-be should meet based on problems by the system-as-is and opportunities provided by new technologies" (van Lamsweerde, 2007, p. 6). Heyer et al. (2014) suggested that employing concepts from SE and RE for Digital Humanities (DH) can help to develop interdisciplinary research designs more systematically.

Picking up this idea, I will conceptualize the methodological framework along the *V-Model* known from SE. The V-Model of the software development cycle distinguishes two phases, the verification phase and the validation phase, to coordinate development and testing activities during the entire process (Bucanac, 1991). By assigning a testing task to each development task around the actual implementation of

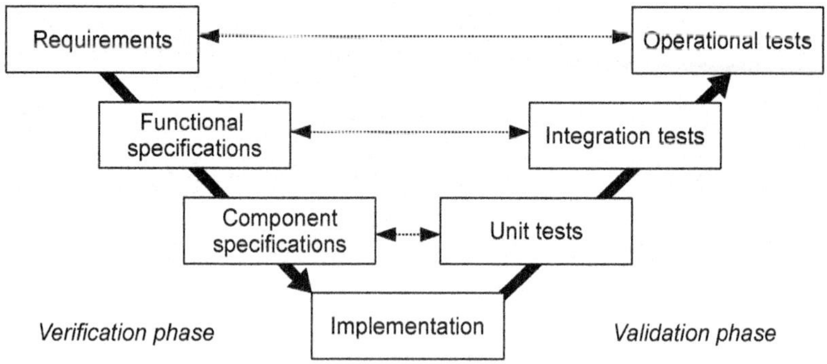

Figure 5.1.: The V-Model of software development process (Liversidge, 2005)

code, the model can be visualized in its typical V-shape (Fig. 5.1). For some years now, there has been much criticism on the V-Model and its predecessor, the *waterfall model*, from a software development perspective because of its rigidity and inflexibility (see for example Liversidge, 2005). Nonetheless, instead of utilizing it for software product management, I rely on strengths of the model as a rough guideline to conceptualize a methodological framework.

The V-Model became attractive due to clear and logic separation of specification phases as well as their close coupling with tests for quality assessment during the development process. We can adapt these ideas and modify the model for our purpose. Figure 5.2 shows the adapted version of the V-Model to guide the methodological framework for TM integration into QDA. For adaption, the verification phase is exchanged with a *research design phase* and the validation phase with an *evaluation phase*. Further, we adapt some of the specific sub-phases and their corresponding tests with processes fitting our domain. Analogue to the V-Model, *requirements* of the analysts, or in business logic terms requirements from the perspective of clients and other stakeholders, have to be identified. But instead of *opera-*

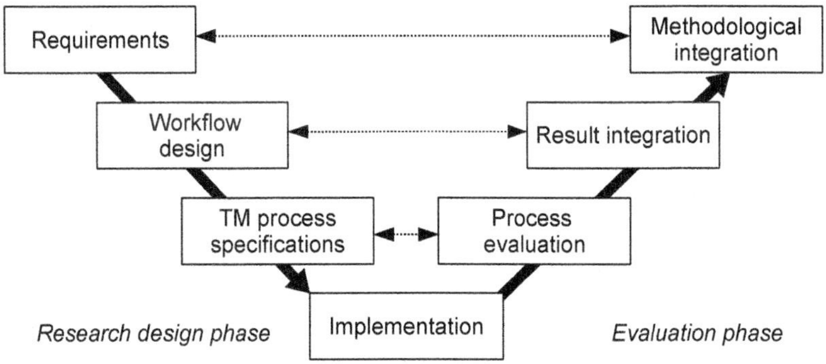

Figure 5.2.: The V-TM framework based on the V-Model to guide the methodological integration of TM into QDA. The upper two levels are discussed in this chapter while the lower two levels were already subject to discussion in Chapter 3.

tional testing in a software development process, social scientists need for integration of their study design with *methodological background* assumptions. The phase of *functional specifications*, sometimes also called high-level design, is exchanged for *workflow design* to define a sequence of analysis methods to answer a social science question. During evaluation phase, it corresponds to *result integration*, i.e. the task of compiling outcomes of different TM processes as input for subsequent processes, or in a final step summarizing outcomes for a comprehensive answer to the research question. The *component specifications* are adapted to *specifications of the selected TM processes*, each corresponding to its own specific *process evaluation* criterion.

This adaption of the V-Model will be named V-TM framework in the following descriptions. Its lower two levels *TM process specifications* and their corresponding *evaluation* followed by suggestions for concrete *implementations* have already been described intensively in Chapter 3. To complete the V-TM framework, descriptions provided in this chapter deliberately concentrate on the upper two levels of the V-formation to elaborate on processual and methodological questions of integrating TM into QDA. In the upcoming sections, I outline on these sub-phases of the V-TM framework in more detail:

- Requirements (Section 5.1)
- Workflow design (Section 5.2)
- Result integration (Section 5.3)
- Methodological integration (Section 5.4).

5.1. Requirements

In order to create a valid and reliable research design integrating a range of computer-assisted analysis procedures for large amounts of qualitative data, we need to identify requirements first. Requirements analysis is an essential sub-task of RE to determine the needs of users, or stakeholders in general. As we deal within an interdisciplinary research environment, it is useful to reflect on two roles of stakeholders: the role of technology providers from a computer science perspective and the role of data analysts from a social science perspective—both with their own interests in research and views on the subject.

Social scientists can rely on a variety of QDA methodologies and procedures to analyze textual data such as interviews, newspapers data, or any other document manually. Surely, depending on their research background, they would like to draft TM integration into their processes as closely to their established procedures as possible. Developers of computer linguistic and NLP procedures, in contrast, have their own standards, established applications and resources to analyze textual data. Probably, both groups do not even share the same theoretical notions of semantics. Different views on the joint task, divergence between analyst requirements and technical capabilities to meet them, should be made clear in an early stage of aspired cooperation processes. Established procedures from both perspectives need to be adapted in order to fit into an integrated research design.

Requirements describe the *what* of a system, but not the *how* of its realization. In this respect, RE distinguishes into functional and non-functional requirements of a project. Functional requirements describe what a system should *do*, while non-functional requirements put emphasis on how a system should *be*. For the V-TM framework, the discipline specific notions, views and demands mentioned above mainly translate into non-functional requirements. For TM supported QDA application in scientific research domains the following **non-functional requirements** can be identified:

- *Compliance with established research quality criteria:* Participating disciplines from social science, linguistics and computer science have their own discourse on quality criteria of their research. Newly introduced methods should strive for compliance with these established criteria to increase acceptance. In quantitative social science these are basically validity, reliability and objectivity (Flick, 2007)—criteria largely compatible with numerical evaluation strategies based on established gold standards dominating in NLP. In QDA on the other hand, there are rather soft criteria such as theoretical contextualization of findings from empirical data, generalizability of findings and inter-subjective traceability of systematically applied methods (Steinke, 1999; Mayring, 2000).

- *Integration with established methodologies:* Although social science procedures of manual QDA are similar in many respects, they mostly differ in their methodological background (see Chapter 2). Integrating TM into QDA should not mean to give up on these methodological reflections. In contrast, through investigation of large amounts of texts, epistemological questions on the character of investigated speech acts as representatives of super-individual knowledge structures or social reality become even more vital.

- *Control over analysis procedures:* Algorithmic extraction of knowledge structures from text should not be a black box to the analyst. Many commercial TM software packages applied in business contexts do not disclose their algorithms and hide key parameters to control the process in favor of usability. Analysts in research domains instead need full control of NLP preprocessing pipelines, single analysis algorithms and their key parameters, as well as chaining them into complex analysis sequences fitting to their research interest.

- *Reliability:* TM algorithms should be deterministic to get reproducible and comparable results complying to the reliability criterion of research. In fact, for many ML applications, reliability is not that easy to achieve, because they rely on random parameter initialization or sampling processes (e.g. LDA topic inference or k-means clustering). Dependent on structures within the data, these moments of chance may result in varying outcomes of the algorithms. Close investigation of the results produced by multiple runs of such algorithms may reveal, if outcomes comprise of stable structures, or instead are rather a product of chance.
- *Reproducibility:* TM workflows can get very complex quickly. Outcomes are influenced by data cleaning, linguistic pre-processing of the text, mathematical pre-processing of DTMs, key parameters of analysis algorithms and chaining of intermediate results with possible filter or selection steps in between. Further, supervised ML processes, e.g. POS-Tagging for linguistic pre-processing, may rely on models built with external training data. To achieve perfect reproducibility of results for other researchers, one would need the raw data, an exact documentation of the entire algorithmic chain and its key parameters, as well as utilized model instances.
- *Usability:* There is a danger that complexity of TM application for QDA is at the expense of the reflection on the social science aspects of the research question. Producing new, hitherto unknown types of results and nifty visualizations of extracted data does not necessarily come with deeper insight. To allow for concentration on discipline specific important aspects of the analysis work, application of TM methods for QDA should give respect to a certain degree of usability.

- *Scalability:* TM usually deals with large amounts of text. Data management procedures, workflows, analysis algorithms and result visualizations should ensure the ability to handle expected amounts of data.

This list may be incomplete. Probably, more non-functional requirements can be identified in the light of concrete analysis scenarios. Nevertheless, this list represents core requirements important to most scenarios of integrating TM into a social science research process.

What may be **functional requirements** of the research design? This highly depends on the concrete research question and its operationalization strategy. They describe which core capabilities of NLP the method design needs to provide. There is, on the one hand, a rather generic requirement of *data management* for large text collections. On the other hand, there are specific functional requirements along with specific *data analysis goals*. The next two sections briefly introduce functional requirements of both aspects.

5.1.1. Data Management

Functional requirements can be identified with respect to data management. To handle large amounts of textual data for TM processes, a system needs efficient storage and retrieval capabilities. For this, relational data bases[1], document oriented data bases[2], or a combination of both might be the right choice. Storage includes the text data itself along with all its metadata further describing the content (e.g. publisher, author, publishing date, or geo-coordinates). However, not only initial texts need to be stored. A solution is also needed for large amounts of data created during several analysis steps, which might serve as intermediate result for subsequent processes or as basis for the final analysis and visualization.

[1]Open source solutions are for example MariaDB (http://mariadb.org) and MySQL (http://www.mysql.com).

[2]Open source solutions are for examples CouchDB (http://couchdb.org) and MongoDB (http://www.mongodb.org).

For context-specific selection of documents as a starting point for any study, fast and convenient access might be provided by specialized full text indexes[3] on a full corpus collection (e.g. entire volumes of a newspaper), which allows for key term search, or more complex queries involving metadata, phrase search and term distance criteria.

To actually analyze textual data by NLP methods, text represented as character strings usually needs to be transformed into vector representations, i.e. Document-Term-Matrices (DTMs). This conversion is achieved by procedures of linguistic preprocessing resulting in a DTM object which might be transformed further by some mathematical preprocessing before computer-linguistic and statistical NLP analyses are applied. To structure and coordinate these processes, the application of an NLP framework is advised.[4] These frameworks provide functions for data reading, preprocessing and chaining of analysis tools. With their help, researchers are enabled to connect to selected data sets and quickly set up workflows for experimentation and analysis.

5.1.2. Goals of Analysis

Functional requirements also can be identified with respect to data analysis. At the beginning, there is a research question and the presumption that answers to that question can be found in a large set of documents. Requirements for analysis may be formulated along with analysis goals which arise directly from the operationalization of the research question. Operationalization of a qualitative research question with the help of TM needs to define units of analysis as a basis for structure identification. These units may be terms or phrases, concepts, actors or locations, activities, statements representing specifically defined categories of content, semantic fields, topics,

[3]Open source solutions are for example Apache Lucene/Solr (http://lucene.apache.org) and Elastic(https://www.elastic.co).

[4]Open source solutions are for example Apache UIMA (https://uima.apache.org.), the *tm*-packge for R (Feinerer et al., 2008) or the Natural Language Toolkit (NLTK; http://nltk.org) for the Python programming language.

or combinations of all these types. Goals of analysis with respect to such analysis units might be

- identification of documents relevant for the research question
- retrieving paradigmatic example texts for manual analysis
- extraction of meaningful vocabulary
- observation of semantic fields by term co-occurrences
- observation of changes in semantic fields over time
- observation of changes in semantic fields between topics, actors etc.
- observation of sentiments in documents or towards semantic units
- identification of actors or other named entities in certain contexts
- identification of topics in document collections
- identification of content analytic categories and semantic concepts
- measuring category proportions
- measuring category frequencies for time series analysis
- measuring correlation and co-occurrence of categories
- correlating quantified structures with external data.

Such analysis goals may be translated into well-defined, traceable and evaluable sub-tasks to prepare the later workflow design.

To give a more precise exemplary description, I recur to the goals of the exemplary study on democratic demarcation (see Chapter 4). The overall research question *'How was democratic demarcation performed in Germany over the past six decades?'* was operationalized two-fold: 1) an inductive step clarified on qualitative changes of topics and language use on democratic demarcation over time; 2) a deductive step measured categories of democratic demarcation derived from political science theory on political spectrums. This operationalization translated into the following analysis goals and corresponding tasks:

1. *Identification of relevant documents:* From a corpus of around 600,000 documents from two newspapers, those relevant to the topic of democratic demarcation needed to be identified. As this topic is not easily definable by a handful of key terms, an IR approach based on language use in reference documents needed to be developed. Further steps were compiling the reference corpus of paradigmatic documents, scoring relevancy of target documents by the IR approach, deciding on the size of relevant document set for subsequent analysis and evaluation of the retrieved set. Requirements of this step are described in Section 3.1.1.

2. *Exploration of contents:* To assess on contents of around 29,000 retrieved documents qualitatively, exploratory methods needed to be applied. Tasks were: identification of meaningful time periods, identification of thematic clusters, visualization of significant meaningful patterns in these thematic clusters, and extraction of paradigmatic sentences representing good examples for identified patterns. Qualitative descriptions can be retrieved from synoptic review of all partial results. Requirements of this step are described in more detail in Section 3.2.1.

3. *Manual annotation of content categories:* Statements on democratic demarcation needed to be classified by a semi-automatic process, which combines steps of manual training set creation and automatic machine classification. For the first step, five categories were derived from theoretical assumptions and defined in a code book. Afterwards, documents for initial coding needed to be selected, and then annotated manually. For manual annotation a user-friendly tool for document retrieval and coding is advised, since there are several hundred documents to read. To ensure coding quality, intercoder-reliability or intracoder-reliability has to be evaluated.

4. *Active learning of content categories:* The initial training set from manual coding is to be extended within an active learning process using supervised machine classification. The classifier needs to be chosen, feature types extracted from the training set, meaningful

features need to be selected. Then, the classifier can start to identify new meaningful text samples from the selected document set to extend the training set. In iterated steps of batch active learning suggestions for new training examples generated by the classifier need to be evaluated manually until evaluation criteria of precision, recall and size of the training set fit to required quality criteria of the process defined beforehand. Requirements of this step are described in more detail in Section 3.3.1.

5. *Final analysis:* The trained classifier from the previous step is applied to the original data set to analyze developments of the measured categories over time and in selected subsets of the data. Results from the final classification process need to be filtered by meta-data, to prepare them for visual and statistic evaluation. Visualizations for time series and co-occurrences of categories need to be provided and statistics for more comprehensive analysis should be computed. Quantified results need to be interpreted in the light of the research question and hypothesis formulated at the beginning of the study. Triangulation of the findings with external literature and qualitative investigation of the classified text units for each category help to assure the quality of the overall process chain and backup the interpretations. An example for such a comprehensive analysis is given in Section 4.3.

This list of analysis goals and corresponding tasks may serve as the basis to define specific analysis workflows in the next step.

5.2. Workflow Design

After having identified analysis goals and further refined them into tasks, we now can start to model the research design on a high level as a chain of workflows.

5.2.1. Overview

The chain of workflows realized in the example study on democratic demarcation can be seen as a specific realization of the V-TM framework to integrate several TM methods for answering a complex research question. Yet, not all steps need to be conducted to generate desired outcomes for other types of studies. Instead, single steps might be combined differently, or just can be omitted if they are considered as unimportant for the analysis. Analogue, new steps might be introduced to augment the workflow chain by other analysis approaches considered as helpful to answer the posed research question.

To visualize workflow patterns in a generic way, Figure 5.3 displays five abstract categories of previously identified analysis goals, which can be chained in varied sequential orders to realize different research designs. In accordance with the relevancy of context in CATA application (see Chapter 2), as a first step, research designs needs to conduct a certain context selection strategy to define the base population of texts for subsequent analyses. Apparently, this is a generic step to be realized by any research strategy. Subsequent steps then may be conducted to realize either inductive or deductive research strategies, or a combination of both. For this, semantic patterns representing desired units of analysis can be conceived as some kind of abstract, rather vaguely defined 'category'. Inductive exploratory analysis steps can be conducted to identify such patterns (step 2). For some research designs, qualitative description of patterns retrieved in a data-driven manner might be the final goal. Alternatively, the workflow chain can be augmented with steps of category specification to fixate identified patterns (step 3). This can be compared to the derivation of real types from empirical data, or to selective coding in GTM. Well-specified categories can be employed in a further deductive analysis step. For this, category representative analysis units can be retrieved in the entire corpus (step 4). This can be done in conjunction with or without previous data exploration and inductive category specification. In a last step of any research design, all generated categorical data from each of the conducted steps has to be evaluated in a synoptic analysis

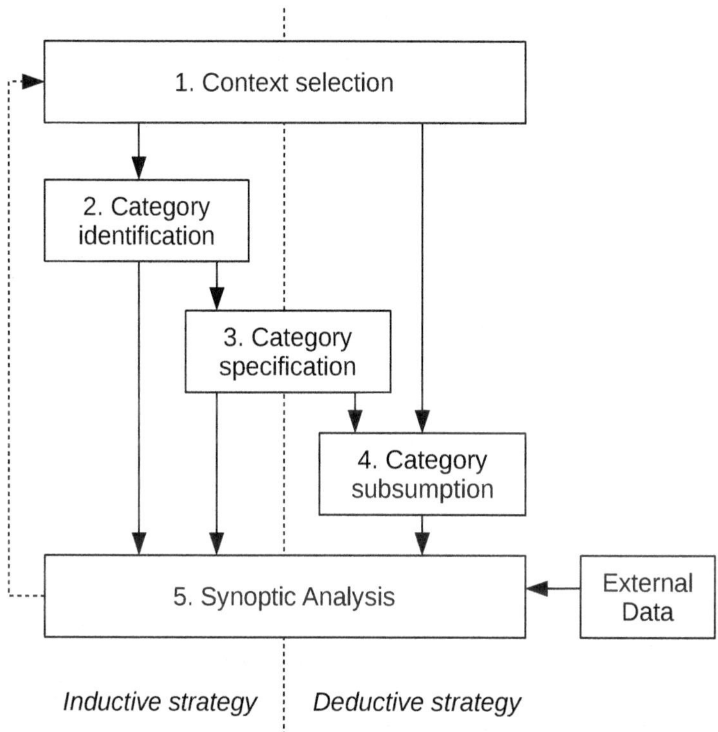

Figure 5.3.: Generic workflow design of the V-TM framework for QDA integrating Text Mining: Single steps might be realized by different technologies and under different methodological assumptions to follow either inductive or deductive research strategies, or a combination of both.

(step 5). Here also certain external data could be taken into account, e.g. for correlating patterns extracted from a document collection with text external observations.[5]

Analogue to the example study, Figure 5.4 presents the schematic visualization of a specific V-TM workflow chain. It can be perceived as an instantiation of the generic workflow design (Fig. 5.3) integrating all analysis steps, both inductive and deductive. Additionally, it shows results as resources produced by one step and utilized as input for subsequent processes to achieve following analysis goals. In accordance with the V-Model's emphasis on testing, each sub-goal needs to be evaluated separately to ensure the overall quality of results within the entire workflow chain. The principle 'garbage in, garbage out' governs any of the applied sub-processes. Serious flaws produced at the beginning of the process cannot be compensated by later processes. To assure quality of the entire analysis process, measures and procedures for quality assessment have to be distinctively defined for each goal. Defining these evaluation procedures and sufficient quality criteria is a decisive part of any workflow design. It guarantees that validity of a procedure depends on its implementation or parameters only, and not on variances in quality of its input. Consequently, the example workflow design presented in Fig. 5.4 mentions types of evaluation procedures and makes suggestions for concrete approaches.

As we are on the second level of the V-TM framework dealing with high-level research design, the following workflow descriptions operate on classes of algorithms rather than mentioning specific algorithms. Input data and outcome of results are given along with substantiated imperative descriptions of analysis tasks as steps to achieve the analysis goal. The decision for specific algorithms and their key parameters would be part of the subsequent level of TM process specifications. Nonetheless, in some cases, I refer to specific algorithmic approaches

[5] Petring (2015), for example, cross-correlates patterns in news coverage related to topics of social justice and inequality with the development of the Gini-coefficient in Germany. In a time series analysis, he can show a significant relationship between economic inequality expressed by the Gini-coefficient and increases of media reports on the topic, peaking after five months.

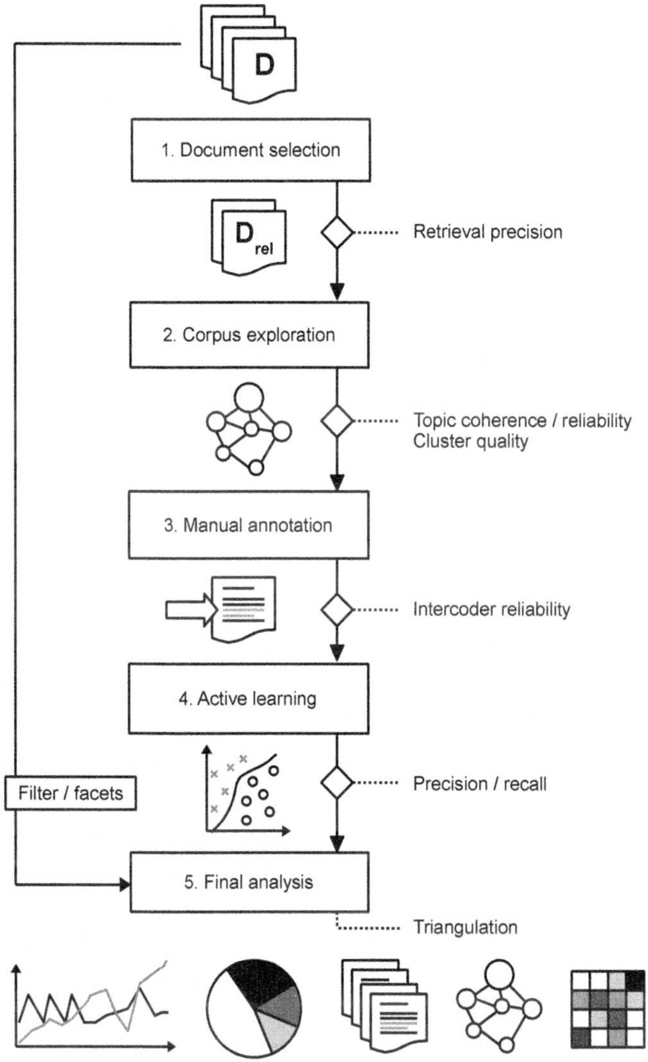

Figure 5.4.: Specific workflow design of the V-TM framework consisting of five integrated tasks. For each task, potential results are given and corresponding evaluation steps are determined to ensure validity of the results of the entire process chain.

used in the exemplary study and also mention alternatives to this design decision. Opting for such alternatives might be a good idea, if requirements change, operationalizations allow for simpler solutions or demand more complex ones.

5.2.2. Workflows

Document Selection

Workflow 1 substantiates on steps for the goal of identifying relevant documents in a population of documents $\mathcal{D}$. In the example study, scoring of relevancy is done by utilizing a contextualized dictionary of key terms extracted from a paradigmatic reference corpus $\mathcal{V}$. This reference corpus consists of five German governmental reports of the BfV on perceived threats for democracy. 'Contextualized dictionary' means the method not only relies on containment of key terms in the target collection, but rewards if key terms occur in similar contexts such as observed in the reference corpus. This proves useful in cases where target collections cannot be identified by a small set of key terms, and relevancy instead is determined by a variety of expressions and contextual language use. But surely there are research problems, where operating with a simple full text index and document selection by key term occurrence would be sufficient. Assume you want to investigate the debate on minimum wages in Germany, then simply selecting all documents containing the term 'Mindestlohn' will deliver an appropriate document set for further studies. For some research designs, retrieval may require additional filtering of certain contexts after selecting the n most relevant documents from a collection. Close reading samples may reveal that the retrieved set contains thematically relevant, yet unwanted elements with respect to the research question. In the example study, I needed to filter out documents concerned with democratic demarcation, but related to foreign countries. If one operates with key terms of ambiguous meaning, it also may be advisable to filter sub-collections with the help of a topic model. Topic models are able to identify coherent latent semantics in the data. Hence, they may be utilized to filter (un-)desired contexts from collections.

Workflow 1: Document selection

Data: $\mathcal{D}$ – corpus of documents; n – number of documents to select

Result: $\mathcal{D}'$ – Sorted list of (potentially) relevant documents

Score each document $d \in \mathcal{D}$ with relevancy function.
Sort $\mathcal{D}$ by decreasing relevancy.
Return list $\mathcal{D}' = (d_1, \ldots, d_n)$ from $\mathcal{D}$ as relevant documents.
Option: Filter $\mathcal{D}'$ for undesired contexts, e.g. by dictionary lists or topic models.
Evaluate retrieval precision.

Evaluation: *Retrieval precision* of document selection should be evaluated to ensure that the selected document set contains a sufficiently large number of relevant documents. For automatic performance evaluation of a retrieval process, a gold standard of relevant documents is helpful. It can be utilized to estimate the share of relevant documents among the top ranks of the retrieved set. If a reference corpus for extraction of a contextualized dictionary is utilized, parts of this corpus could be used as a pseudo-gold set (see Section 3.1.6). Another method is suggested by Nuray and Can (2006), who propose to generate a set of pseudo-gold set by an automatic approach. They aggregate highly ranked result items found by different retrieval systems to define a set of 'pseudo-relevant' documents. The simplest and most reliable method would be to manually determine relevancy of the documents in different ranges of ranks in the retrieval list, also known as 'precision at k' (Baeza-Yates and Ribeiro-Neto, 2011, p. 140).

Corpus Exploration

Workflow 2 substantiates on steps for corpus exploration of the retrieved documents from the previous workflow. It basically relies on data-driven clustering methods for identification of time periods and thematic structures inherent to the collection. Once thematic clusters per time period have been identified, they can be visualized in a 'distant reading' paradigm to give analysts easy access to contents of sub-collections. Section 3.2 proposes Semantically Enriched Co-occurrence Graphs for this goal. Most probable terms for each topic from an LDA topic model are observed in documents containing a topic to a substantial share in a given time period. Co-occurrence of terms in sentences of such documents is then drawn into a graph network and enriched by sentiment and term significance information. The process could be varied in multiple ways, either by relying on other topic models than LDA, other methods for clustering time periods, or modifications of the graph visualization. To provide QDA researchers with concrete text examples to anchor their interpretations, semantic patterns revealed visually on the global context level can be linked back again to the local context level (see Section 2.3). For this, sentences (or any other analysis unit) containing extracted global patterns can be retrieved as paradigmatic references for any temporal and thematic cluster.

Evaluation: As clustering is an unsupervised, data-driven process, there is not really a strict anchor for quality. For analysts it should be possible to bring identified time periods in line with their prior knowledge on important events in history. Cluster quality indices can be utilized to guide the analysist evaluation of clustering outcomes. For clustering of time periods, I utilized the Calinski-Harabasz index (Caliński and Harabasz, 1974) to determine which number of time periods yields best clustering of years. For thematic clustering, inferred topics should contain terms from coherent semantic fields. If needed, semantic coherence of topics could be evaluated experimentally in user studies (Chang et al., 2009).[6] But usually, a close qualitative investigation combined with numeric evaluation measures, such as held out likelihood (Wallach et al., 2009), would be sufficient for optimal model selection. A recommendable evaluation measure for

[6] An established approach is to deliberately insert random terms into lists of high probable topic terms. Topic coherence is high, if human evaluators are able to identify the artificially inserted word.

Workflow 2: Exploratory clustering

Data: A corpus $\mathcal{D}'$ of relevant documents with time stamps
Result: Thematic clusters of documents $d \in \mathcal{D}'$; Time periods with similar thematic structures; Semantically Enriched Co-occurrence Graphs

Compute thematic clusters of documents $d \in \mathcal{D}'$ (e.g. by LDA).
Aggregate thematic cluster assignments of documents per time span (e.g. mean topic probability per year).
Cluster on thematic aggregates per time span to get periods with similar thematic structures.
Split $\mathcal{D}'$ into subsets per thematic and temporal cluster.
for *each time period* **do**
    Rank thematic clusters (e.g. topic probability or $rank\_1$).
    Identify most important clusters by rank and/or manual selection.
    for *m most important thematic clusters* **do**
        Draw SECGs revealing global context patterns in documents of the current temporal and thematic cluster (for details on SECGs see Workflow 6 in the Appendix).
        Extract samples of paradigmatic text snippets containing revealed global context patterns in their local context.
Evaluate cluster quality and topic model reproducibility.

topic coherence is suggested by Mimno et al. (2011) (see Eq. 3.15). Social scientists also should be careful with the reliability of topic models which may produce varying results due to random sampling for topic inference (Koltcov et al., 2014). To determine the reliability of a model, a measure for reproducibility of topics between repeated inferences can be computed by matching topic pairs (Niekler, 2016). Nevertheless, instead of relying on data-driven parameter selection and numeric evaluation only, intuition of analysts appears to be very important for adjustments of exploratory processes to generate the most valuable outcomes with respect to the analysis goal.

Manual Annotation

Workflow 3 substantiates on steps for initial document annotation with semantic categories for content analysis to prepare machine classification. Selecting documents for annotation appropriately at this point is essential for preparation of the following active learning step. Chances that machine classification predicts category trends in a valid and reliable way are much higher, if the initial training samples contain as much variety of category-related expressions as possible. If one wants to analyze documents from a time span of more than sixty years, it is advisable to rely on a training set sampled from the entire time span. Moreover, it is likely that categories occur within certain thematic contexts more frequently than in others. If the topics themselves are not highly frequent in the base population of documents, random sampling from the entire collection will deliver a poor starting point for generating a good training set. Accordingly, Workflow 3 proposes to utilize topics automatically extracted by corpus exploration in the previous step. Documents are selected by their topic probability and faceted by time period. In the example study, I identified five time periods. For each time period, I selected the 10 topics containing most interesting content with respect to the research question. Selecting the five most probable documents per topic and time period produced a list of 250 documents to read and annotate. This document set for initial annotation contains sufficient variety of category relevant language use, in both thematic and temporal manner. Context units for annotation can be of different kind, e.g. sentences, paragraphs or complete documents.

Evaluation: Manual codings of text are evaluated by *intercoder-* or *intracoder-reliability* measures. They measure agreement of codings between human coders or a single coder at different times. Established measurements in QDA are the Holsti index which just calculates the share of codings two coders agree on. Two more elaborated measures, Cohen's κ and Krippendorff's α, correct basic agreement counts for agreement by chance (Krippendorff, 2013). As a rule of thumb, it can be expected that machine classification in the next step will not

Workflow 3: Manual annotation

Data: Ranked thematic clusters of relevant documents in distinct time periods; Category system $\mathcal{C}$ for text annotation

Result: Text samples representing content categories which capture a wide range of language use determining the categories

for *each time period* **do**
- Select the n best ranked thematic clusters.
- **for** *each selected cluster* **do**
  - Select the m most representative documents (e.g. by topic probability).
  - **for** *each selected document* **do**
    - Read through document and annotate units of analysis representing content categories.

Evaluate intercoder-reliability (Cohen's κ, Krippendorff's α, ...).

perform better than humans do. But if categories are defined in a way that allows for reliable coding by humans, machine learning algorithms will probably be able to learn category characteristics for correct classification, too. Conversely, if humans fail to reliably identify categories, algorithms do not stand a good chance either.

Active Learning

Workflow 4 substantiates on steps for active learning of content categories in texts by supervised learning. The goal is to extend the initial training set from manual coding in the previous step with more positive and negative examples. As category systems for content analysis often are not fully complete and disjoint to describe the empirical data, we train a separate binary classifier for each category to decide whether a context unit belongs to it or not. Training examples are generated in an iterated loop of classifier training, classification of the relevant document set, selection of category candidates and manual evaluation of these candidates. This process should be repeated until we have at least $minExamples$ positive training examples identified. It should also run at least $minIter$ times to guarantee that dubious outcomes of classification in early iteration phases are corrected. During early iterations on small training sets, one can observe that the supervised learning algorithm assumes presence of single features as absolute indicator for a specific category. Imagine the term 'right' as feature to determine statements on demarcation against far-right politics. Provided with an initial training set originating from documents of political contexts only, the classifier will learn the feature occurrence of the term 'right' as a good feature. In early active learning steps, we now can expect suggestions of sentences containing the term 'right' in the context of spatial direction or as synonym for 'correct'. Only through manual evaluation of such examples as negative candidates in ongoing iterations, the classifier will learn to distinguish between such contexts by taking dependency of the term 'right' with occurrence of other terms into account. The final training set generated by this workflow will contain valuable positive *and* negative examples to validly identify category trends. Experimentally, I identified $minIter = 6$ and $minExamples = 400$ as a good compromise between prediction performance and annotation cost (see Section 3.3).

Evaluation: Supervised classification usually is evaluated in terms of *precision*, *recall* and their harmonic mean, the F_1-measure (Baeza-Yates and Ribeiro-Neto, 2011, p. 327). To improve comparability to intercoder reliability, Cohen's κ between (human annotated) training data and machine predicted codes would also be a valid evaluation measure. As the number of positive examples often highly deviates from the number of negative examples in annotated training sets of CA categories, the application of *accuracy*, i.e. the simple share of correctly classified positive *and* negative analysis units based on all analysis units, is not advisable as evaluation measure.[7] As training

[7]Imagine a toy example of a test set containing 100 sentences, 10 belonging into the positive and 90 into the negative class. A classifier not learning any feature at all, but always predicting the negative class as outcome, would still achieve an accuracy of 90%.

Workflow 4: Active learning

Data: Corpus $\mathcal{D}'$ of relevant documents; Manually annotated samples $\mathcal{S}$ with $\mathcal{S}_+ \subset \mathcal{S}$ positive examples representative for a content category $c_p \in \mathcal{C}$

Result: *minExamples* or more positive examples $\mathcal{S}_+$ for c_p extracted from $\mathcal{D}'$; a reasonable number of 'good' negative examples $\mathcal{S}_-$ for c_p.

$i \leftarrow 0$
while $|\mathcal{S}_+| < minExamples \ OR \ i < minIter$ **do**
    $i \leftarrow i + 1$
    Train machine learning classification model on $\mathcal{S}$ (e.g. using SVM).
    Classify with trained model on $\mathcal{U} \leftarrow \mathcal{D}' \setminus \mathcal{S}$.
    Select randomly n classified results $u \in \mathcal{U}$ with $P(+|u) >= 0.3$.
    for *each of the n examples* **do**
        Accept or reject classifiers prediction of the class label.
        Add correctly labeled example to $\mathcal{S}$.
Evaluate classifier performance (F_1, Cohen's κ, ...).

sets are rather small, it is advisable to use a process of k-fold cross validation (Witten et al., 2011, p. 152), which splits the training data into k folds, $k-1$ one for training and one for testing. Precision, recall and F_1 are then calculated as the mean of these values out of k evaluation runs, where the test set split is changed in each iteration.

Synoptic Analysis

Workflow 5 substantiates on final analysis steps incorporating results from unsupervised exploration of the retrieved relevant document set $\mathcal{D}'$ and classification of categories on the entire data set $\mathcal{D}$. For generation of final results from supervised learning, a classifier is trained with the training set $\mathcal{S}$ generated in the previous workflow (again, separately for each category). Then, the classifier model is applied to the entire corpus $\mathcal{D}$, our initial starting point in Workflow 1. Predicted label results are assigned to each document $d \in \mathcal{D}$. Labels of the entire collection or subsets of it can be aggregated to frequency counts, e.g. per year or month, to produce time series of category developments. Subsets can be filtered beforehand by any meta-data available to a document, e.g. its publisher. Instead of category frequencies, it is advisable to use document frequencies, i.e. counting documents containing one or more positively classified context units. Document frequencies eliminate the effect of unequal category densities within documents and dampen the influence of unequal document lengths (e.g. between different publications). Further, it is advisable to normalize absolute frequency counts to relative frequencies for time series, since the original document collection may be distributed unequally over time, yielding misleading peaks or trends in the trend line. For visualization of trend lines, using smoothing of curves is advisable, because granularity of data points may produce too complex plots. To reveal more information from the category measurements, pairs of categories can be observed together on an aggregated distant level and on document level. On the distant level, Pearson's correlation between trend lines can identify concurrent, but not necessarily linked, discourse flow patterns. Beyond that, linkage of categories becomes observable by evaluating on their co-occurrence in documents. Co-occurrence can be counted as frequency, but similar to term frequencies is better judged on by a statistic, e.g. the Dice coefficient. Observing conditional probability of categories, i.e. the chance of observing B if having observed A before, can reveal even more insight on (un-)equal usage of categories in documents (see Section 4.3.3).

For synoptic analysis, findings from supervised classification of categories should be reflected in the light of the findings from exploratory analysis. Final results together with intermediate results from each workflow provide the basis for a comprehensive and dense description of the contents in qualitative as well as quantitative manner. Analogue to manual methods such as Critical Discourse Analysis (Jäger, 2004, p. 194), a synoptic analysis of textual material representative

Workflow 5: Synoptic analysis

Data: Corpus $\mathcal{D}$ of all documents; Samples of texts $\mathcal{S}$ representative for a content category $c_p \in \mathcal{C}$ retrieved by active learning

Result: Measures of trends and co-occurrence of categories in $\mathcal{D}$

1 Train ML classification models for all $c_p \in \mathcal{C}$ on S.

2 Classify each $d \in \mathcal{D}$ with the trained models.

3 Option: filter classification results on $\mathcal{D}$ by desired meta data, e.g. 1) time periods identified during exploratory clustering, 2) publication, 3) thematic cluster, or 4) mentioning of a certain actor.

4 Aggregate frequencies of positively classified context units as document frequencies by time span (e.g. years).

5 Option: Normalize absolute frequencies to relative ones. Visualize category trends as frequencies over time.

6 Count co-occurrence of c_p with other categories in documents.

7 Calculate statistic (e.g. Dice) or conditional probability of joint category co-occurrence.

8 Visualize co-occurrence statistic (e.g. as heatmap or graph network).

9 Substantiate on findings from supervised learning with those from unsupervised exploration in the previous workflow.

10 Check on findings in the light of preexisting literature or by triangulation with different QDA methods.

for relevant categories aims at providing deeper understanding of contents and underlying social formations investigated. Quantification of categories and discourse patterns allows for long term observations, comparison between categories and their dependency or relation to certain external factors. Again, the interplay of qualitative and quantitative dimensions of the retrieved data is what makes this approach appealing. A simple close reading of a sample of the extracted positively classified analysis units is very useful to further elaborate on the extracted contents. More systematically, a concept for method *triangulation* could be set up, to compare findings generated by TM supported analysis with findings made by purely qualitative research methods on (samples of) the same data (Flick, 2004).

Of course, classification of CA categories does not have to be the end of the entire workflow chain. Positively classified analysis units easily can be utilized as input to any other TM procedure. For example, automatically classified sentences representing a certain category might be clustered to get deeper insights in types of category representatives. Or documents containing a certain category might be subject to another topic model analysis to reveal more fine-grained thematic structures within a category. In some research designs it might be interesting to identify specific actors related to categories. In this case, applying a process of Named Entity Recognition (NER) to extracted context units can be a very enlightening approach to determine persons or organizations playing a vital role. Once the full range of TM application is at hand to the analyst, there is plenty of room to design extensions and new variants of the workflow chain.

5.3. Result Integration and Documentation

For quality assurance and compliance with rules of scientific work, the validity of the overall research design not only depends on isolated parts of the workflow chain, but also on their interplay. Moreover, reliability and reproducibility requires detailed documentation of analysis steps.

5.3.1. Integration

In the previous section, a TM supported research workflow design has been introduced, together with suggestions for specific algorithmic approaches and evaluation strategies. Thereby, evaluation mainly focused on the quality of encapsulated single analysis goals. In the proposed V-TM framework, such evaluations correspond to the level of unit tests in the V-Model of SE. On the next level up, workflow design corresponds with result integration during the evaluation phase (see Fig. 5.2). This level does not put emphasis on the results of analysis goals in isolated manner. Instead, it judges on the validity of combining intermediate results. Outputs of single analysis workflows often need to be filtered or transformed in a specific way to serve as input for the next workflow. Regarding this, decisions have to be made with respect to the concrete circumstances and requirements of the workflow design.

Document retrieval, for example, produces a ranked list of documents from the entire collection with respect to a relevancy scoring. If this ranking should serve as a basis to select a sub-corpus of relevant documents for the upcoming analysis, there is the need for determining a number n of documents to select from the ranking. This decision should be made carefully by evaluating and investigating the retrieval results. Dependent on the retrieval strategy, it might be absolutely valid to select the entire list containing a single key word (think again of the 'minimum wage' example). But if retrieval was performed by a large list of (contextualized) key terms producing a large list of documents, such as for democratic demarcation in the example study, clearly restricting the selection to the top ranks would be advisable.

After corpus exploration via temporal and thematic clustering of the retrieved document set, there are several ways to rank identified topics per cluster and documents within a cluster, e.g. for close reading or manual coding of categories. These rankings are not inherent to the clustering processes as such and may be even guided by researchers intuition rather than determined by data-driven numeric criteria. In this respect, specified thresholds and steps taken for selection should be justified in a transparent way. For QDA purposes it is decisive to always maintain the connection between patterns identified on the global context level quantitatively and their underlying qualitative local contexts. To anchor interpretations based on exploratory analysis steps, it is advised to extract paradigmatic text examples containing such globally retrieved patterns. Close reading of such paradigmatic examples helps to backup interpretations qualitatively and to much better understand the contents underlying the 'distant reading' procedures.

Final evaluations based on classification of an entire population by a category system may be realized in different ways. If classification identifies sentences as representative statements of a given category, frequencies of positive sentences in all documents could be counted. By adjusting the threshold for positive label probability of the classifier, it is possible to control classified sets for precision or recall. If a study should rather concentrate on high precision of individual sentence classifications, higher thresholds for label probability might be a valid strategy to restrict outcomes.

For time series analysis, instead of sentence frequencies transformation to document frequencies might be preferred, because documents are the more natural context unit in content analysis. To restrict the final set to those documents highly representative for a certain category, it might be a valid approach to only count documents containing at least two or more positively classified sentences. At the same time, we should keep in mind that due to unequal mean lengths of articles in different publications, like in the daily newspaper *FAZ* compared to the weekly paper *Die Zeit*, higher frequency thresholds may lead to distorted measurements.

Last but not least, absolute counts preferably should be converted into relative counts, to make proportional increases and decreases of category occurrence visible independent of the data distribution in the base population. Here, different normalization strategies are applicable, such as normalization by the entire base population, by the retrieved set of relevant documents, or by the set of documents containing at least one of the categories classified. All strategies may provide viable measures, but need to be interpreted differently. Making wrong decisions during this step may lead to false interpretations.

As briefly sketched in this section, there are many pitfalls in combining results of TM processes. Usually, there is no single best practice—only the advice to think carefully about valid solutions and provide reasonable justifications.

5.3.2. Documentation

Integration of isolated TM applications into complex workflows not only needs sound justification. To comply with demands for reliability and reproducibility, researchers need to document data inputs, chains of linguistic and mathematical preprocessing, and TM algorithms used together with settings of key parameters as detailed as possible. For complete reproducibility, it would also be necessary to provide external data utilized during the processes such as stop word lists, models utilized for tokenization and POS-tagging, etc. Strict requirements in this manner pose hard challenges to the applicability of TM methods. Complexity of the overall workflow design makes it almost impossible to completely document all decisive settings, decisions and parameters. Furthermore, there might be severe license issues concerning the disclosure of raw data, like in the case of newspaper data,[8] or issues for passing on data and models from linguistic (pre-)processing.

Hence, a complete fulfillment of the reproducibility requirement is hardly achievable, if it demands for exact reproduction of results. One possible solution could be the utilization of Open Research Computing (ORC) environments which allow for 'active documents' containing verbal descriptions of research designs and results together with scripts and raw data for evaluation.[9] Subject to the condition

[8]For this project I utilized the newspaper data of the project 'ePol – post-democracy and neoliberalism'. Unfortunately, license agreements with the publishers does not allow for data use outside the ePol project.

[9]For example, the platform 'The Mind Research Repository' (openscience.uni-leipzig.de) provides such an integrated environment of data/analysis packages along with research papers for cognitive linguistics.

that raw data can be provided together with these documents, this would allow for perfect reproducibility of published research results.

Unfortunately, until such ways of scientific publication further matured, we need to stick to verbal descriptions of workflows and parameters as systematic and detailed as possible. Hence, reproducibility as quality criterion for empirical research has to be conceptualized somewhat softer. As exact reproduction of measurements and visualizations is too strict, requirement of reproducibility should rather refer to the possibility for secondary studies to generate analysis data of the same kind as produced by the primary study. This would allow to compare whether trends and interpretations based on processed results correspond to each other. To achieve this, method standards for documentation are needed in social science disciplines. Which information at least needs to be specified depends on the concrete workflow design. For example, for linguistic preprocessing (see Section 2.2.2), this means to document the use of tokenization strategies, lower case reduction, unification strategies (e.g. stemming, lemmatization), handling of MWUs, stop word removal, n-gram-concatenation and pruning of low/high frequent terms. For co-occurrence analysis, it is the context window, minimum frequencies and the co-occurrence statistic measure. For LDA topic models, it would be the number of topics K together with the prior parameters α and η (if they are set manually an not estimated automatically by the model process).

For documentation of the realization of a specific research design, I suggest *fact sheets* as part of the V-TM framework. Such specifically formatted tables allow for a comprehensive display of

- the research question,
- the data set used for analysis,
- expected result types,
- analysis goals split up into workflows of specific tasks,
- chains of preprocssing used for task implementation,

- analysis algorithms with their key parameters, and finally,
- analysis results together with corresponding evaluation measures.

Figure 5.5 gives a (mock-up) example for the display of a V-TM fact sheet. Further method debates in social science need to be hold to determine a common set of standards and criteria for documentation and reproducibility as quality criteria.

5.4. Methodological Integration

As Chapter 2 has shown, there is definitely a growing number of studies which exploit several TM techniques for exploration and analysis of larger document collections. Some of them are designed along specific QDA methodologies, but most rather explore potentials of certain technologies, while lacking a methodological embedding. Further, up to now most studies just employ a comparatively small set of analysis techniques—if not just one single TM procedure only. To overcome the state of experimentation with single analysis procedures, the V-TM framework not only asks for integration of various procedures on the high level workflow design, but for methodological integration of the entire study design. Methodological integration not only contributes to interoperability between manual QDA methods and computer-assisted analysis, but also gives guidance for researchers what to expect from their workflow results. Alongside with identification of requirements in the research design phase (see Fig. 5.2), methodological integration of the evaluation phase asks:

1. how input data and (quantified) output of semantic structures identified by TM relate to the overall research question,
2. which parts of knowledge discovery need to be conducted in rather inductive or deductive manner, and
3. whether or how ontological and epistemological premises of the study reflect the concrete method design.

Research question	How accepted is the idea of a statutory minimum wage in the news coverage of the *Frankfurter Allgemeine Zeitung* (FAZ)?					
Data set	Set of 1,1 million FAZ articles from 1991-2015 (D)					
Expected result types	a) Semantic clusters around the minimum wage debate in Germany, 2) time series of acceptance / rejection of a statutory minimum wage (MW), 3) statistical dependency between minimum wage acceptance and employees in the low-wage sector					
Goals	**Tasks**	**Data**	**Preprocessing**	**Algorithms / Param.**	**Results + Evaluation**	**Notes**
1. Document selection	Key term retrieval	Collection of 1,1 million documents between 1991 and 2015 (D)	none	Regular expressions search	12,032 documents containing the string "Mindestlohn" were retrieved. Qualitative evaluation of 100 sample documents shows that 87% of them relate to domestic politics.	Filter for foreign affairs not needed, as 13% of documents relating to foreign countries can be tolerated.
2. Corpus exploration	1. Thematic clustering 2. Remove documents associated with bad clusters	12,032 documents containing the string "Mindestlohn" (D')	Lemmatization, stop word removal, relative pruning (Min. 1%, Max. 99%), DTM: 3012 types in 12,032 documents	LDA with K = 15, $\alpha = 0.2$, $\eta = 0.02$	15 topics, 10 of them of relevance for the question, e.g. related to construction industry, unemployment or economic growth D'' = D' minus 3,201 documents mainly belonging to 5 bad topics Reproducibility of model topics: 73,3% (t = 0.2, n = 100)	LDA was fine, but let us try a non-parametric model next time
3. Manual annotation	1. identify documents to annotate 2. annotate documents	8,831 documents (D'') and Category system with 2 categories "(A) MW supporting", "(B) MW opposing"	Selection of 10 random articles from each year of the investigated time frame for annotation	none	Identification of 272 sentences for A, 301 sentences for B Intercoder reliability Cohen's κ = 0.71	Category system should be augmented by category "MW ambivalent" next time
4. Active learning	Extend training set to at least 400 documents	D'' and 272 (A) / 301 (B) positive sentences, 1926 negative sentences in 250 initially annotated documents	Stemming, no stop word removal, absolute pruning (MinFrq = 1), unigrams/bigrams DTM: 34289 types in 8,831 documents	Features with Chi-Square(c_p) >= 6 SVM, C = 1 7 iterations of active learning	423 (A) / 513 (B) positive sentences, 2701 negative sentences in the final training set for the category system $P = 0.70$, $R = 0.50$, $F_1 = 0.58$	Reached enough examples already after 5 iterations of active learning for (B), category (A) took 7 iterations
5. Final analysis	1. Classification of categories A and B for time series 2. Cross-Correlation of A with external data	D'' and Final training data set Employees in the low-wage sector from 1991-2015	Stemming, absolute pruning (MinFrq = 1), unigrams/bigrams DTM: 34289 types in 8,831 documents	1. Features with Chi-Square(c_p) >= 6, SVM, C = 10 2. Cross-Correlation	A correlates with low-wage employment rate highest in a time lag of 13 month, i.e. 13 month after an increase of employment in the low-wage sector an increase in ML approval is observable (r = 0.46).	Correlation is statistically significant ($p < 0,01$)

Figure 5.5.: Mock-up example of a V-TM fact sheet for documenting a V-TM analysis process.

The example study on democratic demarcation has shown that computer-assisted analysis of qualitative data may become a very complex endeavor. From simple counts of occurrences of character strings in single documents to complex statistical models with latent variables over huge document collections and supervised classification of hundreds of thousands of sentences, a long road has been traveled. The integration of TM revealed that nowadays algorithms are capable to extract quite a bit of meaning from large scale text collections. In contrast to manual methods of QDA, a quantitative perspective is necessarily inherent to these algorithms, either because they reveal structures in unsupervised approaches or classify large quantities of textual units in supervised approaches. Which meaning is expressed within a concrete speech act can only be understood by relating it to context, i.e. comparing it to a large set of other (linguistic) data. Human analysts in manual QDA rely on their expert and world knowledge for that, whereas computer-assisted (semi-)automatic methods need a lot of qualitative data. Thus, analyzing big data in QDA with the help of TM only makes sense as mixed method analysis combining qualitative and quantitative aspects.

In this respect: What kind of resources of large text collections are valuable resources for social science data analysis, and what kinds of research questions can be answered with them? Surely, there are collections of newswire text, as utilized in this example study, covering knowledge from the public media discourse. Other valuable resources are, for instance, web and social media data, parliamentary protocols, press releases by companies, NGOs or governmental institutions. All of these resources encompass different knowledge types and, more important, can be assigned to different actor types on different societal discourse levels. Consequently, they allow for answering of different research questions. What they all have in common is that investigation of this textual material assumes inter-textual links of the contained knowledge structures. Such links can be revealed as structures by human interpretation as well as with the help of TM algorithms.

Identification of structures also is part of any manual QDA methodology to some extent. Yet, the character of structure identification in qualitative social research can follow different logics with respect to underlying epistemological assumptions. Goldkuhl (2012) distinguishes three epistemologies in qualitative research: 1) interpretive, 2) positivist, and 3) critical. He states, the method debate in social science mainly is concerned with the dichotomy between interpretivism and positivism:

> "The core idea of *interpretivism* is to work with [...] subjective meanings already there in the social world; that is to acknowledge their existence, to reconstruct them, to understand them, to avoid distorting them, to use them as building-blocks in theorizing. [...] This can be seen as a contrast to *positivistic* studies, which seem to work with a fixed set of variables." (ibid., p. 138)

In methodological ways of proceeding, this dichotomy translates into two distinct logics: *subsumptive* versus *reconstructive* logic. Subsumptive logic strives for assignment of observations, e.g. speech acts in texts, to categories; in other terms, "subsuming observations under already existing ones" (Lueger and Vettori, 2014, p. 32). In contrast, reconstructive logic aims for deep understanding of isolated cases by "consider as many interpretive alternatives as possible. [...] Methodologically, this means to systematically search for the various latencies a manifest expression may carry out" (ibid.). Nevertheless, even reconstructive logic assumes structure for its dense description of single cases in its small case studies, to reveal typical patterns from the language data investigated. But, in contrast to QDA in subsumptive logic, researchers do not necessarily strive for generalization of identified patterns to other cases.[10] In this characterization, both logics of QDA relate differently to *inductive* and *deductive* research designs. While reconstructive approaches always need to be inductive, subsumptive approaches may be both, either inductive by subsuming under open, undefined categories, or deductive by subsuming under

[10]For me, the main difference between the two logics seems to be the point of time for creation of types or categories during the research process. While subsumptive approaches carry out category assignments in the primary analysis phase directly on the investigated material, reconstructive approaches rather develop types on secondary data based on interpretation of the primary text.

closed, previously defined categories. This brief categorization of QDA methodologies makes clear that mainly subsumptive research logics profit from TM applications on large collections, while strictly reconstructive approaches[11] cannot expect to gain very much interesting insights.

Since TM refers to a heterogeneous set of analysis algorithms, individually adapted variants of the V-TM framework may contribute to a range of methods from subsumptive QDA. It seems obvious that computers will not be able to actually understand texts in ways reconstructivist social scientists strive for. Algorithms may deploy only little contextual knowledge from outside the text they shall analyze, compared to the experience and common sense knowledge a human analyst can rely on. But they can learn to retrieve patterns for any specific category constituted by regular and repetitive language use. Methodologies for QDA which epistemologically assume trans-textual knowledge structures observable in language patterns do have a decent chance to benefit from computer-assisted methods, if they are not shy of quantification. The integration of TM appears to be useful with qualitative methodologies such as Grounded Theory Methodology (Glaser and Strauss, 2005), Qualitative Content Analysis (Mayring, 2010), Frame Analysis (Donati, 2011), and, most promising, variants of (Foucauldian) Discourse Analysis (Foucault, 2010; Jäger, 2004; Mautner, 2012; Blätte, 2011; Bubenhofer, 2008; Keller, 2007).

Especially Discourse Analysis fits with TM because of its theoretical assumption on super-individual knowledge structures determining individual cognition and social power relations to a large extent. Michel Foucault, the french philosopher who described characteristics of his conceptualization of discourse as primary productive power for social reality, sharply distinguished between *utterance* and *statement* (Foucault, 2005). Only by repetition of utterances following certain regularities within a group of speakers, statements emerge which are able to transport social knowledge, hence, power to interfere

[11]For example, Objective Hermeneutics (Oevermann, 2002) or the Documentary Method (Bohnsack, 2010, p. 31ff)

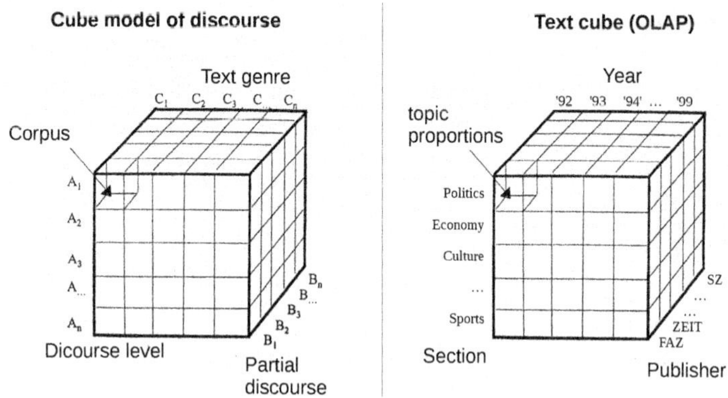

Figure 5.6.: Discourse cube model (Jung, 2011), and OLAP cube for text in the style of (Zhang et al., 2011).

in social reality. Consequently, a quantitative dimension is at least implicitly contained in Discourse Theory, wherefore it sometimes also is labeled a 'quasi-qualitative method' (Angermüller, 2005). Jung (2011) provides an interesting visual model of discourse as a cube (Fig. 5.6). It identifies corpora as slices from an entire discourse D separable along n different dimensions, for instance (topic specific) partial discourses, text genres or discourse levels (e.g. political, academic or media discourse). Every selectable (sub-)corpus comprises of certain distributions of utterances which may follow identifiable patterns, hence, statement formations following certain language regularities interesting for the analysis. By looking for patterns of language constituting important discursive statements, it would be desirable to analyze corpora along the cube dimensions. Normally, discourse analysts manually analyze small corpora of text to identify such patterns (Jäger, 2004, p. 158ff). But, being restricted to small corpora prevents to utilize the clear advantages of this systematic model.

Interestingly, the discourse cube model pretty much resembles data models of Online Analytical Processing (OLAP) cubes in data warehousing. In fact, NLP literature contains of some approaches to model text collections in OLAP cubes, which allow for computation of key figures based on selected sub-collections by specified meta-data along cube dimensions, e.g. time, publisher or section/genre (Keith et al., 2006; Zhang et al., 2009, 2011). The task is to retrieve aggregated data (e.g. term frequencies, mean sentence length or topic proportions) from these selected sub-corpora rapidly, either computed in advance or if possible in real time. Slicing and dicing operations on such cubes allow for fast selection of sub-corpora, and more importantly, for comparison of aggregated key figures. If it is manageable to integrate meaningful data for QDA as atomic facts into such a model, it would allow for great increases of analysis capabilities through comparison of aggregated results from sub-collections easily split along multiple dimensions. The TM applications introduced and integrated in the exemplary study (see Chapter 3) provide interesting data, to be analyzed along such cube dimensions. Chapter 4 conducts analysis of measured content analytic categories together with discourse patterns along the dimensions time, publication and thematic structure. Using OLAP databases and fast indexes for text might be an interesting supplement for implementations of TM analysis infrastructures to conveniently discover semantic patterns. Certainly, equivalences between the two models highlight interesting parallels between models of (inter-)textual semantics in computer science and social science methodologies.

6. Summary: Integrating Qualitative and Computational Text Analysis

In the light of recent research debates on computational social science and Digital Humanities (DH) as meanwhile adolescent disciplines dealing with big data (Reichert, 2014), I strove for answering in which ways Text Mining (TM) applications are able to support Qualitative Data Analysis (QDA) in the social sciences in a manner that fruitfully integrates a qualitative with a quantitative perspective. The guiding assumption was, the more modern Natural Language Processing (NLP) and Machine Learning (ML) algorithms enable us to identify patterns of 'meaning' from global contexts of mass data collections, while at the same time preserving opportunities to retrieve identified patterns again in local contexts of single documents, the more they allow for a fruitful integration of qualitative and quantitative text analysis. By combining extraction of qualitative knowledge from text to buttress understanding of social reality with quantification of extracted knowledge structures to infer on their relevancy, utilizing TM for QDA is inherently a mixed method research design.

This study contributed to a systematic development of such mixed method designs throughout the entire path of the research process. Along with an exemplary study on the public discourse of 'democratic demarcation' investigated in 60 years of German newspaper articles, general problems of integrating QDA with TM have been formulated and discussed. Tailored solutions to such problems and requirement specific extensions of common TM approaches have been developed. Their applicability and validity has been shown with respect to the exemplary research question. Finally, experiences from the conducted study have been generalized into a methodological framework to provide guidance for future TM applications in social sciences. Contributions of this work are summarized in the following sections with respect to three major aspects:

1. requirement-driven adaptation of TM applications,
2. exemplary application of integrated TM procedures, and
3. methodological integration into the V-TM framework.

In a final section on future work, an outlook is given concerned with aspects of technology integration and developments in computational social science which did not fit into this study.

6.1. Meeting Requirements

The social science perspective on QDA demands application of TM for compliance with certain requirements to fit to its standards and procedures. Algorithmic approaches primarily should seek to extract 'meaning', i.e. semantics contributing to understanding of the research subject. Quantification of once identified meaningful structures in varying, but well-defined contexts (e.g. different newspapers, time frames or topics) is only of interest in a subsequent step. Consequently, TM supported research designs need to allow for data-driven, inductive exploration. But instead of pure data-driven ways of proceeding, opportunities for manual intervention are required at some points to integrate background knowledge of the researcher or guide the direction of analysis. Further, research designs need to allow for subsumptive approaches of knowledge codification as a part of deductive methodologies such as Quantitative Content Analysis and Frame Analysis, or abductive methodologies such as Discourse Analysis, GTM or Qualitative Content Analysis, which combine inductive and deductive analysis steps. To support such approaches by computational methods and to enable them to process large data collections, this study identified three consecutive goals of an exemplary research design:

1. *Retrieval*: From the starting point of a complete collection of topic unspecific texts, a set of documents potentially relevant for the research question needs to be identified. For many questions in social science, the research interest does not directly translate into a small set of keywords for document selection. To solve this task, Section 3.1 introduces an approach of retrieval with contextualized dictionaries based on a reference collection. The idea is that an abstract research interest can be described easier by a set of documents containing paradigmatic knowledge of interest than by single key terms arbitrarily defined by an analyst. First, a reference collection is compiled by the researcher, followed by an algorithmic process of key term extraction. Then, extracted key terms are weighted by rank and employed for retrieval. To capture aspired meanings even better than just by single terms, co-occurrence profiles of key terms are extracted from the reference collection as well. Correspondence of these semantic contexts with contexts in target documents is incorporated to the relevancy scoring. Evaluation of the method shows which approach of key term extraction from the reference corpus leads to best results. It also proves that using co-occurrence information for relevancy scoring considerably improves retrieval results for QDA purposes.

2. *Corpus Exploration*: Document collections for analyzing discourses usually are far too large to be explored manually by close reading. To investigate such collections, I introduced a workflow to generate Semantically Enriched Co-occurrence Graphs (SECGs) which allow for context specific 'distant reading'. For this, thematic and temporal clusters are identified with the help of topic models to separate the heterogeneous collection into more coherent sub-parts. Time periods of coherent topic distributions were identified via clustering. Then, meaningful topics with regard to the research question were selected for each identified time period. For each thematic and temporal cluster, key terms and their co-occurrence patterns in sentences of corresponding documents are extracted. These co-occurrences then are visualized together with their contex-

tual sentiments (i.e. polarity of their contexts ranging from negative to positive) in network graphs. Graphs combine information from multiple TM applications providing insight into complex patterns of meaningful structures which allow for deeper understanding of contained contents across topical and temporal dimensions. Finally, paradigmatic sentences containing propositional patterns identified from global contexts in SECGs are retrieved to anchor qualitative interpretations of graph visualization on representative text examples.

3. *Category classification*: Several experiments introduce on issues of applying supervised ML for classification of content categories, which in QDA scenarios has to deal with rather hard conditions: Mostly, context units are smaller than complete documents (e.g. paragraphs, or just sentences) resulting in very sparse training data. Additionally, training data sets are small because manual annotation of categories is costly. What is more, categories often are rather abstract and contain great language variety. To deal with such challenges, I apply topic models in a kind of semi-supervised learning scenario to augment sparse training data instances by latent semantic features. Further, to generate training data of sufficient quality at low cost, I introduce a workflow of active learning which iteratively integrates machine classification with manual evaluation of intermediate results to extend training sets efficiently. The good news is, quality requirements on classification for social science can be formulated less restrictive. Rather than correct classification of as many as possible individual cases, it aims for valid and reliable prediction of proportions and trends of the categories classified. For this goal, with the help of a large manually annotated collection of party manifestos, I show that even under hard conditions of classification for QDA leading to rather mediocre results in individual classification, proportion and trend prediction still achieves valid results.

6.2. Exemplary Study

In Chapter 3, I introduced three major analysis goals for QDA to be supported by a variety of TM applications: 1) Retrieval of relevant documents, 2) inductive exploration of retrieved contents, and 3) deductive classification for determining on quantities of relevant categories. The workflows developed to achieve these goals have been in applied in Chapter 4 for analyzing an complex political science question on 'democratic demarcation'. For this exemplary study, a corpus consisting of roughly 600,000 German newspaper articles needed to be narrowed down to such documents relating to (perceived) domestic threats of democracy. From the initial news collection, around 29,000 articles have been selected, (potentially) consisting of statements on democratic demarcation. This collection is then described in an exploratory way by temporally and thematically clustered co-occurrence graphs. Visualizations of 50 SECGs reveal multiple interesting aspects on subjects related to the overall research question centered around right-wing extremism, historical national socialism, (anti-)communist activities, student protests, or the changing role of workers unions in the FRG. Finally, classification of sentences with content analytic categories was utilized to determine on discursive distribution of patterns of demarcation from far right-wing and far left-wing politics over the last decades. Results point to the fact that conservative and liberal newspapers have different focal points on these categories and, more surprisingly, that demarcation from right-wing politics differs from left-wing politics in discursive strategies. The far-right is excluded by moral and legal arguments referring to democratic ideals and repressive measures of 'fortified democracy', while demands for left-wing demarcation often lack of the legal component. Instead, leftist politics more often is discredited by equating it to its right counterpart or 'extremism' as generic concept. The interplay of qualitative and quantitative information extracted from hundreds of thousands of newspaper documents allowed a deep and insightful analysis. It gave answers to a complex, qualitative research question which could not have been generated by conventional approaches alone.

6.3. Methodological Systematization

The opposition between interpretivism and positivism (Goldkuhl, 2012), or reconstructivist and subsumptive research paradigms is prevalent in QDA (Donati, 2011; Schönfelder, 2011). Using TM in a reflected, systematically integrated research design contributes to conceptualize these paradigms as rather subsequent than opposing. In general, the proposed workflow allows for reconstructive exploration of contents without all too much preformation of results by previous knowledge of the researcher or theoretically derived category concepts. Instead, structures and categories emerging from the data can be identified inductively, intensively described in the first place, and transformed into well-defined measurable categories for quantification afterwards.

The typology of Computer Assisted Text Analysis (CATA) in social sciences (see Section 2.3) revealed that studies usually apply single TM methods in isolated manner with mixed benefit for QDA research interests. The example study on 'democratic demarcation' has shown that integration of a variety of lexicometric and ML applications into a coherent workflow provides true benefits for QDA. At the same time, it showed that integrated TM application may quickly become a very complex undertaking.

To systematically describe aspects of methodological integration of QDA with TM, I introduced the V-TM framework in Chapter 5. In analogy to the V-model, it borrows from software engineering the idea of consequent entanglement of requirements specification with validation procedures, to describe the need for correspondence between research design and evaluation in empirical social research. For this, it distinguishes in different levels for requirements analysis, workflow design and specification of single TM processes before the actual implementation and application of computer-assisted tools begins. To ensure validity of the research design, three conditions have to be met in correspondence to the framework levels: 1) validity of every single sub-task evaluated in its own process with respect to quality standards from NLP and from social science alike, 2) validity of using output data from one process as input data to the subsequent process, and 3) methodological fit of data sources and analysis procedures with the research question. As integral parts of the V-TM framework, guidance for complex research designs is given by identification of generic *goals* together with descriptions of corresponding analysis *workflows* and *evaluation* strategies. For comprehensive documentation of the analysis proceeding, the framework suggests *fact sheets* displaying tasks, algorithms and their key parameters together with evaluation results for each accomplished (sub-)goal separately.

Slowly emerging discipline-specific debates on methodological standards and procedures will contribute to mature TM method application in the near future (Schaal and Kath, 2014; Wiedemann and Lemke, 2015). Nonetheless, for a discipline-wide agreement on best practices for empirical social research there is a long road ahead. Therefore, the proposed V-TM framework should be seen as a first approach to systematically integrate Text Mining technology with QDA methods and requirements in order to make an important contribution to this debate.

6.4. Further Developments

Of course, not the full range of existing TM application types has been assessed for suiting QDA needs and, consequently, some applications have not been integrated into the V-TM framework. Future work on extensions and improvement of the framework for best practices of TM application may not be hesitant to exchange certain technologies with equivalents on the level of workflow design specifications, or even to include completely new workflows. Some possible extensions are given in the following.

Formulating different requirements on the highest V-TM framework level may even lead us to new goals for workflow designs. The workflow chain presented in this study, left out methods of Named Entity Recognition (NER) and sentiment analysis for person or organization identification and their attribution to certain categories. This would definitely be an interesting extension to study discourses on democratic demarcation more closely from the perspective of (speech) actors. Methods to capture syntactic structures, such as parsing (van Atteveldt et al., 2008), semantic role labeling or unsupervised template-based information extraction (Chambers and Jurafsky, 2009, 2011) are promising candidates to extend the TM toolbox for social scientists on their hunt for semantic patterns. In political protest research, for instance, information extraction to collect well-defined, structured data sets from text is an appealing application for TM. The Prodat project (Rucht, 2001) manually extracted information on places, dates, topics and numbers of participants of political protest events in Germany from newspaper data of several decades. Much of this work could be done automatically (Wiedemann, 2016). For such information extraction goals, the integration of external knowledge resources appears to be very promising. For example, integration of large semantic knowledge bases, such as Wikidata[1], Linked Open Data (LOD)[2] and DBpedia[3], or linguistic knowledge bases, such as WordNet[4] or FrameNet[5] could provide valuable extensions for QDA studies. Also the systematic integration of quantified semantic information extracted from text with quantitative data from external resources, such as country statistics or survey data, still is open to discussion in the methodological debate.

On the levels of workflow design and TM process specifications a variety of alterations of the suggested workflows and algorithms could be interesting. For example, to identify topics in exploratory workflows, Mimno et al. (2011) introduced the 'polya urn model' which is supposed to model coherent structures better than LDA and, hence, may better support inductive steps of the research design (see Section 3.2). Also, it would be interesting to integrate time dynamic topic

[1]https://www.wikidata.org
[2]http://linkeddata.org
[3]http://dbpedia.org
[4]https://wordnet.princeton.edu
[5]https://framenet.icsi.berkeley.edu

models into the analysis which are able to model semantic shifts of topics in diachronic corpora (Dubey et al., 2012; Wang et al., 2012).

For deductive workflow steps, classification of content analytic categories can be altered in manifold aspects provided by NLP literature. To overcome the simple 'bag-of-words' assumption in feature engineering, Mikolov et al. (2013b) introduced with 'word2vec' a highly efficient model of semantic word embeddings which represent meaning of words in continuous vectors. Such meaning vectors are learned by neural networks from very large corpora and can even be composed with each other to represent meaning of phrases or sentences (Mikolov et al., 2013a). Further experiments need to demonstrate, whether 'word2vec' representations can improve classification in real world QDA scenarios. To improve the workflow for batch mode active learning, Hoi et al. (2006) suggest a query selection strategy based on Fisher-information matrices which potentially increases efficiency of training data generation. More work could also be done to include features for classification which depict specific syntactic structures contributing to semantics.

However, not only analytical capabilities are a decisive part to successfully implant TM in the social science method repertoire. Equally important is the debate on presentation, documentation and publication of results for complying with reproducibility as research quality criterion. In best cases, raw data and analysis scripts would be published along with the verbal descriptions written in research papers. Web based Open Research Computing (ORC) infrastructures allowing for documentation, server-side execution and sharing of analysis code may contribute to this goal in the near future. For keeping research reproducible, a combination of centralized and decentralized science infrastructures together with standardized software tools may be helpful. Promising attempts have been made by the development of free R packages for various text analysis tasks (Feinerer et al., 2008; Jurka et al., 2013). A directory of tools for text and data mining together with capabilities to enhance their interoperability is built by the project OpenMinTeD[6] which probably will provide useful guidance through the jungle of tools and services in the near future. Moreover, software projects focusing on usability such as the "Leipzig Corpus Miner"[7] provide analysis capabilities for very large corpora without the need for coding skills of the analysts (Niekler et al., 2014). Last but not least, the European DH research infrastructure projects such as CLARIN, DARIAH and DASISH provide technologies and methods which can establish standards for Text Mining-enhanced QDA one day. For this to happen, social scientists need to contribute actively to formulation of requirements, implementation of workflows, development of best practices and education of academic colleagues and students to make the most of the new technological opportunities.

[6] http://openminted.eu

[7] http://lcm.informatik.uni-leipzig.de

A. Data Tables, Graphs and Algorithms

In this Appendix, topics selected for distinct time periods of the exploratory analysis in the example study are given together with a selection of their corresponding Semantically Enriched Co-occurrence Graphs (SECGs). In addition, a workflow description for generating SECGs is presented. For supervised classification, time series plots of absolute frequencies of documents containing left-wing demarcation or right-wing-demarcation are given for the *FAZ* and *Die Zeit* separately.

Table A.1.: Manually selected topics from the LDA topic model ($K = 100$, $\alpha = 0.2$) of the retrieved collection on democratic demarcation. $\theta_{c,k}$ is the probability of topic k in cluster c, $\overline{s}$ is the mean sentiment score of $\mathbf{s}$, i.e. all sentiment scores of the top 200 terms of a topic.; $var(\mathbf{s})$ is their variance, also to be interpreted as 'controversy score'. For each table row, a Semantically Enriched Co-occurrence Graph (SECG) has been generated. A selection of SECGs is presented below.

Cluster	ID	Terms	Docs	$\boldsymbol{\theta}_{c,k}$	$\overline{\mathbf{s}}$	var(s)
	54	erklären regierung französisch außenminister amerikanischen	256	0.070	-0.806	0.262
	78	deutschland adenauer deutschen zone westlich	240	0.058	-1.510	0.529
	4	volk mensch welt leben groß	177	0.038	0.657	0.895
	58	gewerkschaft arbeitnehmer arbeiter dgb streik	44	0.012	-0.372	1.352
Cluster 1:	33	jahr leben werden tod freund	61	0.017	-1.457	2.395
1950-1956	39	abgeordnete parlament bundestag partei wahl	50	0.017	0.050	1.306
	90	ddr sed ulbricht sozialistisch honecker	45	0.012	0.202	1.264
	10	grundgesetz verfassung land gesetz artikel	41	0.013	-2.312	0.594
	49	bundeswehr soldat militärisch armee general	31	0.012	-0.246	1.247
	62	partei dkp kommunistisch politisch kommunist	31	0.010	-2.095	1.370
	59	bundesrepublik deutschen ddr wiedervereinigung deutschland	495	0.025	-0.060	0.629
	4	volk mensch welt leben groß	385	0.023	0.708	0.777
	64	kritik meinung werden öffentlich frage	360	0.023	-3.313	1.048
	90	ddr sed ulbricht sozialistisch honecker	372	0.018	0.292	0.605
Cluster 2:	12	politisch gesellschaft gesellschaftlich system sozial	287	0.017	-0.237	0.706
1957-1970	13	student universität hochschule schule professor	204	0.012	1.017	1.241
	76	richter gericht urteil justiz jahr	196	0.011	-5.141	1.558
	62	partei dkp kommunistisch politisch kommunist	156	0.010	-3.456	1.292
	63	polizei demonstration gewalt demonstrant aktion	154	0.010	-3.481	1.234
	58	gewerkschaft arbeitnehmer arbeiter dgb streik	148	0.009	0.095	0.394

	12	politisch gesellschaft gesellschaftlich system sozial	503	0.020	-0.225	0.475
	62	partei dkp kommunistisch politisch kommunist	353	0.016	-2.403	0.649
	58	gewerkschaft arbeitnehmer arbeiter dgb streik	395	0.014	-0.451	0.562
	17	sozialismus sozialistisch revolution kommunistisch kommunist	314	0.014	-1.233	0.588
Cluster 3:	42	terrorist terrorismus anschlag raf mord	360	0.013	-4.307	1.103
1971-1988	63	polizei demonstration gewalt demonstrant aktion	314	0.013	-3.055	1.247
	90	ddr sed ulbricht sozialistisch honecker	361	0.012	1.436	0.755
	13	student universität hochschule schule professor	272	0.010	0.589	0.798
	20	grüne grün fischer partei grünen	227	0.009	-0.947	0.967
	29	hitler deutschen reich nationalsozialismus widerstand	221	0.008	-2.344	1.304
	74	ddr weste osten einheit alt	655	0.026	0.264	0.299
	68	europa europäisch europas gemeinsam politisch	395	0.018	0.562	0.222
	52	sozial gesellschaft mensch politik staat	313	0.016	0.284	0.609
	30	nation national geschichte kultur kulturell	298	0.015	0.220	0.466
Cluster 4:	51	npd republikaner rechtsradikal rechen gewalt	331	0.014	-3.325	1.875
1989-2000	83	krieg international militärisch deutschland nation	329	0.014	-1.517	0.723
	73	pds partei spd gysi osten	299	0.013	0.285	0.576
	95	ausländer deutschland flüchtling land bundesrepublik	275	0.013	-1.187	1.251
	20	grüne grün fischer partei grünen	196	0.010	0.091	1.496
	29	hitler deutschen reich nationalsozialismus widerstand	233	0.011	-2.419	0.911
	83	krieg international militärisch deutschland nation	455	0.023	-1.820	1.026
	25	politisch gesellschaft öffentlich lassen bild	363	0.021	-1.440	0.994
	52	sozial gesellschaft mensch politik staat	281	0.017	0.659	0.885
	73	pds partei spd gysi osten	296	0.016	0.344	0.826
Cluster 5:	68	europa europäisch europas gemeinsam politisch	280	0.015	0.673	0.433
2001-2011	96	türkei türkisch islam türke muslime	254	0.014	-0.613	1.016
	51	npd republikaner rechtsradikal rechen gewalt	257	0.013	-2.537	2.111
	65	verfassungsschutz polizei behörde information geheimdienst	237	0.013	-2.491	1.662
	42	terrorist terrorismus anschlag raf mord	217	0.012	-3.847	1.365
	57	jude jüdisch israel antisemitismus israelisch	131	0.008	-1.096	0.967

Table A.2.: Selected Semantically Enriched Co-occurrence Graphs (cluster 1).

Cluster 1: 1950–1956 #54

Cluster 1: 1950–1956 #78

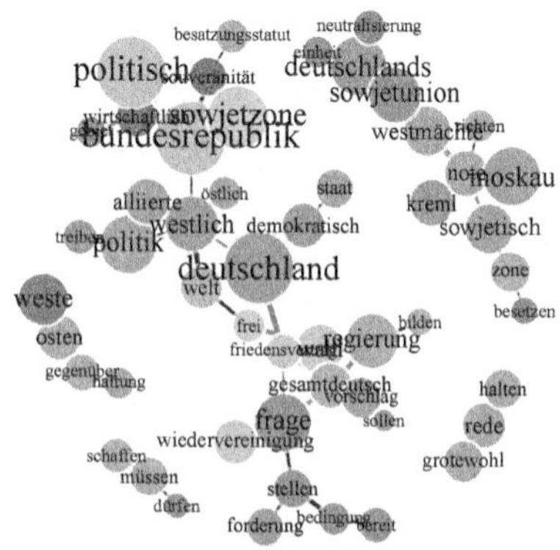

Cluster 1: 1950–1956 #58

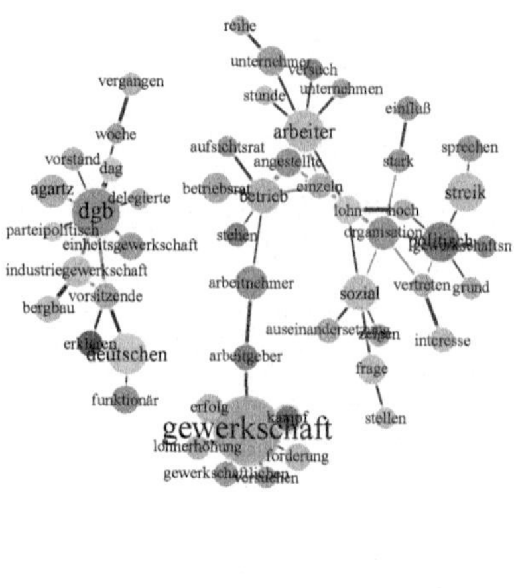

Cluster 1: 1950–1956 #62

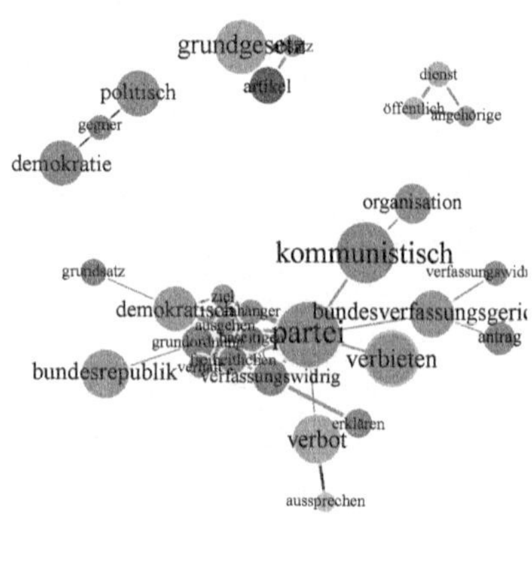

Table A.3.: Selected Semantically Enriched Co-occurrence Graphs (cluster 2).

Cluster 2: 1957–1970 #12

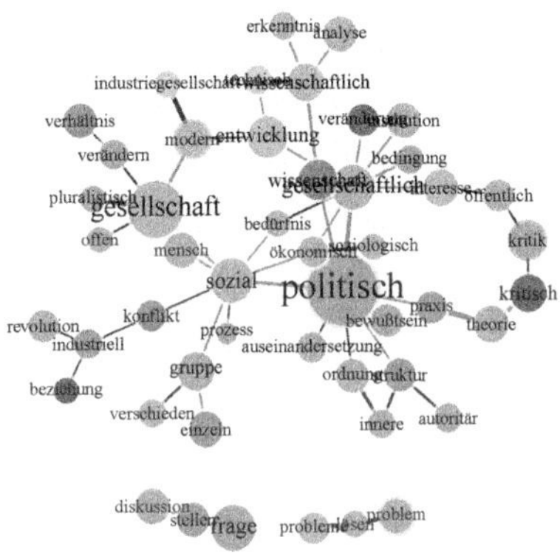

Cluster 2: 1957–1970 #4

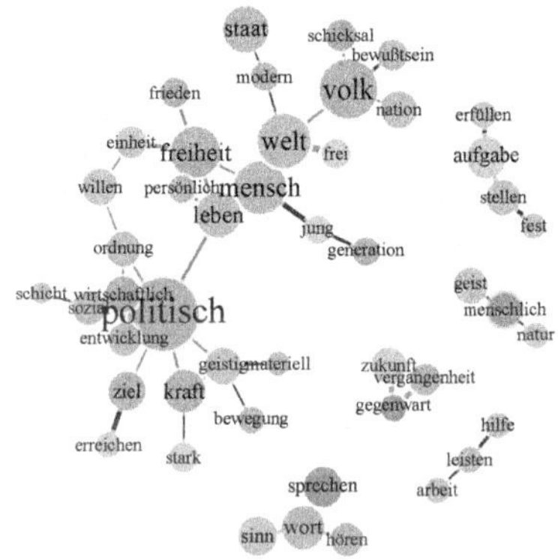

Cluster 2: 1957–1970 #64

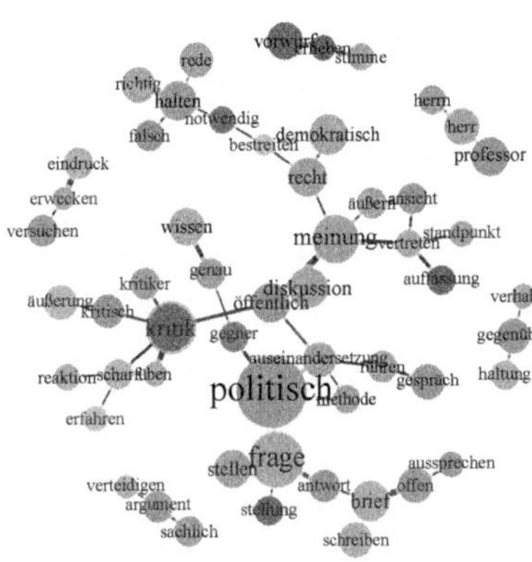

Cluster 2: 1957–1970 #63

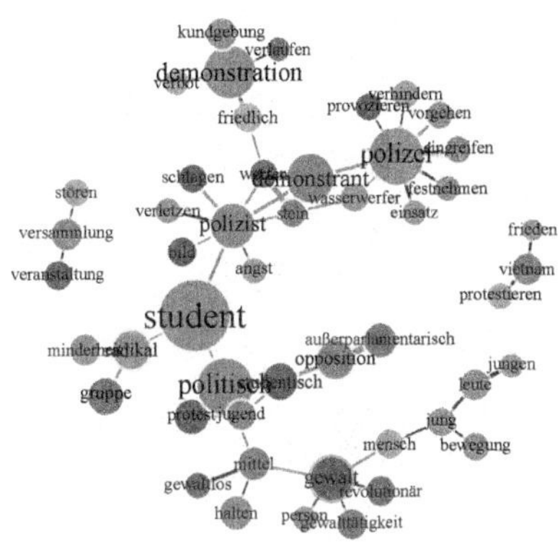

Table A.4.: Selected Semantically Enriched Co-occurrence Graphs (cluster 3).

Cluster 3: 1971–1988 #20

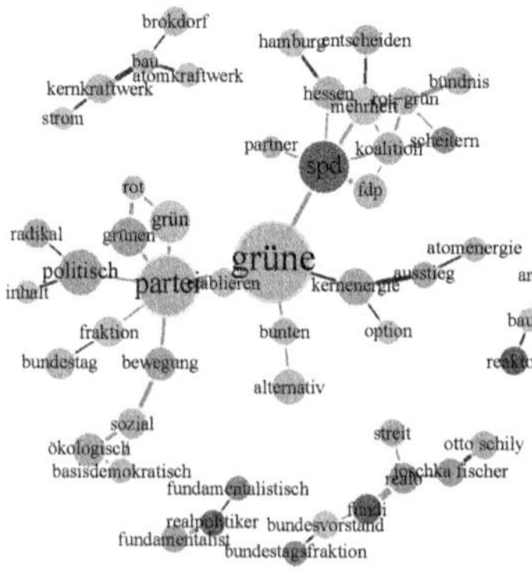

Cluster 3: 1971–1988 #42

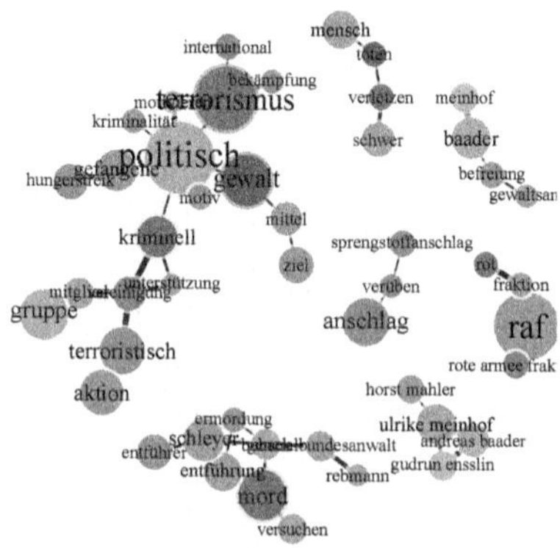

Cluster 3: 1971–1988 #63

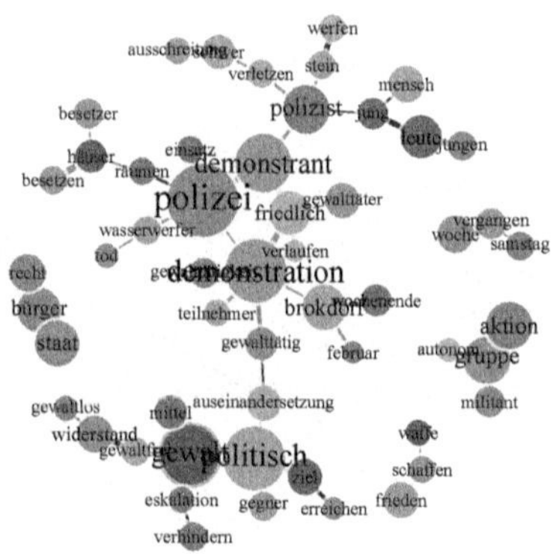

Cluster 3: 1971–1988 #29

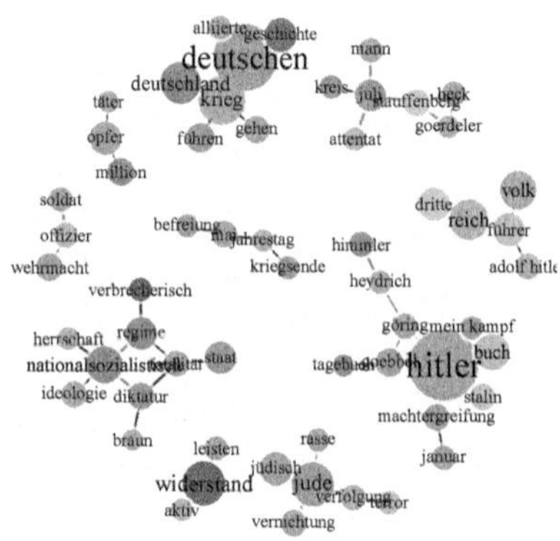

Table A.5.: Selected Semantically Enriched Co-occurrence Graphs (cluster 4).

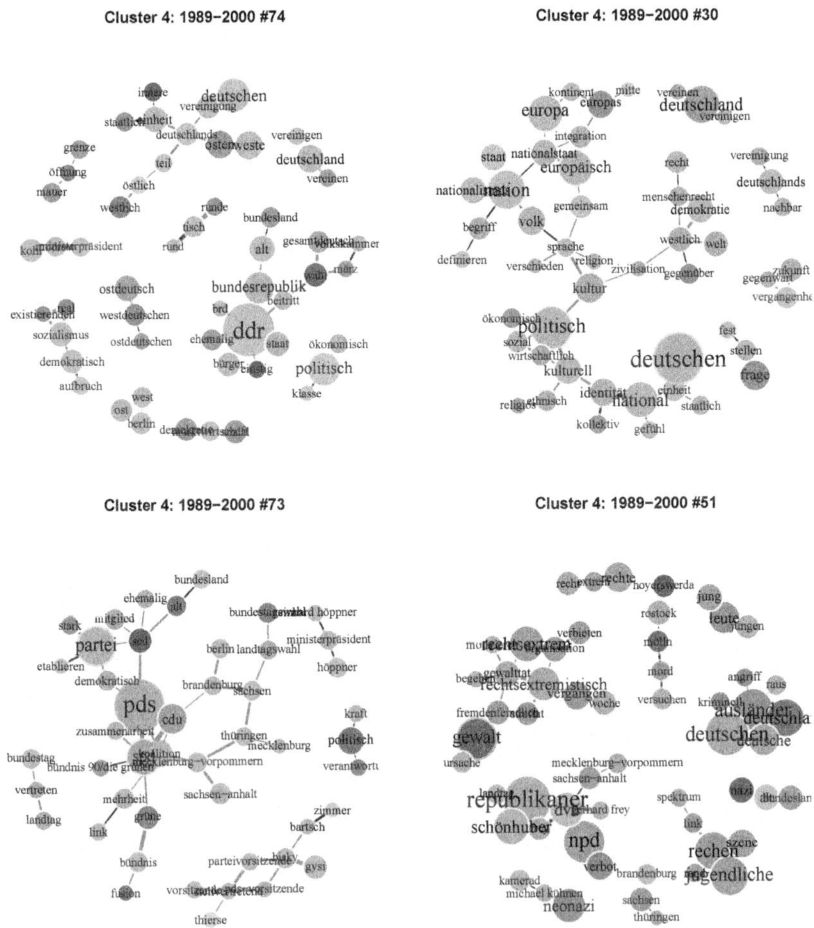

Table A.6.: Selected Semantically Enriched Co-occurrence Graphs (cluster 5).

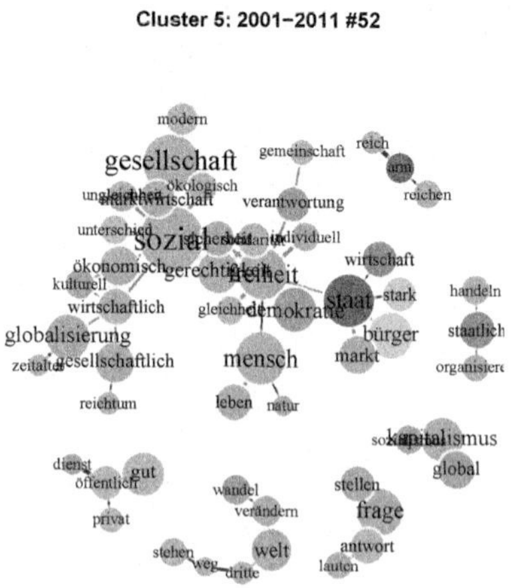

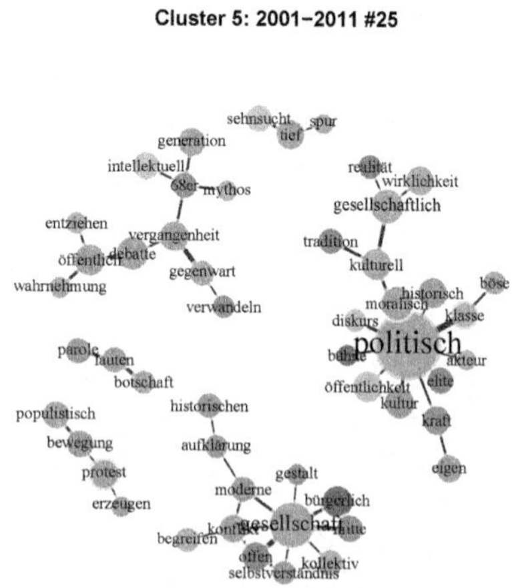

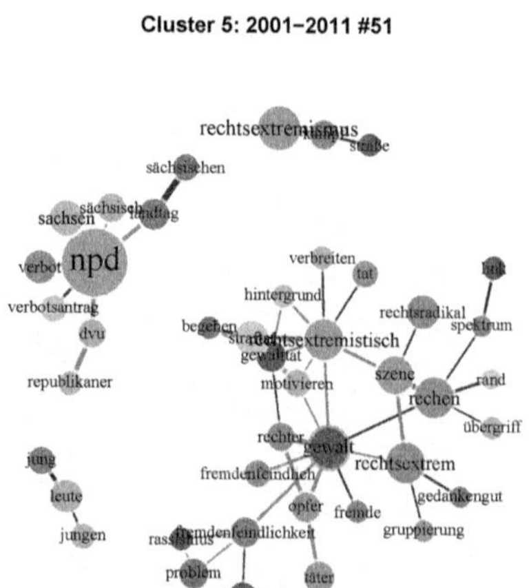

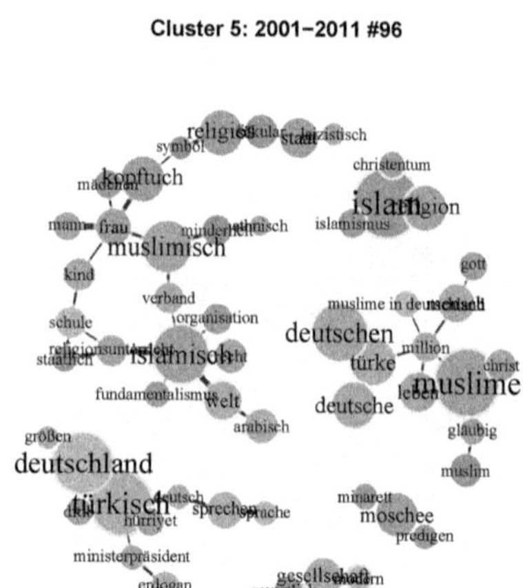

Workflow 6: Extracting terms co-occurring significantly in sentences from documents of different time periods and topics.

Input:
$\mathcal{D}$ – set of documents including sentence type counts and time stamps,
$\boldsymbol{\theta}$ – Topic probability per document from global topic model on $\mathcal{D}$,
$\mathcal{C}$ – list of sets of K' topics per time period,
$minP$ – threshold of probability for a topic in a document,
$minC, minSig$ – thresholds of minimum co-occurrence counts/statistic,
$V^k = (v_1^k, \cdots, v_N^k)$ – a list of the N most probable words for topic k
M – number of co-occurrence pairs to retrieve per cluster and topic
Output:
$cPairs$: $|\mathcal{C}| \times K'$ lists of M most significant co-occurrence pairs

```
for c ∈ 1 : |C| do
    T ← C_c ;                                  // Select topics per time period
    D_c ← getDocumentsForTimeFrame(D, c)
    for k' ∈ 1 : K' do
        S ← {}; k ← T_{k'} ;                   // Init sentence set, get global topic id
        for d ∈ D_c do
            // Get sentences of documents containing topics
               above a minimum share
            if θ_{d,k} >= minP then
                s ← getSentencesFromDocument(d)
                S ← S ∪ s
        // Count how often pairs of terms from V^{k'} appear
           together in S
        counts ← countTypeCooccurrences(S, V^{k'})
        for i ∈ 1 : N do
            for j ∈ 1 : N do
                significance ←
                logLikelihood(counts_i, counts_j, counts_ij, |S|)
                if counts_ij < minC | significance < minSig then
                    significances_ij ← 0 ;     // ignore this pair
                else
                    significances_ij ← significance
        cPairs_{c,k} ← getMostSignificantPairs(significances, M)
```

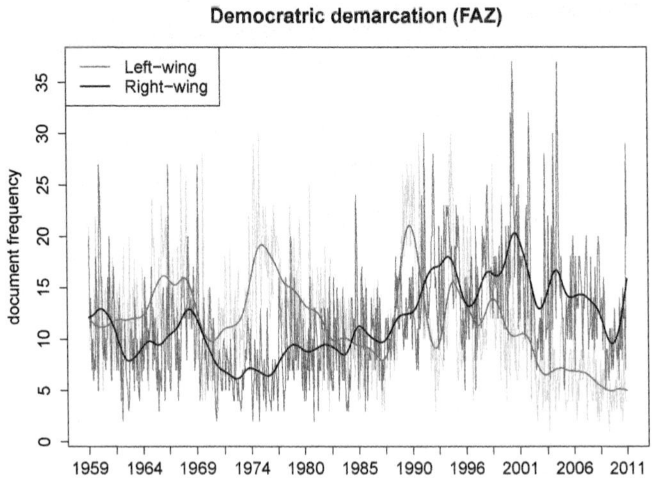

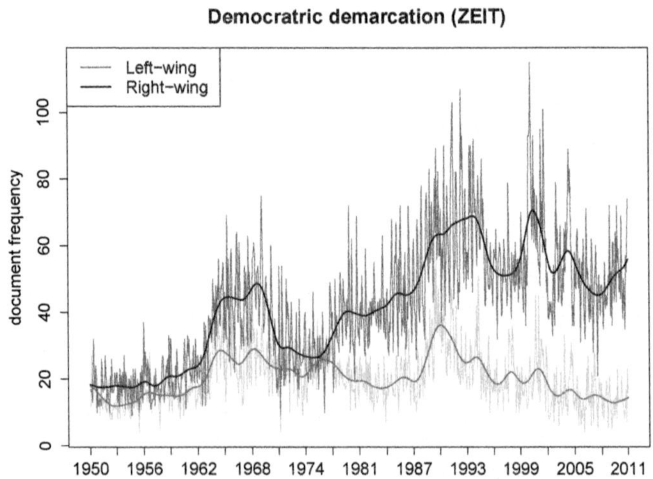

Figure A.1.: Absolute frequencies of documents containing expressions of democratic demarcation in both publications, *FAZ* and *Die Zeit.* Frequencies are aggregated per month. A spline-smoothed line is plotted to visualize trends ($spar = 0.5$).

Bibliography

AlSumait, Loulwah; Barbará, Daniel; Gentle, James and Domeniconi, Carlotta. Topic significance ranking of LDA generative models. In Buntine, Wray; Grobelnik, Marko; Mladenić, Dunja and Shawe-Taylor, John, editors, *Machine Learning and Knowledge Discovery in Databases*, pages 67–82. Springer, Berlin, 2009. URL http://dx.doi.org/10.1007/978-3-642-04180-8_22.

Angermüller, Johannes. Qualitative methods of social research in France: reconstructing the actor, deconstructing the subject. *Forum Qualitative Sozialforschung / Forum: Qualitative Social Research*, 6(3), 2005. URL http://nbn-resolving.de/urn:nbn:de:0114-fqs0503194.

Archer, Dawn, editor. *What's in a word-list? Investigating word frequency and keyword extraction.* Ashgate, Aldershot, 2008.

Arendt, Hannah. *Elemente und Ursprünge totaler Herrschaft: Antisemitismus, Imperialismus, Totalitarismus.* Piper, Zürich, 1998.

Asch, Vincent van. Macro- and micro-averaged evaluation measure, 2013. URL http://www.cnts.ua.ac.be/~vincent/pdf/microaverage.pdf.

Backes, Uwe. *Politische Extreme: Eine Wort- und Begriffsgeschichte von der Antike bis in die Gegenwart.* Vandenhoeck & Ruprecht, Göttingen, 2006.

Baeza-Yates, Ricardo and Ribeiro-Neto, Berthier. *Modern information retrieval: The concepts and technology behind search.* Addison Wesley, New York, 2 edition, 2011.

Baharudin, Baharum; Lee, Lam Hong and Khan, Khairullah. A review of machine learning algorithms for text-documents classification. *Journal of Advances in Information Technology*, 1(1), 2010.

Baker, Paul; Gabrielatos, Costas; KhosraviNik, Majid; Krzyzanowski, Michael; McEnery, Tony and Wodak, Ruth. A useful methodological synergy?

Combining critical discourse analysis and corpus linguistics to examine discourses of refugees and asylum seekers in the UK press. *Discourse & Society*, 19(3):273–306, 2008.

Banerjee, Somnath. Improving text classification accuracy using topic modeling over an additional corpus. In *Proceedings of the 31st Annual International Conference on Research and Development in Information Retrieval (ACM SIGIR '08)*, pages 867–868, New York, 2008. URL http://doi.acm.org/10.1145/1390334.1390546.

Büchler, Marco. *Medusa: Performante Textstatistiken auf großen Textmengen: Kookkurrenzanalyse in Theorie und Anwendung.* VDM, Saarbrücken, 2008.

Benoit, Kenneth and Laver, Michael. The dimensionality of political space: Epistemological and methodological considerations. *European Union Politics*, 13(2):194–218, 2012.

Bergmann, Gustav. Two types of linguistic philosophy. *The Review of Metaphysics*, 5(3):417–438, 1952.

Biemann, Chris; Heyer, Gerhard; Quasthoff, Uwe and Richter, Matthias. The Leipzig Corpora Collection: Monolingual corpora of standard size. In *Proceedings of Corpus Linguistic 2007*, Birmingham, 2007.

Blei, David M. Probabilistic topic models: Surveying a suite of algorithms that offer a solution to managing large document archives. *Communications of the ACM*, 55(4):77–84, 2012.

Blei, David M. and Lafferty, John D. Correlated topic models. In *Proceedings of the 23rd International Conference on Machine Learning (ICML)*, pages 113–120. MIT Press, 2006.

Blei, David M.; Ng, Andrew Y. and Jordan, Michael I. Latent Dirichlet Allocation. *Journal of Machine Learning Research*, 3:993–1022, 2003. URL http://www.cs.princeton.edu/~blei/papers/BleiNgJordan2003.pdf.

Blätte, Andreas. Korpusbasierte Diskursforschung: Ausgabe 3 / 2011, 2011. URL http://www.uni-due.de/imperia/md/content/gesellschaftswissenschaften/profilschwerpunkt/newsletter_juni2011_wandel.pdf.

Blätte, Andreas. Unscharfe Grenzen von Policy-Feldern im parlamentarischen Diskurs: Messungen und Erkundungen durch korpusunterstützte Politikforschung. *Zeitschrift für Politikwissenschaft*, 22(1):35–68, 2012.

BMBF. Bekanntmachung des Bundesministeriums für Bildung und Forschung von Richtlinien zur Förderung von Forschungs- und Entwicklungsvorhaben aus dem Bereich der eHumanities, 2011. URL http://www.bmbf.de/foerderungen/16466.php.

Bobbio, Norberto. *Rechts und Links: Gründe und Bedeutungen einer politischen Unterscheidung*. Wagenbach, Berlin, 1994.

Bohnsack, Ralf. *Rekonstruktive Sozialforschung: Einführung in qualitative Methoden*. Budrich, Opladen, 8 edition, 2010.

Bonzio, Roberto. Father Busa, pioneer of computing in humanities with Index Thomisticus, dies at 98, 2011. URL http://www.forbes.com/sites/robertobonzio/2011/08/11/father-busa-pioneer-of-computing-in-humanities-dies-at-98.

Bordag, Stefan. A comparison of co-occurrence and similarity measures as simulations of context. In Gelbukh, Alexander, editor, *Computational Linguistics and Intelligent Text Processing*, Lecture notes in computer science, pages 52–63. Springer, Berlin, 2008.

Boulis, Constantinos and Ostendorf, Mari. Text classification by augmenting the bag-of-words representation with redundancy-compensated bigrams. In *Proceedings of the International Workshop in Feature Selection in Data Mining*, pages 9–16, 2005.

Boyd, Danah and Crawford, Kate. Critical questions for big data. *Information, Communication & Society*, 15(5):662–679, 2012.

Bubenhofer, Noah. Diskurse berechnen? Wege zu einer korpuslinguistischen Diskursanalyse. In Warnke, Ingo and Spitzmüller, Jürgen, editors, *Methoden der Diskurslinguistik*, pages 407–434. de Gruyter, Berlin and New York, 2008.

Bubenhofer, Noah. *Sprachgebrauchsmuster: Korpuslinguistik als Methode der Diskurs- und Kulturanalyse*. de Gruyter, Berlin and New York, 2009.

Bucanac, Christian. The V-Model, 1991. URL http://www.bucanac.com/documents/The_V-Model.pdf.

Buck, Elena. Keine Gesellschaft ohne Grenzen, keine Politik ohne Gegner_innen. Auf dem Weg zu Kriterien demokratischer Grenzziehungen. In Forum für Kritische Rechtsextremismusforschung, editor, *Ordnung. Macht. Extremismus*, pages 263–285. VS Verlag für Sozialwissenschaften, Wiesbaden, 2011.

Bundesministerium des Innern. Verfassungsschutzbericht 1969/70, 1971.

Bundesministerium des Innern. Verfassungsschutzbericht 1979, 1980.

Bundesministerium des Innern. Verfassungsschutzbericht 1989, 1990.

Bundesministerium des Innern. Verfassungsschutzbericht 1998, 1999.

Bundesministerium des Innern. Verfassungsschutzbericht 2009, 2010.

Busa, Roberto A. Foreword: Perspectives on the digital humanities. In Schreibman, Susan; Siemens, Raymond George and Unsworth, John, editors, *A Companion to Digital Humanities*, pages xvi–xxi. Blackwell, Malden, 2004.

Caliński, Tadeusz and Harabasz, Joachim. A dendrite method for cluster analysis. *Communications in Statistics*, 3(1):1–27, 1974.

Chambers, John M. and Hastie, Trevor. *Statistical models in S*. Chapman & Hall, Boca Raton, 1992.

Chambers, Nathanael and Jurafsky, Dan. Unsupervised learning of narrative schemas and their participants. In *Proceedings of the Joint Conference of the 47th Annual Meeting of the ACL and the 4th International Joint Conference on Natural Language Processing of the AFNLP*, pages 602–610, Stroudsburg, 2009. ACL. URL http://dl.acm.org/citation.cfm?id=1690219.1690231.

Chambers, Nathanael and Jurafsky, Dan. Template-based Information Extraction Without the Templates. In *Proceedings of the 49th Annual Meeting of the Association for Computational Linguistics: Human Language Technologies (HTL '11)*, pages 976–986, Stroudsburg, 2011. ACL. URL http://dl.acm.org/citation.cfm?id=2002472.2002595.

Chang, Chih-chung and Lin, Chih-jen. LIBSVM: A library for support vector machines. *ACM Transactions on Intelligent Systems and Technology*, 2 (3):27:1–27:27, 2011.

Chang, Jonathan; Gerrish, Sean; Wang, Chong; Boyd-graber, Jordan L. and Blei, David M. Reading tea leaves: how humans interpret topic models. In Bengio, Yoshua; Schuurmans, Dale; Lafferty, John D.; Williams, Christopher K. and Culotta, Aron, editors, *Advances in Neural Information Processing Systems 22*, pages 288–296. Curran, 2009. URL http://papers.nips.cc/paper/3700-reading-tea-leaves-how-humans-interpret-topic-models.pdf.

Cimiano, Philipp. *Ontology learning and population from text: algorithms, evaluation and applications*. Springer, Boston, 2006.

Clough, Paul and Sanderson, Mark. Evaluating the performance of information retrieval systems using test collections. *Information Research*, 18(2), 2013.

Crane, Gregory. What do you do with a million books? *D-Lib Magazine*, 12 (3), 2006.

Csardi, Gabor and Nepusz, Tamas. The igraph software package for complex network research. *InterJournal*, Complex Systems:1695, 2006. URL http://igraph.org.

Deerwester, Scott; Dumais, Susan T.; Furnas, George W.; Landauer, Thomas K. and Harshman, Richard. Indexing by latent semantic analysis. *Journal of the American Society for Information Science*, 41(6):391–407, 1990.

Dinu, Georgiana and Lapata, Mirella. Measuring distributional similarity in context. In *Proceedings of the 2010 Conference on Empirical Methods in Natural Language Processing (EMNLP '10)*, pages 1162–1172, Stroudsburg, 2010. ACL. URL http://dl.acm.org/citation.cfm?id=1870658.1870771.

Donati, Paolo R. Die Rahmenanalyse politischer Diskurse. In Keller, Reiner; Hirseland, Andreas; Schneider, Werner and Viehöver, Willy, editors, *Handbuch sozialwissenschaftliche Diskursanalyse 1*, pages 159–193. VS Verlag für Sozialwissenschaften, Wiesbaden, 2011.

Dubey, Avinava; Hefny, Ahmed; Williamson, Sinead and Xing, Eric P. A non-parametric mixture model for topic modeling over time. *ArXiv e-prints*, 2012. URL http://arxiv.org/abs/1208.4411.

Dunning, Ted. Accurate methods for the statistics of surprise and coincidence. *Computational Linguistics*, 19(1):61–74, 1993. URL http://dl.acm.org/citation.cfm?id=972450.972454.

Dzudzek, Iris. *Hegemonie kultureller Vielfalt: Eine Genealogie kultur-räumlicher Repräsentationen in der UNESCO*, volume 5 of *Forum Politische Geographie*. LIT, Münster, 2013.

Dzudzek, Iris; Glasze, Georg; Mattissek, Annika and Schirmel, Henning. Verfahren der lexikometrischen Analyse von Textkoprora. In Glasze, Georg and Mattissek, Annika, editors, *Handbuch Diskurs und Raum*, pages 233–260. transcript, Bielefeld, 2009.

Ebling, Sarah; Scharloth, Joachim; Dussa, Tobias and Bubenhofer, Noah. Gibt es eine Sprache des politischen Extremismus? In Liedtke, Frank, editor, *Die da oben. Texte, Medien, Partizipation*, pages 43–68. Hempen, Bremen, 2014.

Endres, Dominik M. and Schindelin, Johannes E. A new metric for probability distributions. *IEEE Transactions on Information Theory*, 49(7):1858–1860, 2003.

Ester, Martin; Kriegel, Hans-Peter; Xu, Xiaowei and Sander, Jörg. A density-based algorithm for discovering clusters in large spatial databases with noise. In Simoudis, Evangelos; Han, Jiawei and Fayyad, Usama M., editors, *Proceedings of the Second International Conference on Knowledge Discovery and Data Mining (KDD-96)*, pages 226–231. AAAI Press, 1996.

Evans, Michael S. A computational approach to qualitative analysis in large textual datasets. *PloS one*, 9(2), 2014.

Evers, Jeanine C.; Silver, Christina; Mruck, Katja and Peeters, Bart. Introduction to the KWALON experiment: discussions on qualitative data analysis software by developers and users. *Forum Qualitative Sozialforschung / Forum: Qualitative Social Research*, 12(1), 2011. URL http://nbn-resolving.de/urn:nbn:de:0114-fqs1101405.

Feinerer, Ingo; Hornik, Kurt and Meyer, David. Text mining infrastructure in R. *Journal of Statistical Software*, 25(5):1–54, 2008. URL http://www.jstatsoft.org/v25/i05.

Feustel, Robert. Entropie des Politischen. Zur strategischen Funktion des Extremismusbegriffs. In Forum für Kritische Rechtsextremismusforschung, editor, *Ordnung. Macht. Extremismus*, pages 117–139. VS Verlag für Sozialwissenschaften, Wiesbaden, 2011.

Fielding, Nigel and Lee, Raymond M. *Computer analysis and qualitative research.* SAGE, London, 1998.

Finkel, Jenny Rose; Grenager, Trond and Manning, Christopher. Incorporating non-local information into information extraction systems by Gibbs sampling. In *Proceedings of the 43rd Annual Meeting on Association for Computational Linguistics (ACL '05)*, pages 363–370, Stroudsburg, 2005. ACL.

Firth, John R. A synopsis of linguistic theory 1930-1955. *Studies in Linguistic Analysis*, pages 1–32, 1957.

Fisahn, Andreas. Überwachung und Repression: Logiken der Herrschaftssicherung. In Leipziger Kamera. Initiative gegen Überwachung, editor, *Kontrollverluste*, pages 34–48. Unrast, Münster, 2009.

Flick, Uwe. *Triangulation: Eine Einführung.* VS Verlag für Sozialwissenschaften, Wiesbaden, 1 edition, 2004.

Flick, Uwe. Zur Qualität qualitativer Forschung: Diskurse und Ansätze. In Kuckartz, Udo, editor, *Qualitative Datenanalyse computergestützt*, pages 188–209. VS Verlag für Sozialwissenschaften, Wiesbaden, 2007.

Forman, George and Cohen, Ira. Learning from little: comparison of classifiers given little training. In Boulicaut, Jean-François; Esposito, Floriana; Giannotti, Fosca and Pedreschi, Dino, editors, *Knowledge Discovery in Databases (PKDD '04)*, volume 3202, pages 161–172. Springer, Berlin, 2004.

Foucault, Michel. *Archäologie des Wissens.* Suhrkamp, Frankfurt am Main, 2005.

Foucault, Michel. *Die Ordnung des Diskurses.* Fischer, Frankfurt am Main, 11 edition, 2010.

Fraas, Claudia and Pentzold, Christian. Big Data vs. Slow Understanding? *Zeitschrift für Germanistische Linguistik*, 43(1), 2015.

Friese, Susanne. Using ATLAS.ti for analyzing the financial crisis data. *Forum Qualitative Sozialforschung / Forum: Qualitative Social Research*, 12(1), 2011. URL http://nbn-resolving.de/urn:nbn:de:0114-fqs1101397.

Glaser, Barney G. and Strauss, Anselm L. *Grounded theory: Strategien qualitativer Forschung*. Huber, Bern, 2 edition, 2005.

Glasze, Georg. Vorschläge zur Operationalisierung der Diskurstheorie von Laclau und Mouffe in einer Triangulation von lexikometrischen und interpretativen Methoden. *Forum Qualitative Sozialforschung / Forum: Qualitative Social Research*, 8(2), 2007. URL http://nbn-resolving.de/urn:nbn:de:0114-fqs0702143.

Goldkuhl, Göran. Pragmatism vs interpretivism in qualitative information systems research. *European Journal of Information Systems*, 21(2):135–146, 2012.

Gray, Jane. Qualitative data workshop report: Data service infrastructure for the social sciences and humanities, 2013. URL http://dasish.eu/publications/projectreports/D8.7_-_Qualitative_Data_Workshop_Report__1_.pdf.

Grimmer, Justin. A bayesian hierarchical topic model for political texts: Measuring expressed agendas in senate press releases. *Political Analysis*, 18(1):1–35, 2010.

Grün, Bettina and Hornik, Kurt. Topicmodels: an R package for fitting topic models. *Journal of Statistical Software*, 40(13):1–30, 2011. URL http://www.jstatsoft.org/v40/i13/.

Guilhaumou, Jacques. Geschichte und Sprachwissenschaft: Wege und Stationen (in) der 'analyse du discours'. In Keller, Reiner; Hirseland, Andreas; Schneider, Werner and Viehöver, Willy, editors, *Handbuch sozialwissenschaftliche Diskursanalyse 2*, pages 21–67. VS Verlag für Sozialwissenschaften, Wiesbaden, 2008.

Hall, David; Jurafsky, Daniel and Manning, Christopher D. Studying the history of ideas using topic models. In *Proceedings of the Conference on Empirical Methods in Natural Language Processing (EMNLP '08)*, pages 363–371, Stroudsburg, 2008. ACL. URL http://dl.acm.org/citation.cfm?id=1613715.1613763.

Harris, Zellig. Distributional structure. *Word*, 10(23):146–162, 1954.

Helsloot, Niels and Hak, Tony. Pêcheux's contribution to discourse analysis. *Forum Qualitative Sozialforschung / Forum: Qualitative Social Research*, 8(2), 2007. URL http://nbn-resolving.de/urn:nbn:de:0114-fqs070218.

Heyer, Gerhard. Introduction to TMS 2009. In Heyer, Gerhard, editor, *Text mining services*, volume 14 of *Leipziger Beiträge zur Informatik*, pages 1–14, Leipzig, 2009. LIV.

Heyer, Gerhard; Quasthoff, Uwe and Wittig, Thomas. *Text Mining: Wissensrohstoff Text: Konzepte, Algorithmen, Ergebnisse.* W3L, Bochum, 2006.

Heyer, Gerhard; Keim, Daniel; Teresniak, Sven and Oelke, Daniela. Interaktive explorative Suche in großen Dokumentbeständen. *Datenbank-Spektrum*, 11(3):195–206, 2011.

Heyer, Gerhard; Niekler, Andreas and Wiedemann, Gregor. Brauchen die Digital Humanities eine eigene Methodologie? Überlegungen zur systematischen Nutzung von Text Mining Verfahren in einem politikwissenschaftlichen Projekt, 2014. URL http://asv.informatik.uni-leipzig.de/publication/file/255/Heyer-Brauchen_die_Digital_Humanities_eine_eigene_Methodologie__berlegungen-1451050.pdf.

Hillard, Dustin; Purpura, Stephen and Wilkerson, John. Computer-assisted topic classification for mixed-methods social science research. *Journal of Information Technology & Politics*, 4(4):31–46, 2008.

Hoi, Steven C.; Jin, Rong and Lyu, Michael R. Large-scale text categorization by batch mode active learning. In *Proceedings of the 15th International Conference on World Wide Web (WWW '06)*, pages 633–642, New York, 2006. ACM. URL http://doi.acm.org/10.1145/1135777.1135870.

Holger Billhardt; Daniel Borrajo and Victor Maojo. Using term co-occurrence data for document indexing and retrieval. In *Proceedings of the 22nd Annual Colloquium on Information Retrieval Research (BCS-IRSG)*, pages 105–117, 2000.

Hopkins, Daniel J. and King, Gary. A method of automated nonparametric content analysis for social science. *American Journal for Political Science*, 54(1):229–247, 2010.

Hösl, Maximilian and Reiberg, Abel. Das gemeinsame Verständnis vom Feld – Eine Annäherung an ein Kriterium der Politikfeldentstehung durch Themenexploration und feldbezeichnende Begriffe am Beispiel Netzpolitik. In Lemke, Matthias and Wiedemann, Gregor, editors, *Text Mining in den Sozialwissenschaften*, Kritische Studien zur Demokratie. VS Verlag für Sozialwissenschaften, Wiesbaden, 2015.

Janasik, Nina; Honkela, Timo and Bruun, Henrik. Text mining in qualitative research application of an unsupervised learning method. *Organizational Research Methods*, 12(3):436–460, 2009.

Jaschke, Hans-Gerd. *Politischer Extremismus.* Bundeszentrale für Politische Bildung, Bonn, 2007.

Jesse, Eckhard. Formen des politischen Extremismus. In Bundesministerium des Innern, editor, *Extremismus in Deutschland.* Berlin, 2004.

Jäger, Siegfried. *Kritische Diskursanalyse: Eine Einführung.* Unrast, Münster, 4 edition, 2004.

Joachims, Thorsten. Text categorization with support vector machines: learning with many relevant features, 1998. URL http://www.cs.cornell.edu/people/tj/publications/joachims_98a.pdf.

Johnson, Christopher; Shukla, Parul and Shukla, Shilpa. On classifying the political sentiment of tweets, 2011. URL http://citeseerx.ist.psu.edu/viewdoc/summary?doi=10.1.1.229.3927.

Jung, Matthias. Diskurshistorische Analyse: Eine linguistische Perspektive. In Keller, Reiner; Hirseland, Andreas; Schneider, Werner and Viehöver, Willy, editors, *Handbuch sozialwissenschaftliche Diskursanalyse 1*, pages 35–59. VS Verlag für Sozialwissenschaften, Wiesbaden, 2011.

Jurka, Timothy P. maxent: An R package for low-memory multinomial logistic regression with support for semi-automated text classification. *The R Journal*, 4(1):56–59, 2012.

Jurka, Timothy P.; Collingwood, Loren; Boydstun, Amber E.; Grossman, Emiliano and van Atteveldt, Wouter. RTextTools: A Supervised Learning Package for Text Classification. *The R Journal*, 5(1):6–12, 2013. URL http://rjournal.github.io/archive/2013-1/collingwood-jurka-boydstun-etal.pdf.

Kantner, Cathleen. The European public sphere and the debate about humanitarian military interventions. *European Security*, 23(4):409–429, 2014.

Keith, Steven; Kaser, Owen and Lemire, Daniel. Analyzing large collections of electronic text using OLAP, 2006. URL http://arxiv.org/abs/cs/0605127.

Kelle, Udo. Theory building in qualitative research and computer programs for the management of textual data. *Sociological Research Online*, 2(2), 1997. URL http://www.socresonline.org.uk/2/2/1.html.

Kelle, Udo. Computergestützte Analyse qualitativer Daten. In Flick, Uwe, editor, *Qualitative Forschung*, pages 485–502. Rowohlt, Reinbek bei Hamburg, 2008.

Kelle, Udo. Computerunterstützung in der qualitiativen Forschung. In Bohnsack, Ralf; Marotzki, Winfried and Meuser, Michael, editors, *Hauptbegriffe Qualitativer Sozialforschung*, pages 29–31. Budrich, Opladen, 2011.

Keller, Reiner. *Diskursforschung: Eine Einführung für SozialwissenschaftlerInnen*. VS Verlag für Sozialwissenschaften, Wiesbaden, 3 edition, 2007.

Kleinnijenhuis, Jan and van Atteveldt, Wouter. Political positions and political cleavages in texts. In Kaal, Bertie; Maks, Isa and Van Elfrinkhof, Annemarie, editors, *From Text to Political Positions*. John Benjamins, Amsterdam, 2014.

Kohlstruck, Michael. Thesen zur Diskussionsveranstaltung „Verfassungsschutz durch Aufklärung?“ am 21.3.2012, 2012. URL http://www.djb-ev.de/sites/djb-ev.de/files/verfassungsschutz_kohlstruck.pdf.

Koltcov, Sergei; Koltsova, Olessia and Nikolenko, Sergey. Latent dirichlet allocation: stability and applications to studies of user-generated content. In *Proceedings of the 2014 ACM Conference on Web Science (WebSci '14)*, pages 161–165, New York, 2014. ACM. URL http://doi.acm.org/10.1145/2615569.2615680.

Kracauer, Siegfried. The challenge of qualitative content analysis. *Public Opinion Quarterly*, 16(4):631–642, 1952. URL http://www.jstor.org/stable/2746123.

Krippendorff, Klaus. *Content analysis: An introduction to its methodology*. SAGE, Los Angeles, 3 edition, 2013.

Kuş Saillard, Elif. Systematic versus interpretive analysis with two CAQDAS packages: NVivo and MAXQDA. *Forum Qualitative Sozialforschung / Forum: Qualitative Social Research*, 12(1), 2011. URL http://nbn-resolving.de/urn:nbn:de:0114-fqs1101345.

Kuckartz, Udo. QDA-Software im Methodendiskurs: Geschichte, Potenziale, Effekte. In Kuckartz, Udo, editor, *Qualitative Datenanalyse computergestützt*, pages 15–31. VS Verlag für Sozialwissenschaften, Wiesbaden, 2007.

Kuckartz, Udo. *Einführung in die computergestützte Analyse qualitativer Daten*. VS Verlag für Sozialwissenschaften, Wiesbaden, 3 edition, 2010.

Laclau, Ernesto and Mouffe, Chantal. *Hegemony and socialist strategy*. Verso, London and New-York, 2 edition, 2001.

Lancichinetti, Andrea; Sirer, M. Irmak; Wang, Jane X.; Acuna, Daniel; Körding, Konrad and Amaral, A. Nunes. High-Reproducibility and High-Accuracy Method for Automated Topic Classification. *Physical Review X*, 5(1):11007, 2015. URL http://link.aps.org/doi/10.1103/PhysRevX.5.011007.

Landwehr, Achim. *Historische Diskursanalyse*. Campus, Frankfurt am Main, 2008.

Laver, Michael; Benoit, Kenneth and Garry, John. Extracting policy positions from political texts using words as data. *American Political Science Review*, 97(2):311–331, 2003.

Lazer, D.; Pentland, A.; Adamic, L.; Aral, S.; Barabasi, A.-L; Brewer, D.; Christakis, N.; Contractor, N.; Fowler, J.; Gutmann, M.; Jebara, T.; King, G.; Macy, M.; Roy, D. and van Alstyne, M. Computational Social Science. *Science*, 323(5915):721–723, 2009.

Lee, Steven. A paradox of democracy. *Public Affairs Quarterly*, 15(3): 261–269, 2001. URL http://www.jstor.org/stable/40441297.

Lejeune, Christophe. From normal business to financial crisis ... and back again: An illustration of the benefits of Cassandre for qualitative analysis. *Forum Qualitative Sozialforschung / Forum: Qualitative Social Research*, 12(1):52–83, 2011. URL http://nbnresolving.de/urn:nbn:de:0114-fqs1101247.

Lemke, Matthias and Stulpe, Alexander. Text und soziale Wirklichkeit: Theoretische Grundlagen und empirische Anwendung von Text-Mining-Verfahren in sozialwissenschaftlicher Perspektive. *Zeitschrift für Germanistische Linguistik*, 43(1):52–83, 2015.

Lemke, Matthias; Niekler, Andreas; Schaal, Gary S. and Wiedemann, Gregor. Content analysis between quality and quantity: Fulfilling blended-reading requirements for the social sciences with a scalable text mining infrastructure. *Datenbank-Spektrum*, 15(1):7–14, 2015.

Lewis, Seth C.; Zamith, Rodrigo and Hermida, Alfred. Content analysis in an era of big data: A hybrid approach to computational and manual methods. *Journal of Broadcasting & Electronic Media*, 57(1):34–52, 2013. URL http://dx.doi.org/10.1080/08838151.2012.761702.

Link, Jürgen. *Versuch über den Normalismus: Wie Normalität produziert wird.* Vandenhoeck & Ruprecht, Göttingen, 3 edition, 2006.

Liversidge, Ed. The Death of the V-Model, 2005. URL http://www.harmonicss.co.uk/index.php/hss-downloads/doc_download/12-death-of-the-v-model.

Lowe, Will. The statistics of text: New methods for content analysis, 2003. URL http://citeseerx.ist.psu.edu/viewdoc/download?doi=10.1.1.129.5225\&rep=rep1\&type=pdf.

Lowe, Will. Understanding Wordscores. *Political Analysis*, 16(4):356–371, 2008.

Lowe, Will; Benoit, Kenneth; Mikhaylov, Slava and Laver, Michael. Scaling policy preferences from coded political texts. *Legislative Studies Quarterly*, 36(1):123–155, 2011.

Lueger, Manfred and Vettori, Oliver. A social hermeneutics approach to higher education research. In Huisman, Jeroen and Tight, Malcolm, editors, *Theory and method in higher education research II*, volume 10, pages 23–43. Emerald, Bingley, 2014.

Luhn, Hans Peter. Key word-in-context index for technical literature (KWIC index). *American Documentation*, 11(4):288–295, 1960.

Manovich, Lev. Computational humanities vs. digital humanities, 2012. URL http://lab.softwarestudies.com/2012/03/computational-humanities-vs-digital.html.

Mautner, Gerlinde. Checks and balances: how corpus linguistics can contribute to CDA. In Wodak, Ruth and Meyer, Michael, editors, *Methods of critical discourse analysis*, pages 122–143. SAGE, London, 2009.

Mautner, Gerlinde. Die kritische Masse: Korpuslinguistik und kritische Diskursanalyse. In Felder, Ekkehard; Müller, Marcus and Vogel, Friedemann, editors, *Korpuspragmatik*, pages 83–114. de Gruyter, Berlin, 2012.

Mayring, Philipp. Qualitative Inhaltsanalyse. *Forum Qualitative Sozialforschung / Forum: Qualitative Social Research*, 1(2), 2000. URL http://nbn-resolving.de/urn:nbn:de:0114-fqs0002204.

Mayring, Philipp. *Qualitative Inhaltsanalyse: Grundlagen und Techniken.* Beltz, Weinheim and Basel, 11 edition, 2010.

Mcauliffe, Jon D. and Blei, David M. Supervised Topic Models. In Platt, John C.; Koller, Daphne; Singer, Yoram and Roweis, Sam T., editors, *Advances in Neural Information Processing Systems 20 (NIPS 2007)*, pages 121–128. Curran, 2008. URL http://papers.nips.cc/paper/3328-supervised-topic-models.pdf.

McNamara, Danielle S. Computational methods to extract meaning from text and advance theories of human cognition. *Topics in Cognitive Science*, 3(1):3–17, 2011.

Meeks, Elijah and Weingart, Scott B. The digital humanities contribution to topic modeling. *Journal of Digital Humanities*, 2(1), 2012. URL http://www.journalofdigitalhumanities.org/2-1/dh-contribution-to-topic-modeling.

Meyer, David. Support vector machines: The interface to libsvm in package e1071, 2014. URL http://cran.r-project.org/web/packages/e1071/vignettes/svmdoc.pdf.

Mühlmeyer-Mentzel, Agnes. Das Datenkonzept von ATLAS.ti und sein Gewinn für Grounded-Theory-Forschungsarbeiten. *Forum Qualitative Sozialforschung / Forum: Qualitative Social Research*, 12(1), 2011. URL http://nbn-resolving.de/urn:nbn:de:0114-fqs1101325.

Mikolov, Tomas; Chen, Kai; Corrado, Greg and Dean, Jeffrey. Efficient estimation of word representations in vector space, 2013a. URL http://arxiv.org/abs/1301.3781.

Mikolov, Tomas; Sutskever, Ilya; Chen, Kai; Corrado, Greg and Dean, Jeffrey. Distributed representations of words and phrases and their compositionality, 2013b. URL http://arxiv.org/abs/1310.4546v1.

Mimno, David; Wallach, Hanna M.; Talley, Edmund; Leenders, Miriam and McCallum, Andrew. Optimizing semantic coherence in topic models. In *Proceedings of the Conference on Empirical Methods in Natural Language Processing (EMNLP '11)*, pages 262–272, Stroudsburg, 2011. ACL. URL http://dl.acm.org/citation.cfm?id=2145432.2145462.

Mitchell, Tom M. *Machine Learning*. McGraw-Hill, New York, 1997.

Moretti, Franco. Conjectures on World Literature. *New Left Review*, (1): 54–68, 2000.

Moretti, Franco. *Graphs, maps, trees: Abstract models for literary history*. Verso, London and New York, 2007.

Mouffe, Chantal. *The democratic paradox*. Verso, London and New York, 2009.

Murswiek, Dietrich. Die meisten Verfassungsschutzberichte sind verfassungswidrig, 2009. URL http://www.pr.uni-freiburg.de/pm/2009/pm.2009-12-04.420.

Ng, Andrew Y. and Jordan, Michael I. On discriminative vs. generative classifiers: A comparison of logistic regression and naive Bayes. In *Advances in Neural Information Processing Systems 14 (NIPS '01)*, pages 841–848. MIT Press, 2002.

Niehr, Thomas. *Einführung in die Politolinguistik: Gegenstände und Methoden*. Vandenhoeck & Ruprecht, Göttingen, 1 edition, 2014.

Niekler, Andreas. Automatisierte Verfahren für die Themenanalyse nachrichtenorientierter Textquellen: Dissertation zur Erlangung des akademischen Grades Doktor-Ingenieur (Dr.-Ing.) im Fachgebiet Informatik, 2016. URL http://asv.informatik.uni-leipzig.de/publication/file/350/Niekler_Diss.pdf.

Niekler, Andreas and Jähnichen, Patrick. Matching results of latent dirichlet allocation for text. In *Proceedings of the 11th International Conference on Cognitive Modeling (ICCM 2012)*, pages 317–322. Universitätsverlag der TU Berlin, 2012.

Niekler, Andreas; Wiedemann, Gregor and Heyer, Gerhard. Leipzig Corpus Miner: A Text Mining Infrastructure for Qualitative Data Analysis. In *Terminology and Knowledge Engineering (TKE '14)*, 2014. URL https://hal.archives-ouvertes.fr/hal-01005878.

Nigam, Kamal; Lafferty, John D. and McCallum, Andrew. Using maximum entropy for text classification. In *Workshop on Machine Learning for Information Filtering (IJCAI '99)*, pages 61–67, 1999.

Nonhoff, Martin. Einleitung: Diskurs - radikale Demokratie - Hegemonie: Zum politischen Denken von Ernesto Laclau und Chantal Mouffe. In Nonhoff, Martin, editor, *Diskurs – radikale Demokratie – Hegemonie*, pages 7–23. transcript, Bielefeld, 2007.

Nonhoff, Martin. Hegemonieanalyse: Theorie, Methode und Forschungspraxis. In Keller, Reiner; Hirseland, Andreas; Schneider, Werner and Viehöver, Willy, editors, *Handbuch sozialwissenschaftliche Diskursanalyse 2*, pages 299–311. VS Verlag für Sozialwissenschaften, Wiesbaden, 2008.

Nuray, Rabia and Can, Fazli. Automatic ranking of information retrieval systems using data fusion. *Information Processing & Management*, 42(3): 595–614, 2006.

Oevermann, Ulrich. Klinische Soziologie auf der Basis der Methodologie der objektiven Hermeneutik: Manifest der objektiv hermeneutischen Sozialforschung, 2002. URL http://publikationen.ub.uni-frankfurt.de/frontdoor/deliver/index/docId/4958/file/ManifestWord.pdf.

Oppenhäuser, Holger. Das Extremismus-Konzept und die Produktion von politischer Normalität. In Forum für Kritische Rechtsextremismusforschung, editor, *Ordnung. Macht. Extremismus*, pages 35–58. VS Verlag für Sozialwissenschaften, Wiesbaden, 2011.

Pang, Bo and Lee, Lillian. Opinion mining and sentiment analysis. *Foundations and Trends in Information Retrieval*, 2(1-2):1–135, 2008. URL http://dx.doi.org/10.1561/1500000011.

Pêcheux, Michel. *Analyse automatique du discours.* Dunod, Paris, 1969.

Pêcheux, Michel; Hak, Tony and Helsloot, Niels, editors. *Automatic discourse analysis.* Rodopi, Amsterdam and Atlanta, 1995.

Peat, Helen J. and Willett, Peter. The limitations of term co-occurrence data for query expansion in document retrieval systems. *Journal of the American Society for Information Science*, 42(5):378–383, 1991.

Petring, Alexander. Die drei Welten des Gerechtigkeitsjournalismus? Text-Mining in FAZ, TAZ und SZ zu sozialer Gerechtigkeit und Ungleichheit. In Lemke, Matthias and Wiedemann, Gregor, editors, *Text Mining in den Sozialwissenschaften*, Kritische Studien zur Demokratie. VS Verlag für Sozialwissenschaften, Wiesbaden, 2015.

Phan, Xuan-Hieu; Nguyen, Cam-Tu; Le, Dieu-Thu; Nguyen, Le-Minh; Horiguchi, Susumu and Ha, Quang-Thuy. A hidden topic-based framework toward building applications with short web documents. *IEEE Transactions on Knowledge and Data Engineering*, 23(7):961–976, 2011.

Platt, John C. Probabilities for SV machines. In Smola, Alexander J.; Bartlett, Peter; Schölkopf, Bernhard and Schuurmans, Dale, editors, *Advances in large margin classifiers*, pages 61–74. MIT Press, 2000.

Pollak, Senja; Coesemans, Roel; Daelemans, Walter and Lavrac, Nada. Detecting contrast patterns in newspaper articles by combining discourse analysis and text mining. *Pragmatics*, 21(4):647–683, 2011.

Prüwer, Tobias. Zwischen Skylla und Charybdis: Motive von Maß und Mitte: Über die merkwürdige Plausibilität eines Welt-Bildes – eine genealogische Skizze. In Forum für Kritische Rechtsextremismusforschung, editor, *Ordnung. Macht. Extremismus.* VS Verlag für Sozialwissenschaften, Wiesbaden, 2011.

Rayson, Paul and Garside, Roger. Comparing corpora using frequency profiling. In *Proceedings of the workshop on Comparing Corpora (ACL 2000)*, 2000. URL http://www.comp.lancs.ac.uk/~paul/publications/rg_acl2000.pdf.

Rayson, Paul; Berridge, Damon and Francis, Brian. Extending the Cochran rule for the comparison of word frequencies between corpora. In *Proceedings of the 7th International Conference on Statistical analysis of textual data (JADT '04)*, pages 926–936, 2004.

Reichert, Ramón, editor. *Big Data: Analysen zum digitalen Wandel von Wissen, Macht und Ökonomie.* transcript, Bielefeld, 2014.

Remus, Robert; Ahmad, Khurshid and Heyer, Gerhard. Sentiment in German language news and blogs, and the DAX. In Heyer, Gerhard, editor, *Text mining services*, volume 14 of *Leipziger Beiträge zur Informatik*, pages 149–158, Leipzig, 2009. LIV.

Remus, Robert; Quasthoff, Uwe and Heyer, Gerhard. SentiWS: A publicly available German-language resource for sentiment analysis. In *Proceedings of the 7th International Language Resources and Evaluation (LREC '10)*, pages 1168–1171, 2010.

Reynar, Jeffrey C. and Ratnaparkhi, Adwait. A maximum entropy approach to identifying sentence boundaries. In *Proceedings of the Fifth Conference on Applied Natural Language Processing (ANLC '97)*, pages 16–19, Stroudsburg, 1997. ACL. URL http://dx.doi.org/10.3115/974557.974561.

Reynolds, Alan P.; Richards, Graeme; de la Iglesia, B., Beatriz and Rayward-Smith, Victor J. Clustering rules: A comparison of partitioning and hierarchical clustering algorithms. *Journal of Mathematical Modelling and Algorithms*, 5(4):475–504, 2006. URL http://dx.doi.org/10.1007/s10852-005-9022-1.

Rohrdantz, Christian; Koch, Steffen; Jochim, Charles; Heyer, Gerhard; Scheuermann, Gerik; Ertl, Thomas; Schütze, Hinrich and Keim, Daniel A. Visuelle Textanalyse. *Informatik-Spektrum*, 33(6):601–611, 2010.

Rucht, Dieter, editor. *Protest in der Bundesrepublik: Strukturen und Entwicklungen.* Campus, Frankfurt am Main, 2001.

Salton, Gerard; Wong, Andrew and Yang, Chungshu. A vector space model for automatic indexing. *Communications of the ACM*, 18(11):613–620, 1975.

Saussure, Ferdinand de. *Grundfragen der allgemeinen Sprachwissenschaft.* de Gruyter, Berlin, 3 edition, 2001.

Schaal, Gary S. and Kath, Roxana. Zeit für einen Paradigmenwechsel in der politischen Theorie? In Brodocz, André; Herrmann, Dietrich; Schmidt, Rainer; Schulz, Daniel and Schulze Wessel, Julia, editors, *Die Verfassung des Politischen*, pages 331–350. Springer, Wiesbaden, 2014. URL http://dx.doi.org/10.1007/978-3-658-04784-9_20.

Scharkow, Michael. *Automatische Inhaltsanalyse und maschinelles Lernen.* epubli, Berlin, 2012.

Scharkow, Michael. Thematic content analysis using supervised machine learning: An empirical evaluation using German online news. *Quality and Quantity*, 47(2):761–773, 2013.

Scharloth, Joachim; Eugster, David and Bubenhofer, Noah. Das Wuchern der Rhizome: Linguistische Diskursanalyse und Data-driven Turn. In Busse, Dietrich and Teubert, Wolfgang, editors, *Linguistische Diskursanalyse.* VS Verlag für Sozialwissenschaften, Wiesbaden, 2013.

Schmidt, Benjamin M. Words alone: dismantling topic models in the humanities. *Journal of Digital Humanities*, 2 (1), 2012. URL http://journalofdigitalhumanities.org/2-1/words-alone-by-benjamin-m-schmidt/.

Schönfelder, Walter. CAQDAS and qualitative syllogism logic: NVivo 8 and MAXQDA 10 compared. *Forum Qualitative Sozialforschung / Forum: Qualitative Social Research*, 12(1), 2011. URL http://nbn-resolving.de/urn:nbn:de:0114-fqs1101218.

Schreibman, Susan; Siemens, Raymond George and Unsworth, John, editors. *A Companion to Digital Humanities.* Blackwell, Malden, 2004.

Schubert, Frank. Die Extremismus-Polizei. Eine Kritik des antiextremistischen Denkens mit Jacques Rancière. In Forum für Kritische Rechtsextremismusforschung, editor, *Ordnung. Macht. Extremismus*, pages 102–116. VS Verlag für Sozialwissenschaften, Wiesbaden, 2011.

Sebastiani, Fabrizio. Machine learning in automated text categorization. *ACM Computing Surveys*, 34(1):1–47, 2002.

Settles, Burr. Active Learning Literature Survey, 2010. URL http://burrsettles.com/pub/settles.activelearning.pdf.

Singhal, Amit; Buckley, Chris and Mitra, Mandar. Pivoted document length normalization. In *Proceedings of the 19th Annual International Conference on Research and Development in Information Retrieval (SIGIR '96)*, pages 21–29, New York, 1996. ACM. URL http://doi.acm.org/10.1145/243199.243206.

Slapin, Jonathan B. and Proksch, Sven-Oliver. A scaling model for estimating time-series party positions from texts. *American Journal of Political Science*, 52(3):705–722, 2008.

Steinke, Ines. *Kriterien qualitativer Forschung: Ansätze zur Bewertung qualitativ-empirischer Sozialforschung.* Juventa, Weinheim, 1999.

Stone, Phillip J. Thematic text analysis: New agendas for analyzing text content. In Roberts, Carl W., editor, *Text analysis for the social sciences*, pages 35–54. Erlbaum, Mahwah NJ, 1997.

Stone, Phillip J.; Dunphy, Dexter C.; Smith, Marshall S. and Ogilvie, Daniel M. *The General Inquirer: A computer approach to content analysis.* MIT Press, Cambridge, 1966.

Stöss, Richard. *Rechtsextremismus im Wandel.* Friedrich-Ebert-Stiftung, Berlin, 2005. URL http://www.gbv.de/dms/sub-hamburg/496475088.pdf/http://www.loc.gov/catdir/toc/fy0710/2006370240.html.

Tamayo Korte, Miguel; Waldschmidt, Anne; Dalman-Eken, Sibel and Klein, Anne. 1000 Fragen zur Bioethik: Qualitative Analyse eines Onlineforums unter Einsatz der quantitativen Software MAXDictio. In Kuckartz, Udo, editor, *Qualitative Datenanalyse computergestützt*, pages 163–174. VS Verlag für Sozialwissenschaften, Wiesbaden, 2007.

Teh, Yee W.; Jordan, Michael I.; Beal, Matthwe J. and Blei, David M. Hierarchical dirichlet processes. *Journal of the American Statistical Association*, 101(476):1566–1581, 2006.

Teubert, Wolfgang. Korpuslinguistik, Hermeneutik und die soziale Konstruktion der Wirklichkeit. *Linguistik Online*, 28(3), 2006. URL http://www.linguistik-online.de/28_06/teubert.html.

Teubert, Wolfgang. Provinz eines föderalen Superstaates, regiert von einer nicht gewählten Bürokratie? Schlüsselbegriffe des europaskeptischen Diskurses in Großbritannien. In Keller, Reiner; Hirseland, Andreas; Schneider, Werner and Viehöver, Willy, editors, *Handbuch sozialwissenschaftliche Diskursanalyse 2*, pages 387–421. VS Verlag für Sozialwissenschaften, Wiesbaden, 2008.

Tiqqun. *Kybernetik und Revolte.* Diaphanes, Zürich, 2007.

Tsuruoka, Yoshimasa. A simple C++ library for maximum entropy classification, 2011. URL http://www.nactem.ac.uk/tsuruoka/maxent.

Tumasjan, Andranik; Sprenger, Timm O.; Sandner, Philipp G. and Welpe, Isabell M. Predicting elections with twitter: What 140 characters reveal about political sentiment. In *Proceedings of the 4th International AAAI Conference on Weblogs and Social Media*, pages 178–185, 2010.

Turney, Peter D. and Pantel, Patrick. From frequency to meaning: Vector space models of semantics. *Journal of Artificial Intelligence Research*, 37: 141–188, 2010. URL http://www.jair.org/media/2934/live-2934-4846-jair.pdf.

van Atteveldt, Wouter; Kleinnijenhuis, Jan and Ruigrok, Nel. Parsing, semantic networks, and political authority using syntactic analysis to extract semantic relations from Dutch newspaper articles. *Political Analysis*, 16 (4):428–446, 2008.

van Lamsweerde, Axel. *Requirements engineering: From system goals to UML models and software specifications*. Wiley, Hoboken, 2007.

van Rijsbergen, Cornelis J. A theoretical basis for the use of co-occurrence data in information retrieval. *Journal of Documentation*, 33(2):106–119, 1977.

Vlachos, Andreas. A stopping criterion for active learning. *Computer Speech and Language*, 22(3):295–312, 2008. URL http://dx.doi.org/10.1016/j.csl.2007.12.001.

Volkens, Andrea; Bara, Judith; Budge, Ian; McDonald, Michael and Klingemann, Hans-Dieter, editors. *Mapping policy preferences from texts: Statistical solutions for manifesto analysts*. Oxford University Press, Oxford, 2013.

Volkens, Andrea; Lehmann, Pola; Merz, Nicolas; Regel, Sven and Werner, Annika. *The Manifesto Data Collection. Manifesto Project (MRG/CMP/MARPOR). Version 2014b*. Wissenschaftszentrum Berlin für Sozialforschung, Berlin, 2014.

Voorhees, Ellen. Overview of the TREC 2005 robust retrieval track. In Voorhees, Ellen and Buckland, Lori, editors, *Proceedings of the Fourteenth Text REtrieval Conference (TREC 2005)*. NIST, 2005. URL http://trec.nist.gov/pubs/trec14/papers/ROBUST.OVERVIEW.pdf.

Voorhees, Ellen and Harman, Donna. Overview of the sixth Text REtrieval Conference (TREC-6). *Information Processing and Management*, 36(1): 3–35, 2000. URL http://dx.doi.org/10.1016/S0306-4573(99)00043-6.

Wallach, Hanna M.; Murray, Iain; Salakhutdinov, Ruslan and Mimno, David. Evaluation methods for topic models. In *Proceedings of the 26th Annual International Conference on Machine Learning (ICML '09)*, pages 1105–1112, New York, 2009. ACM. URL http://doi.acm.org/10.1145/1553374.1553515.

Wang, Chong; Blei, David M. and Heckerman, David. Continuous time dynamic topic models. *ArXiv e-prints*, 2012. URL http://arxiv.org/abs/1206.3298.

Werner, Annika; Lacewell, Onawa and Volkens, Andrea. Manifesto coding instructions: 4th fully revised edition, 2011. URL https://manifesto-project.wzb.eu/down/papers/handbook_v4.pdf.

Wettstein, Martin. Best of both worlds: Die halbautomatische Inhaltsanalyse. In Sommer, Katharina; Wettstein, Martin; Wirth, Werner and Matthes, Jörg, editors, *Automatisierung in der Inhaltsanalyse*, pages 16–39. Halem, Köln, 2014.

Wiedemann, Gregor. *Regieren mit Datenschutz und Überwachung: Informationelle Selbstbestimmung zwischen Sicherheit und Freiheit*, volume 41 of *Wissenschaftliche Beiträge aus dem Tectum-Verlag*. Tectum, Marburg, 2011.

Wiedemann, Gregor. Opening up to big data: computer-assisted analysis of textual data in social sciences. *Forum Qualitative Sozialforschung / Forum: Qualitative Social Research*, 14(2), 2013. URL http://nbn-resolving.de/urn:nbn:de:0114-fqs1302231.

Wiedemann, Gregor. Vertrauen und Protest: Eine exemplarische Analyse des Demonstrationsgeschehens in der BRD mit Hilfe von Text Mining in diachronen Zeitungskorpora. In Haller, Michael, editor, *Wandel und Messbarkeit des öffentlichen Vertrauens im Zeitalter des Web 2.0*. Herbert van Halem, Köln. [In print], 2016.

Wiedemann, Gregor and Lemke, Matthias. Text Mining für die Analyse qualitativer Daten – Auf dem Weg zu einer Best Practice? In Lemke, Matthias and Wiedemann, Gregor, editors, *Text Mining in den Sozialwissenschaften*, Kritische Studien zur Demokratie. VS Verlag für Sozialwissenschaften, Wiesbaden, 2015.

Wiedemann, Gregor and Niekler, Andreas. Document retrieval for large scale content analysis using contextualized dictionaries. In *Terminology and Knowledge Engineering (TKE '14)*, 2014. URL http://hal.archives-ouvertes.fr/hal-01005879/.

Wiedemann, Gregor; Lemke, Matthias and Niekler, Andreas. Postdemokratie und Neoliberalismus – Zur Nutzung neoliberaler Argumentationen in der Bundesrepublik Deutschland 1949–2011: Ein Werkstattbericht. *Zeitschrift für politische Theorie*, 4(1):99–116, 2013.

Witten, Ian H.; Frank, Eibe and Hall, Mark A. *Data mining: Practical machine learning tools and techniques.* Morgan Kaufmann, Burlington, 3 edition, 2011.

Wong, Michael; Ziarko, Wojciech and Wong, Patrick. Generalized vector spaces model in information retrieval. In *Proceedings of the 8th annual international conference on Research and development in information retrieval (SIGIR '85)*, pages 18–25, 1985.

Xiaojin Zhu. Semi-supervised learning literature survey, 2008. URL http://pages.cs.wisc.edu/~jerryzhu/pub/ssl_survey.pdf.

Yang, Yiming and Pedersen, Jan O. A comparative study on feature selection in text categorization. In *Proceedings of the Fourteenth International Conference on Machine Learning (ICML'97)*, pages 412–420. Morgan Kaufmann Publishers, 1997.

Yao, Limin; Mimno, David and McCallum, Andrew. Efficient methods for topic model inference on streaming document collections. In *Proceedings of the 15th International Conference on Knowledge Discovery and Data Mining (KDD '09)*, pages 937–946, New York, 2009. ACM. URL http://doi.acm.org/10.1145/1557019.1557121.

Zhang, Chao; Wang, Xinjun and Peng, Zhaohui. Extracting dimensions for OLAP on multidimensional text databases. In Gong, Zhiguo; Luo, Xiangfeng; Chen, Junjie; Lei, Jingsheng and Wang, Fu Lee, editors, *International Conference on Web Information Systems and Mining (WISM '11)*. Springer, Berlin and Heidelberg, 2011.

Zhang, Duo; Zhai, Chengxiang and Han, Jiawei. Topic cube: Topic modeling for OLAP on multidimensional text databases, 2009. URL http://www.siam.org/proceedings/datamining/2009/dm09_103_zhangd.pdf.

Zhou, Xiaohua; Zhang, Xiaodan and Hu, Xiaohua. Semantic smoothing for Bayesian text classification with small training data, 2008. URL http://citeseerx.ist.psu.edu/viewdoc/summary?doi=10.1.1.140.6319.

Zižek, Slavoj. *Totalitarismus: Fünf Interventionen zum Ge- oder Missbrauch eines Begriffs*, volume 2. LAIKA, Hamburg, 2011.

Züll, Cornelia and Mohler, Peter. Computerunterstützte Inhaltsanalyse: Codierung und Analyse von Antworten auf offene Fragen, 2001. URL http://www.gesis.org/fileadmin/upload/forschung/publikationen/gesis_reihen/howto/how-to8cz.pdf.

CPSIA information can be obtained
at www.ICGtesting.com
Printed in the USA
LVOW04s0032300816
502338LV00026B/369/P